The Epistemology of Desire and the Problem of Nihilism

The Epistemology of Desire and the Problem of Nihilism

ALLAN HAZLETT

Great Clarendon Street, Oxford, OX2 6DP,
United Kingdom

Oxford University Press is a department of the University of Oxford.
It furthers the University's objective of excellence in research, scholarship,
and education by publishing worldwide. Oxford is a registered trade mark of
Oxford University Press in the UK and in certain other countries

© Allan Hazlett 2024

The moral rights of the author have been asserted

All rights reserved. No part of this publication may be reproduced, stored in
a retrieval system, or transmitted, in any form or by any means, without the
prior permission in writing of Oxford University Press, or as expressly permitted
by law, by licence or under terms agreed with the appropriate reprographics
rights organization. Enquiries concerning reproduction outside the scope of the
above should be sent to the Rights Department, Oxford University Press, at the
address above

You must not circulate this work in any other form
and you must impose this same condition on any acquirer

Published in the United States of America by Oxford University Press
198 Madison Avenue, New York, NY 10016, United States of America

British Library Cataloguing in Publication Data
Data available

Library of Congress Control Number: 2023946444

ISBN 9780198889830

DOI: 10.1093/9780191995583.001.0001

Printed and bound in the UK by
Clays Ltd, Elcograf S.p.A.

Links to third party websites are provided by Oxford in good faith and
for information only. Oxford disclaims any responsibility for the materials
contained in any third party website referenced in this work.

For my children, even if they don't matter

Contents

Acknowledgments	xi

1.	Introduction	1
	1.1 The Thought That Nothing Matters	1
	1.2 The Humean Solution	4
	1.3 The Problem of Nihilism and the Nature of Desire	5
	1.4 Desire as Non-Instrumental	7
	1.5 The Practical Theory of Desire	10
	1.6 Desire as Evaluation	13
	1.7 The Evaluative Belief Theory of Desire	15
	1.8 The Evaluative Perception Theory of Desire	18
	1.9 The Prospective Theory of Desire	19
	1.10 AD Is Not a Theory of Desire	20
	1.11 Desire and the Emotions	21
	1.12 The Epistemology of Desire	24
	1.13 Synopsis	26
2.	Accurate Desire	27
	2.1 Truth as the Accuracy Condition for Belief	27
	2.2 Goodness as the Accuracy Condition for Desire	30
	2.3 Desire as Propositional	34
	2.4 Propositional Goodness	37
	2.5 Aversion	38
	2.6 "Good" vs. "Good For"	39
	2.7 Degrees of Goodness and Strength of Desire	40
	2.8 Axial Gaps	43
	2.9 Axial Gluts?	45
	2.10 Desiring the Bad	47
	2.11 Conclusion	49
3.	Why Criticize Desires for the Bad?	50
	3.1 Axial Criticism of Desires	51
	3.2 Desires for the Bad Are Inaccurate	53
	3.3 Desires for the Bad Depend on False Beliefs	56
	3.4 Desires for the Bad Are Abnormal	56
	3.5 Desires for the Bad Are Vicious	58
	3.6 Desires for the Bad Might Have Bad Consequences	60

viii CONTENTS

3.7	Desires for the Bad Are Bad	62
3.8	Desires for the Bad Are Unfitting	64
3.9	Desires for the Bad Are Unreasonable	68
3.10	Desires for the Bad Are Desires There Is a Reason Not to Have	69
3.11	Conclusion	74

4. Desire That Amounts to Knowledge — 75

4.1	Orectic Knowledge as Knowledge of Goodness	76
4.2	The Ethical Importance of Orectic Knowledge	77
4.3	Knowledge as Apt Mental Representation	80
4.4	An Account of Orectic Knowledge	84
4.5	Sources of Orectic Knowledge	86
4.6	Orectic Knowledge and Epistemic Luck	90
4.7	Conclusion	93

5. Irrational Desire — 94

5.1	Irrationality and Deliberation	95
5.2	Desire and Deliberation	99
5.3	Doxastic Deliberation	100
5.4	Attitude Formation through Deliberation	101
5.5	Orectic Deliberation Is Not Practical Deliberation	106
5.6	Orectic Deliberation Is Not Instrumental Doxastic Deliberation	106
5.7	A Case	108
5.8	Orectic Deliberation	109
5.9	Acedia	112
5.10	Is Acedia Irrational?	114
5.11	Orectic Deliberation Is Not (the Same Thing as) Evaluative Doxastic Deliberation	115
5.12	Why Is Desire Susceptible to Deliberation?	118
5.13	Conclusion	120

6. The Problem — 121

6.1	Statement of the Problem	121
6.2	The Realist Solution	122
6.3	The Expressivist Solution	125
6.4	The Humean Solution, Again	127
6.5	The Egoistic Solution	129
6.6	The Relativistic Solution	130
6.7	The Perspectival Solution	133
6.8	The Naturalist Solution	135
6.9	Conclusion	139

CONTENTS ix

7.	Desiring the Neutral	140
	7.1 Strong Incoherence	140
	7.2 The Risk of Contradiction	142
	7.3 Weak Incoherence	144
	7.4 James' Two Intellectual Duties	148
	7.5 Non-Accurate Representation	149
	7.6 Why Weak Incoherence Is Rationally Permissible	152
	7.7 Preference	155
	7.8 Why It Matters That We Already Have Desires	157
	7.9 Conclusion	158

Bibliography   161
Index   177

Acknowledgments

I started working on this material in 2008, and consequently this book has been a long time coming. It began with an analogical insight, or what I take to have been an insight, that desire is to goodness as belief is to truth. It took me a long time to figure out what this might mean, exactly, and what its consequences might be. I learned a great deal, although you might think not nearly enough, from what others had written on this topic. There remain a lot of loose ends. Paul Valéry observed that, for the anxious, a work of art is never finished, but only abandoned,[1] and although this book is nothing like a work of art, I anxiously acknowledge that it is more abandoned than finished. However, I do not think I abandoned it too soon, or at least not far too soon.

This book incorporates material from three previously published papers: "The Guise of the Good and the Problem of Partiality" (*Canadian Journal of Philosophy* 49(6) (2019), pp. 851–72), "Desire that Amounts to Knowledge" (*Philosophical Quarterly* 71(1) (2021), pp. 56–73), and "Desire and Goodness" (*Philosophy and Phenomenological Research* 105 (2022), pp. 160–80). I am grateful to Cambridge University Press, Oxford University Press, and Wiley for their permission to use material from those papers here.

I presented versions of this material in 2009 at a conference on *Epistemic Goodness* at the University of Oklahoma; in 2011 at the University of Edinburgh; in 2013 at the University of York; in 2014 at the University of California, Riverside, New Mexico State University, and the University of New Mexico; in 2015 and 2016 at a summer seminar (at the University of Missouri) and a conference (in San Antonio) on *The Value and Evaluation of Faith* (which were funded by the Templeton Religious Trust); in 2017 at the University of Nevada, Las Vegas; in 2018 at NYU-Shanghai, Southern Methodist University, the Midwest Epistemology Workshop at the University of Notre Dame, and the University of Edinburgh; in 2019 at Iowa State University and the University of Richmond; and in 2020 at the American Philosophical Association Central Division Meeting and the University of

---

[1] "Au sujet du Cimetière marin," *Nouvelle Revue Française* 234 (March 1933), pp. 399–411, at p. 399.

Glasgow. Thanks to all those audiences, as well as to Anne Baril, Bob Beddor, Selim Berker, Eric Brown, Jessica Brown, Matthew Chrisman, Akshan deAlwis, Daniel Drucker, Billy Dunaway, John Greco, Robert Howell, Zoe Jenkin, Jon Kvanvig, Kathryn Lindeman, Matt McGrath, Ron Mallon, Aaron Meskin, Peter Momtchiloff, Casey O'Callaghan, Christian Piller, Lewis Powell, Geoff Pynn, Rebekah Rice, Mike Ridge, Joe Salerno, Henry Schiller, Roy Sorensen, Jonathan Weinberg, Gabby Zhang, and to a great number of anonymous readers and referees.

If we can't help taking ourselves so seriously, perhaps we just have to put up with being ridiculous.

—Thomas Nagel, *What Does It All Mean?*

1
Introduction

At least at some point in your life, you have probably wondered whether anything matters, and, like Macbeth, you may have come to think, at least temporarily, that nothing matters—or, as he put it, that life is "a tale told by an idiot, full of sound and fury, signifying nothing."[1] This is an unsettling thought—we are not merely curious about the possibility that nothing matters; we worry about it. We rightly associate the thought that nothing matters with existential crises, incidents of loss and grief, and episodes of romantic despair. This is because thinking that nothing matters seems to put rational pressure on you to become indifferent to everything. It seems irrational to care about something while at the same time thinking that it does not matter. The thought that nothing matters seems to mandate total indifference. However, most people who come to think that nothing matters do not become indifferent to everything. Are those who both think that nothing matters and yet care about some things irrational? Or can we make sense of rationally caring about something while thinking that it does not matter? This is a very brief articulation of the problem—the "problem of nihilism"—that I want to investigate in this book.

1.1 The Thought That Nothing Matters

What exactly are you thinking, when you think that nothing matters? What is this thought, the thought that nothing matters, that most of you have considered and that some of you have at least temporarily endorsed? When you think that nothing matters, what exactly are you thinking?

Here are three things that you are surely not thinking. First, you are not thinking that nothing matters *to you*. You are not thinking that you do not care about anything.[2] The thought that nothing matters is unsettling

---

[1] *Macbeth* 5.5.29–31.
[2] That thought would also be unsettling, of course, but it isn't the thought that nothing matters.

2 THE EPISTEMOLOGY OF DESIRE AND THE PROBLEM OF NIHILISM

precisely because you do care about certain things, but if nothing matters, it seems like there is some sense in which you ought not care about them. If you find yourself thinking that nothing matters, you will not be comforted by the fact that you care about your kids getting into a good college or about the survival of the endangered snow leopard. Rather, you will be disturbed by the thought that those things do not really matter. Moreover, it is more or less obvious that some things matter to you. If what you were thinking when you think that nothing matters were that you do not care about anything, it would be weird to wonder about whether anything matters, much less to conclude that nothing does.[3]

Second, you are not thinking that nothing is good or bad for you, i.e. that nothing benefits or harms you. You are neither thinking that you are invincible or self-sufficient, like a god who flourishes no matter what happens, nor thinking that you are not a welfare subject in the first place, something more like a rock or inanimate part of nature that neither flourishes nor languishes.[4] The thought that nothing matters is unsettling, at least in part, because, if nothing matters, then one of the things that does not matter is your welfare. If nothing matters, then things going well or badly for you does not matter either. If you find yourself thinking that nothing matters, you will not be comforted by the fact that mindfulness meditation would improve your quality of life or that being without food and shelter would make it impossible for you to live well. Rather, you will be disturbed by the fact that such changes to your well-being would not really matter. Moreover, it is more or less obvious that some things are good for you and some things bad for you. If what you were thinking when you think that nothing matters were that nothing is good or bad for you, it would be weird to wonder about whether anything matters, much less to conclude that nothing does.[5]

Third, you are not thinking that no individual is a good or bad instance of its kind. You are not thinking that there are no good or bad hotels, no good or bad movies, no good or bad non-stick frying pans. What makes the thought that nothing matters unsettling to the cigar aficionado is the fact that it does not really matter if the cigars they smoke are any good. If you find yourself thinking that nothing matters, you will not be comforted by

---

[3] For the same reasons, when you think that nothing matters you are not thinking that nothing matters to anyone.

[4] That thought would also be unsettling, of course, but it isn't the thought that nothing matters.

[5] For the same reasons, when you think that nothing matters you are not thinking that nothing is good or bad for anyone.

the fact that the Hôtel de Crillon serves an excellent brunch or that Toyota makes the best minivan. Rather, you will be disturbed by the fact that no matter how many good things you acquire and no matter how many bad things you avoid, none of that will really matter. Moreover, it is more or less obvious that some individuals are good or bad instances of their kind. If what you were thinking when you think that nothing matters were that no individual is a good or bad instance of its kind, it would be weird to wonder about whether anything matters, much less to conclude that nothing does.

These last two possibilities, however, point in the right direction, for they point in the direction of an essential connection between the idea of something mattering and the idea of its being good or bad. I propose that, when you think that nothing matters, you are thinking that nothing is good or bad. The thought that nothing matters is a kind of *nihilism about value*. Nihilism of this sort goes by many names in philosophy, including "subjectivism," "moral anti-realism," "moral skepticism," and "moral error theory."[6] As this suggests, it is not only something that some of us are sometimes tempted to think, but a position endorsed and defended by some philosophers.

More precisely, on my proposal, when you think that nothing matters, you are thinking that, for any proposition that p, it is neither good nor bad that p. You are not thinking that, for any proposition that p, you do not care whether p. Nor are you thinking that, for any proposition that p, it is neither good for you nor bad for you that p. Nor are you thinking that, for any individual, it is neither a good instance of its kind nor a bad instance of its kind. You are thinking that it just does not matter whether p—in other words, on my proposal, that it is neither good nor bad that p. It just does not matter either way.

Above, I said that thinking that nothing matters seems to put rational pressure on you to become indifferent to everything. Why? Because it seems incoherent to care about something that you think is neither good nor bad. For example, it seems incoherent to want something to happen when you think it would not be good if it were to happen and incoherent to want something not to happen when you think it would not be bad if it were to happen. If it is neither good nor bad that p, caring about whether p seems like some kind of mistake, such that you cannot rationally care about whether p while at the same time thinking that it is neither good nor bad

---

[6] See e.g. Mackie 1977, Joyce 2001, Olson 2014.

4 THE EPISTEMOLOGY OF DESIRE AND THE PROBLEM OF NIHILISM

that p. If you think it does not matter either way, so the argument goes, you cannot rationally come down on one side or the other.

1.2 The Humean Solution

Nihilism about value, you might think, is a distinctively Modern idea, something only a Modern subject would worry about and something only a Modern philosopher would defend. When I said that most of "us" have wondered whether anything matters and that some of "us" have thought that nothing matters, I had the context of Modernity in mind. So, the problem of nihilism that I consider here may not be a universal one, but it is one that we Moderns have to deal with.

However, you might think that this distinctively Modern problem was solved early on in the Modern period. Hume famously argued that "passions," unlike "judgments of the understanding," cannot be rational or irrational.[7] The problem of nihilism arises only if we assume otherwise. Consider the idea that you cannot rationally care about whether p while at the same time thinking that it is neither good nor bad that p. If passions cannot be rational or irrational, it cannot be rational or irrational to care about something. As Hume famously concluded, it is "not contrary to reason to prefer the destruction of the whole world to the scratching of my finger."[8] If reason is the slave of the passions, the fact that you think it is neither good nor bad that p cannot make it irrational to care about whether p. That would give reason precisely the kind of control that Hume denies it can have.

Hume's conclusion is popular in contemporary analytic philosophy. It motivates the formal decision theory that informs the way many contemporary philosophers, economists, political scientists, and others think about practical rationality. It is a central tenet of what is known as the Humean theory of practical rationality,[9] although it is doubtful that Hume subscribed to that theory.[10] According to the Humean theory of practical rationality, practical rationality is instrumental rationality, i.e. the rationality of taking the means to your ends. Your ends themselves—what you care about, want,

---

[7] *Treatise of Human Nature*, 2.3.3.5 and 3.1.1.9; cf. *Enquiry concerning the Principles of Morals*, App1.21.

[8] *Treatise*, 2.3.3.6.

[9] Cf. Williams 1980/1981, Smith 1993, Drier 1996, 2001, Lewis 1996; see also Railton 2007.

[10] Cf. Millgram 1995, Brink 2008, pp. 9–11, Railton 2012, 2017.

prefer, value, and so on—cannot be rational or irrational, only your selection of means to those ends. On this view, passions provide the inputs for practical reasoning and are not themselves subject to evaluation as rational or irrational.

It is no accident that the Humean theory of practical rationality provides a solution to the problem of nihilism. The Humean theory is a distinctively Modern philosophical position, a position that emerges and becomes popular just as people start worrying about nihilism about value.[11] It is easy to understand how metaphysical doubts about the existence of values coincided with the development of an instrumental conception of practical rationality.

1.3 The Problem of Nihilism and the Nature of Desire

Whether the Humean solution to the problem of nihilism (§1.2) succeeds depends entirely on the plausibility of the claim that passions cannot be rational or irrational, and the plausibility of this claim depends on the nature of the passions. However, the passions, at least in Hume's sense, comprise a relatively heterogeneous category—they include desires, preferences, intentions, emotions, feelings, and moods.[12] In this book we are going to focus on desire. This is partly for the sake of simplicity, but it is also an acknowledgment of the standard way of understanding Hume's conclusion, as affirming a fundamental difference between desire and belief. Hume's conclusion, on this understanding, is that desires, unlike beliefs, cannot be rational or irrational. Whether this is plausible depends on the nature of desire.

"Desire" is ambiguous, perhaps even more ambiguous than other terms frequently used in contemporary analytic philosophy. I am going to treat "desire" and "want" as synonyms, but that doesn't address the ambiguity: "want" is likewise ambiguous. I want to begin to address this ambiguity by contrasting my intended sense of "desire" with both a narrower and a broader sense of the word.[13] My aim here is not to give an account of desire, nor even to say anything substantive about it, but merely to indicate the sense of "desire" I have in mind for the subsequent discussion.

---

[11] Note that, although the Stoics sometimes seem to recommend indifference about things that are neither good nor bad, they are not nihilists about value.

[12] *Treatise of Human Nature*, 2.3.3.5 and 3.1.1.9, but see in general *Treatise of Human Nature*, Book II, and *Dissertation on the Passions*.

[13] Cf. Schroeder 2004, p. 132.

6   THE EPISTEMOLOGY OF DESIRE AND THE PROBLEM OF NIHILISM

First, there is a narrow sense of "desire" on which desiring contrasts with wishing, hoping, and being glad.[14] In this sense, you cannot desire something that you know has already occurred or that you know has already not occurred. Those who chose to use "desire" in this way have a point. If you know that the Lakers lost last night, a Laker fan would say "I wish the Lakers had won" rather than "I desire that the Lakers won" or "I want the Lakers to have won." Likewise, a Laker-hater would say "I'm glad the Lakers lost" rather than "I desire that the Lakers lost" or "I want the Lakers to have lost."[15] However, it seems to me that wishing, hoping, and being glad have something important in common, something which is usefully labeled "desire." So, I am going to treat wishing, hoping, and being glad as species of desiring.

Above, I articulated the problem of nihilism in terms of *caring*, e.g. by asking whether you can coherently care about something that you think is neither good nor bad. I am going to assume that caring is a species of desiring. To care about something is at least in part to have certain desires. You cannot care about whether p without at a minimum either desiring that p or desiring that not-p. Caring may involve more than merely desiring, but it shares the aforementioned common element with wishing, hoping, and being glad.

Second, there is a broad sense of "desire" on which anything capable of motivation is a desire.[16] A desire, in this sense, is the same as what Donald Davidson (1963/2001) calls a "pro-attitude," where pro-attitudes include such things as "moral views" and "aesthetic principles" (p. 4). Those who chose to use "desire" in this way have a point. There is something puzzling about the idea of someone being motivated to do something that they did not at all want to do. There is something right about the following thought: if you were motivated to do it, there must have been something about doing it that attracted you, some way in which doing it was appealing to you, something about doing it that made you *want* to do it. However, it seems to me that there is an important difference between those actions that we would ordinarily describe as motivated by desire and those actions that we would ordinarily describe as motivated only by belief. In the former case, we act because there is something we want—perhaps simply to act in that way,

[14] Cf. Smith 1994, p. 117, Velleman 1992, p. 17.

[15] However, it seems like you can desire something that you know is impossible, even in the present narrow sense of "desire." "I want the Lakers to have won" sounds weird; "I want to have my cake and eat it, too" doesn't.

[16] Cf. Nagel 1970, pp. 29–30, Drier 2001, pp. 31–2.

or perhaps to do something that we believe we will do if we act in that way. In the latter case, by contrast, we act in spite of everything we want—although we do not want to do so, we do something because we believe it is our duty, or our responsibility, or our calling, or otherwise something that must be done. I want to reserve "desire" for the former kind of motivation. So, I am not going to assume, as a conceptual matter, that anything capable of motivation is a desire. (If it turns out that the latter kind of motivation also involves desire, that will be a substantive discovery, not a conceptual truth.)

1.4 Desire as Non-Instrumental

I characterized the thought that nothing matters as the thought that nothing is good or bad (§1.1). However, consider the following argument. There is a familiar sense of "instrumentally good" on which something is *instrumentally good* if and only if it is a means to something that you want.[17] Given that there are things that you want, there are things that are instrumentally good, in this sense. Therefore, it is false that nothing is good or bad.

Obviously, if you find yourself thinking that nothing matters, you will not be comforted by the fact that there are means to things that you want.[18] When you think that nothing matters, you are not thinking that nothing is instrumentally good for you, in the sense of being a means to something else that you want. When you think that nothing matters, what you are thinking is that nothing is non-instrumentally good or bad.

Just as values are said to be either instrumental or non-instrumental, philosophers standardly distinguish between instrumental and non-instrumental desires. You have an instrumental desire for something when you desire it as a means to something else that you want. I intend a broad sense of "means" here, on which the means to an end might either cause, realize, or constitute said end.[19] If you want to take an exercise class because taking the class will make you fitter and you antecedently want to be fitter, then your desire to take an exercise class is instrumental. If you want to

---

[17] More precisely: something is instrumentally good relative to S if and only if it is a means to something S wants. There is obviously a non-relative sense of "instrumentally good" as well, on which something is instrumentally good if and only if it is a means to something that is non-instrumentally good.

[18] Again (§1.1), that thought would be unsettling, but it isn't the thought that nothing matters.

[19] Cf. Arpaly and Schroeder 2014, p. 6.

8 THE EPISTEMOLOGY OF DESIRE AND THE PROBLEM OF NIHILISM

drink Alphonse Mellot because Alphonse Mellot is a good Sancerre and you antecedently want to drink a good Sancerre, then your desire to drink Alphonse Mellot is instrumental. If you want to visit Seoul because visiting Seoul would make for a pleasant vacation and you antecedently want to take a pleasant vacation, then your desire to visit Seoul is instrumental.

This is sometimes put by saying that, when you desire something instrumentally you desire it "for the sake of something else." By contrast, when you desire something non-instrumentally you desire it, but not "for the sake of something else." This is sometimes put by saying that, when you desire something non-instrumentally, you desire it "for its own sake."

What exactly does it mean to desire something "as a means" to something else that you want? When you have an instrumental desire for something, what makes your desire instrumental is the fact that it depends on your desire for something else. Moreover, when you instrumentally desire something, your desire depends on your belief that it is a means to something else that you want. That is what it means to desire something "as a means" to something else that you want.

Because this is a relatively broad conception of instrumental desire, it is worthwhile to consider an example of non-instrumental desire. Imagine that you want to take a walk. The sun is shining, the weather is mild, and there is a nice breeze. However, your desire to take a walk does not depend on your belief that going for a walk is a means to something else that you want. You just want to take a walk. You want to take a walk "for its own sake" and not "for the sake of something else." You desire to take a walk is a non-instrumental desire. We can, of course, imagine someone with an instrumental desire to take a walk. Someone might believe that walking is a means to lowering their blood pressure (which they antecedently want to do) or a means to fulfilling their prior resolution to walk once a day (which they antecedently want to do) or a means to avoiding working on a book manuscript (which they are antecedently desperate to do). Someone might antecedently have a kind of standing desire to take walks when the conditions are good for walking, such that their desire to take a walk depends on their belief that the conditions are presently good for walking. Your desire, however, is like none of these instrumental desires. It is a spontaneous attraction to the prospect of walking that is not conditioned on any prior desire of yours.

You might object that you want to take a walk because you would enjoy taking a walk. That seems plausible, given the case as described, but I don't think this means that your desire is instrumental. We enjoy doing the things we enjoy doing because we want to do them. But that does not mean that we want to do those things as a means to something else that we want, namely, enjoyment. Enjoyment is not something *else* that we want, such that doing enjoyable things is a means to that end. You do not want to take a walk as a means to something *else* that you want. You just want to take a walk. Contrast the person who wants to take a walk as a means to lowering their blood pressure. Taking a walk will not lower their blood pressure because they want to take a walk. Taking a walk will lower their blood pressure—or so they presume—whether they want to take a walk or not. They intuitively want two things: first, to lower their blood pressure, and, second, to take a walk, because taking a walk will lower their blood pressure. You, who non-instrumentally want to take a walk, only want one thing: to take a walk. This is consistent with the claim that you want to take a walk because you would enjoy taking a walk.

This illustrates something important. I said that, when you instrumentally desire something, your desire depends on your belief that it is a means to something else that you want. However, non-instrumental desires depend on beliefs as well. In the case of non-instrumental desires, these will not be beliefs about whether the thing desired is a means to something else that you want, but rather beliefs about what the thing is like. Your desire to take a walk depends on your beliefs about what it would be like were you to take a walk, e.g. that you would be walking in the sun, in mild weather, with a nice breeze. In this way, non-instrumental desires depend on beliefs. What is distinctive of instrumental desires is not that they depend on beliefs, but that they depend on antecedent desires. When you want one thing "for the sake of" another thing, you antecedently want the second thing, to which you believe the first thing is a means.

To put this another way, non-instrumental desires need not be unconditional. You might non-instrumentally want to take a walk, but only on the condition that the sun is shining, the weather is mild, and there is a nice breeze. Indeed, you might non-instrumentally want to take a walk because the sun is shining, the weather is mild, and there is a nice breeze. In the same way, you might non-instrumentally want to take a walk only on the condition that you will enjoy taking a walk, and, indeed, non-instrumentally want to take a walk because you will enjoy taking a walk.

Now, recall the idea that thinking that nothing matters seems to put rational pressure on you to become indifferent to everything. In this way, nihilism about value (§1.1) seems to threaten our desires. However, if this is right, it is surely because thinking that nothing matters puts rational pressure on you to give up your non-instrumental desires. In as much as your instrumental desires are threatened by the thought that nothing matters, it is because your non-instrumental desires are threatened by the thought that nothing matters. If you want x on the premise that it is a means to y, the thought that nothing matters puts rational pressure on you to stop desiring x only insofar as it puts rational pressure on you to stop desiring y. It does nothing to call into question the premise that x is a means to y.

Thus, insofar as the problem of nihilism has to do with desire, it has to do with non-instrumental desire. For this reason, at this point I am going to assume that all desires are non-instrumental. In what follows, "desire," without qualification, always refers to non-instrumental desire.

We could understand this merely as a stipulation about "desire." Such a stipulation would be entirely warranted: in as much as desire admits of two species, instrumental desire and non-instrumental desire seem like very different sorts of things. It would be perfectly reasonable to focus our attention on non-instrumental desire and set instrumental desire aside. However, I think we could also, with some plausibility, understand the present assumption as the substantive claim that strictly speaking there are no "instrumental desires," because what we call "instrumental desires" are actually complexes of non-instrumental desire and belief. Your instrumental desires depend on your antecedent desires. Your desire to take an exercise class depends on your desire to get fitter, your desire to drink a bottle of Alphonse Mellot depends on your desire to drink a good Sancerre, and your desire to visit Seoul depends on your desire to take a nice vacation. On the view I want to suggest, to "instrumentally desire" x is to be in a complex state of mind that incorporates a desire for y and a belief that x is a means to y. Your desire for the means is not wholly distinct from your desire for the end. As I said, I find this fairly plausible. But the present assumption does not depend on this eliminative account of instrumental desire; it can be understood merely as a stipulation.

1.5 The Practical Theory of Desire

We want to understand the nature of desire (§1.3). Many philosophers have been inspired by G.E.M. Anscombe's (1963) example involving two different lists:

> Let us consider a man going round a town with a shopping list in his hand. Now it is clear that the relation of this list to the things he actually buys is

one and the same whether his wife gave him the list or it is his own list; and that there is a different relation when a list is made by a detective following him. [I]f the [shopping] list and the things that the man actually buys do not agree... then the mistake is not in the list but in the man's *performance*... whereas if the detective's record and what the man actually buys do not agree, then the mistake is in the record. (p. 56)

This example seems to illustrate something important about the nature of desire, and in particular about the essential difference between desire and belief. Here is John Searle (1983):

If my beliefs turn out to be wrong, it is my beliefs and not the world which is at fault, as is shown by the fact that I can correct the situation simply by changing my beliefs. It is the responsibility of the belief, so to speak, to match the world, and where the match fails I repair the situation by changing the belief. But if... my desires are unfulfilled I cannot in that way correct the situation by simply changing the... desire. In these cases it is, so to speak, the fault of the world if it fails to match... the desire, and I cannot fix things up by saying it was a mistaken... desire in the way that I can fix things up by saying it was a mistaken belief. Beliefs like statements can be true or false, and we might say they have the "mind-to-world" direction of fit. Desires... on the other hand, cannot be true or false, but can be... fulfilled... and we might say that they have the "world-to-mind" direction of fit. (p. 8)

Of course, the problem is with the "so to speak." False beliefs are mistaken, in virtue of failing to fit the world. But frustrating worlds, those that fail to fit our desires, are not mistaken—they are simply frustrating. However, some of the aforementioned philosophers have provided rigorous interpretations of "direction of fit" that avoid this worry.[20] For example, Michael Smith (1994) argues that the difference between desire and belief is a matter of their functional role or dispositional profile, and, in particular, that "a belief that p tends to go out of existence in the presence of a perception with the content that not p, whereas a desire that p tends to endure, disposing the subject to bring it about that p" (p. 115). And a natural move at this point is to conclude that desiring something is nothing other than such a disposition. As Robert Stalnaker (1987) proposes, "[t]o desire that *P* is to be disposed to

---

[20] For further discussion, see Schueler 1991, Humberstone 1992, Zangwill 1998, Sobel and Copp 2001, Coleman 2008, Gregory 2012, Frost 2014.

12 THE EPISTEMOLOGY OF DESIRE AND THE PROBLEM OF NIHILISM

act in ways that would tend to bring it about that P in a world in which one's beliefs, whatever they are, were true" (p. 15). Desire, on this view, is essentially a disposition to try to bring something about—or, as Anscombe (1963) puts it, "[t]he primitive sign of wanting is *trying to get*" (p. 68). This is what I am going to call the *practical theory of desire*.[21]

The practical theory of desire sits comfortably with the Humean solution to the problem of nihilism (§1.2). Desires are simply dispositions to try to bring things about. How could such dispositions be rational or irrational?

It seems to me that the practical theory of desire is profoundly mistaken. Imagine that you want the Celtics to the win the NBA Championship. Does this mean that you are disposed to try to bring it about that the Celtics win the NBA Championship? Does wanting the Celtics to win mean that you would do something to help them if you could, as in the loyal fan's fantasy of being called upon to help in some improbable way? Does your wanting the Celtics to win really amount to *that* disposition? Any emphasis on your disposition to bring it about that the Celtics win seems to have badly misidentified what makes it the case that you want them to win. As Anscombe (1963) herself discusses, there are idle wishes, where "a chief mark of an idle wish is that a man does nothing – whether he could or no – towards the fulfillment of the wish" (p. 67), and we sometimes hope that something will happen without our doing anything to bring it about (ibid.).[22]

Moreover, given that desiring includes wishing and being glad (§1.3), desires can be directed towards the past. Wishing the Celtics had won—or that Troy had not fallen (ibid.)—and being glad that they won do not entail dispositions to bring it about that they won.[23] Indeed, once we include wishing, it is clear that we can desire things that are impossible, e.g. you might wish that π were rational or that the sun would blow up (ibid.), which involves no disposition to try to bring anything about. Galen Strawson (2010, chapter 9) goes further, imagining organisms with no capacity for action at all, but nevertheless endowed with powers of perception and, it is easy to imagine, the capacity for desire.[24] It is possible to desire something

---

[21] See also Dretske 1988, chapter 5, Hulse et al. 2004, Brink 2008, p. 31.

[22] C.C.W Taylor (1986) says it is "peculiar" to want something to happen without wanting to act so as to bring it about (p. 221). Some cases like this are peculiar. Imagine that I want to drink a pint of beer but do not want to act so as it bring it about that I drink a pint of beer—suppose I want the beer to be poured down my throat without my consent. That's weird. But wanting the Celtics to win the NBA Championship, without wanting to act so as to bring it about that they win, is not weird.

[23] Cf. Kenny 1963, p. 115n.   [24] Cf. Searle 1992, pp. 65–70.

and yet not be disposed to try to bring it about. The practical theory of desire is false.[25]

However, there is a deeper problem with the practical theory. Desires are evaluations. The practical theory treats them as mere practical dispositions. This, I shall argue, is what is wrong, not only with the practical theory of desire, but with the Humean solution to the problem of nihilism.

1.6 Desire as Evaluation

In defense of the view that passions cannot be rational or irrational, Hume argued that passions cannot be accurate or inaccurate. As he put it: "[a] passion is an original existence...and contains not any representative quality"[26] and "passions are not susceptible of any...agreement or disagreement either to the *real* relations of ideas, or to *real* existence and matter of fact...being original facts and realities, compleat in themselves."[27] From this, Hume concluded that passions cannot be rational or irrational, apparently assuming that only things that can be accurate or inaccurate can be rational or irrational.

In so arguing, Hume initiated a tradition on which belief and desire fundamentally differ when it comes to accuracy: belief has an accuracy condition—namely, truth—and desire doesn't. For Hume and defenders of the Humean theory of practical rationality (§1.2), this fundamental difference between belief and desire is essential to explaining why beliefs can be rational or irrational and desires can't.

I am going to argue that desire has an accuracy condition. There is an intuitive, if difficult to articulate, connection between desire and goodness. We have a concept of something being desirable, which seems equivalent to the concept of its being good in some way or other. On my view, Anscombe (1963) gets the connection between desire and goodness exactly right when she writes that:

---

[25] There is, let us concede, a practical *sense* of "desire." This is yet another way in which "desire" is ambiguous. This seems to be Anscombe's view. She says that "we are not concerned with idle wishing" (1963, p. 67) and that "[t]he wanting that concerns us...is neither wishing nor hoping nor the feeling of desire" (ibid.). As this suggests, the practice sense of "desire" will be useful for certain theoretical purposes, e.g. theorizing intention (which is essentially practical; see Marks 1986, pp. 139–41, Schroeder 2004, pp. 16–20, Railton 2012, p. 33, Arpaly and Schroeder 2014, pp. 111–16).

[26] *Treatise*, 2.3.3.5.   [27] *Treatise*, 3.1.1.9.

14   THE EPISTEMOLOGY OF DESIRE AND THE PROBLEM OF NIHILISM

> The conceptual connection between 'wanting'...and 'good' can be compared
> to the conceptual connection between 'judgment' and 'truth'. (p. 76)

Swapping desire for 'wanting' and belief for 'judgment,' Anscombe's claim is
that the conceptual connection between desire and goodness is the same as
the conceptual connection between belief and truth. Donald Davidson
(1970/2001) similarly suggests an analogy between the relationship between
belief and truth and the relationship between desire and goodness.
Explaining the principle of charity as an essential constraint on interpretation, he writes that:

> In our need to make sense of [someone], we will try for a theory that finds
> him consistent, a believer of truths, and a lover of the good (all by our own
> lights, it goes without saying). (p. 222; see also 1978/2001, p. 86 and p. 97)

Well, what is the conceptual connection between belief and truth? It seems
to me that it is simply that truth is the accuracy condition for belief. Thus,
given Anscombe's claim, it follows that goodness is the accuracy condition
for desire. As Anscombe puts it, "[t]ruth is the object of judgment, and
good the object of wanting" (1963, p. 76).[28]

More precisely, here is what I am going to defend in this book:

> AD   A desire that p is accurate if and only if (and because) it is good
> that p and inaccurate if and only if (and because) it is bad that p.[29]

AD is the most plausible formulation of the idea that we desire things
"under the guise of the good,"[30] which itself is a formulation of the idea that
everyone desires the good.[31] I will have quite a bit more to say about how

---

[28] For other defenses and suggestions of AD, see Brentano 1889/1969, pp. 14–18, 1956,
pp. 175–6, Norman 1971, De Sousa 1974, pp. 538–9, 1987, p. 122, Quinn 1993, Helm 2001,
chapter 3, Thompson 2008, pp. 117–18, Hawkins 2008, Zagzebski 2012, pp. 75–6, Friedrich
2017, Lauria 2017, and those cited below as defenders of the evaluative belief (§1.7) and evaluative perception (§1.8) theories of desire.

[29] AD says that goodness is the accuracy condition for desire and that badness is the inaccuracy condition for desire. In what follows, I'll use "goodness is the accuracy condition for
desire" to mean both of these things, i.e. to express what AD says.

[30] Aquinas, *Summa Theologica* I-II, Q1, Art. 1, Kant, *Critique of Practical Reason* 5:59–60;
see also Raz 1999, chapter 2, 2010.

[31] Plato, *Gorgias* 466e–468d, *Meno* 77c–78b, *Symposium* 205a, *Protagoras* 358c–d, Aristotle,
De Anima III.10 433a27–29, *Nicomachean Ethics* III.4 1113a15–1113b1, V.9 1136b7–8, VIII.2
1155b21–27, IX.3 1165b14–15, *Eudemian Ethics* VII.2 1235b25–29. For further discussion, see
Moss 2012, Pearson 2012, Callard 2017.

INTRODUCTION 15

AD is to be understood in Chapter 2. For now, note not only that AD is not only incompatible with Hume's claim that desires cannot be accurate or inaccurate, but that AD nicely explains why the problem of nihilism is a problem in the first place. If goodness is the accuracy condition for desire, wanting something you believe is not good seems analogous to believing something you think it is not true, which is patently irrational. Isn't it then clear that wanting something you believe is not good is, in the same way, irrational?

1.7 The Evaluative Belief Theory of Desire

Some philosophers argue that desire is a species of belief, e.g. that desires are beliefs about reasons[32] or that desires are beliefs about goodness.[33] Let's say that an *evaluative belief* is a belief that it is good that p. Consider the view that you desire that p if and only if you believe that it is good that p. This is what I am going to call the *evaluative belief theory of desire*. The evaluative belief theory of desire is compatible with AD. Indeed, given that truth is the accuracy condition for belief (§1.6), the view that desires are evaluative beliefs entails that a desire that p is accurate if and only if it is good that p.[34] However, AD does not entail that desires are evaluative beliefs. AD says that goodness is the accuracy condition for desire, in the same way that truth is the accuracy condition for belief, but the fact that truth is the accuracy condition for belief does not entail that you believe that p if and only if you believe that it is true that p.

Intuitively, desire and evaluative belief are distinct: you can desire something without believing that it is good—as in the case of someone who has an inexplicable desire to drink a can of paint[35]—and you can believe that something is good without desiring it—as when someone overcome with depression or malaise finds themselves unmoved by what they believe is good.

Given AD, and given that truth is the accuracy condition for belief (§1.6), desire and evaluative belief have the same accuracy condition.[36] A desire that p and a belief that it is good that p are both accurate if and only if it is

---

[32] Gregory 2013, 2017, 2018, 2021.   [33] Humberstone 1987.
[34] Assuming, also, that it is true that p if and only if p.
[35] Davidson 1963/2001, p. 4; see also Anscombe 1963, §37, Quinn 1993, p. 32, Scanlon 1998, p. 40.
[36] Assuming, again, that it is true that p if and only if p.

16 THE EPISTEMOLOGY OF DESIRE AND THE PROBLEM OF NIHILISM

good that p. But this does not mean that desire is evaluative belief. Mental representations are not individuated (only) by their accuracy conditions.[37] Distinct mental representations with the same accuracy condition can differ in at least three ways.

First, distinct mental representations with the same accuracy condition can differ in their phenomenology—think here of the difference between perceiving that p and (non-perceptually) believing that p. However, neither desire nor evaluative belief has a distinctive phenomenology, so this kind of difference does not explain the distinctness of desire and evaluative belief.

Second, distinct mental representations with the same accuracy condition can differ in their functional role or dispositional profile—think here of the difference between believing that p and supposing that p. Desire and belief plausibly differ when it comes to functional role or dispositional profile. That is the insight that motivates the practical theory of desire (§1.5): desiring that p tends to cause you to act so as to bring it about that p and acquiring evidence that not-p tends to cause us to stop believing that p. However, desire and *evaluative* belief do not seem to differ in these ways, at least not in such a way that would explain their distinctness.[38] It seems like evaluative belief can motivate action—your believing that it is good that p might cause you to act so as to bring it about that p. And it seems like counter-evidence can destroy desire—possessing strong, undefeated evidence that it would not be good if it were the case that p might cause you not to desire that p, although I will have more to say in defense of this possibility in Chapter 5.

Now, there do seem to be various ways in which desire and evaluative belief differ in their functional role or dispositional profile. Desire seems connected to emotion in a way that evaluative belief isn't: it is typically frustrating or unsatisfying to know that not-p while desiring that p, but it might easily happen that you know that not-p while believing that it would be good if it were the case that p and yet feel nothing at all. And evaluative belief seems connected to other beliefs in a way that desire isn't: someone who believes that it is good that p will typically be disposed to believe the consequences of the proposition that it is good that p—simply because someone who believes something will typically be disposed to believe its consequences—but it might easily happen that you desire that p and yet are not disposed to believe that it is good that p (cf. §7.2).[39] Finally, recalcitrant

---

[37] Cf. Velleman 2000.   [38] Cf. Price 1989, pp. 119–21.
[39] Cf. Oddie 2005, chapters 3–5.

desire (i.e. desire that remains despite strong, undefeated evidence that its object is not good) is a far more familiar phenomenon than recalcitrant evaluative belief (i.e. evaluative belief that remains despite strong, undefeated evidence that its object is not true) (cf. §5.10). However, it seems to me that all of these differences are only a matter of degree, and thus not suitable to explain the in-kind distinction between desire and evaluative belief. I conclude that a difference in functional role or dispositional profile does not explain the distinctness of desire and evaluative belief.

Third, distinct mental representations with the same accuracy condition can differ in their content—think here of the difference between believing that p and believing that it is true that p. Believing that it is true that p requires deploying the concept of truth, because truth is part of the content of such a belief. Believing that p, by contrast, does not require deploying the concept of truth, because truth may be no part of the content of such a belief. Nevertheless, both a belief that p and a belief that it is true that p are accurate if and only if it is true that p.[40] Even though they have the same accuracy condition, a belief that it is true that p is more conceptually sophisticated than a belief that p.

The difference between desire and evaluative belief, I propose, is a difference in content. Believing that it is good that p requires deploying the concept of goodness, because goodness is part of the content of such a belief. Desiring that p, by contrast, does not require deploying the concept of goodness, because goodness may be no part of the content of such a desire (cf. §2.2). Even though they have the same accuracy condition, a belief that it is good that p is more conceptually sophisticated than a desire that p. This account of the difference between desire and evaluative belief vindicates the intuitive view that desire and evaluative belief are distinct. It certainly seems like you can desire something without believing that it is good and believe that something is good without desiring it. That desire and evaluative belief differ in content explains why.[41]

---

[40] Assuming, again, that it is true that p if and only if p.

[41] David Lewis (1988, 1996) argues against what he calls the "desire-as-belief thesis." But his argument does not target the claim that you desire all and only what you believe to be good, which we have been considering here, but rather the claim that *rationality requires* desiring all and only what you believe to be good (cf. Broome 1991, p. 265, Byrne and Hájek 1997, p. 411, Piller 2000, p. 210; Hájek and Pettit 2004, p. 77, Bradley and Stefánsson 2016, p. 691). Thus, Lewis' argument will not help us refute the evaluative belief theory of desire. However, you might think that Lewis' argument makes as much trouble for AD as it does for the view that rationality requires desiring all and only what you believe to be good. All the better, then, that its soundness is controversial (Oddie 1994, 2001, Piller 2000, Bradley and List 2009, Stefánsson 2014, Bradley and Stefánsson 2016).

18 THE EPISTEMOLOGY OF DESIRE AND THE PROBLEM OF NIHILISM

To put all this another way, AD says that goodness is the *formal* object of desire, not that goodness is the *particular* object of desire.[42] If you want to take a walk, the particular object of your desire is your going for a walk. What AD says is that your desire is accurate if and only if your going for a walk would be good, i.e. that goodness is the formal object of your desire. This is just another way of saying that the goodness of the proposition that p is no part of the content of a desire that p. And to put all this yet another way, AD is a claim about the *force* of desire, not a claim about its *content*.[43] It is a claim about how desired things are represented, in virtue of being desired, and not a claim about what things are desired.

1.8 The Evaluative Perception Theory of Desire

Some philosophers argue that desires are, or are analogous to, perceptions or appearances of goodness.[44] As I understand it, on this view desire is a species of perceptual experience. This is what I am going to call the *evaluative perception theory of desire*. The evaluative perception theory of desire is compatible with AD. Consider the view that perceptual experience has an accuracy condition, such that a perceptual experience of a as F is accurate if and only if a is F and inaccurate otherwise.[45] If this is right, and if desire is a species of perceptual experience, then AD would be a natural and elegant way of capturing the idea that desires are perceptions or appearances of goodness.[46]

In this book I'm going to remain neutral on the question of whether perceptual experience has an accuracy condition.[47] But I am happy to grant it for the sake of argument. The problem with the view that desire is a species

---

[42] Cf. De Sousa 1974.

[43] Cf. Brentano 1874/1973, pp. 201–2, 1889/1969, pp. 15–17; see also Frege 1918–19/1956, pp. 293–5, Searle 1983, pp. 5–7.

[44] Stampe 1986, 1987, Johnston 2001, Tenenbaum 2003, 2007, Oddie 2005, 2017, Schafer 2013; see also Noordhof 2018, pp. 103–7.

[45] Cf. Johnston 2011, Siegel 2011, Byrne 2015, Jenkin 2020.

[46] The evaluative perception theory of desire entails, but is not entailed by, the view that there is such a thing as evaluative perception, on which see McGrath 2004, 2018, Chappell 2008, Cullison 2009, Dancy 2010, Audi 2010, 2013, 2018, McBrayer 2010a, 2010b, Cowan 2015, Werner 2016, Noordhof 2018. Note that some but not all defenders of evaluative perception treat it as a species of sense perception.

[47] As well as on the question of whether all species of experience have accuracy conditions. You might think that some species of experience—e.g. mere sensation—have no accuracy condition.

INTRODUCTION   19

of perceptual experience is that desire, unlike perceptual experience, is susceptible to deliberation. To say that a kind of mental representation is susceptible to deliberation is to say that instances of that kind can be formed through deliberation. Belief is susceptible to deliberation, in the sense that beliefs can be formed through deliberation. Perceptual experience, by contrast with belief, is not susceptible to deliberation. It is impossible to form a perceptual experience through deliberation. If desire is a species of perceptual experience, then desire is not susceptible to deliberation. However, desire is susceptible to deliberation. I articulate and defend this claim in Chapter 5.

1.9 The Prospective Theory of Desire

Lloyd Humberstone (1987), in his defense of a version of the evaluative belief theory of desire (§1.7), considers and rejects the view that you desire that p if and only if you believe that you would be happy if it were the case that p (p. 49). Peter Railton (2012, 2017) defends something in this neighborhood. On his (2012) "prospective account of desire" (p. 43), to desire that p is in part to have "a degree of positive evaluation (affective forecast)…toward the act or state of affairs that p" (p. 45), or, alternatively (2017), "a degree of expectation that [the act or state of affairs that] p will be satisfying or beneficial" (p. 262). The common idea here is that your desiring something incorporates a representation of its predicted effects on you—your happiness or well-being or pleasure.[48] Let's call this view, following Railton, but without going into the other details of his account, the *prospective theory of desire.*

On the prospective theory of desire there is a sense in which desire is a species of evaluation: on this view, desires are prudential evaluations. The prospective theory is therefore at least superficially similar to AD, which also implies that desire is a species of evaluation (§1.6). However, as will

---

[48] On Timothy Schroeder's (2004) "reward theory of desire," to desire that P is to "use the capacity to perceptually or cognitively represent that P to constitute P as a reward" (p. 131), and (psychologically speaking) something is a reward for an organism when it "tends to contribute to the production of a reinforcement signal in the organism" (p. 66; see also 2017, Arpaly and Schroeder 2014, chapter 6, Schroeder and Arpaly 2014). If constituting something as a reward involves representing its predicted effects on you, then his account is also in the neighborhood of the prospective theory of desire. However, if constituting something as a reward is merely a functional or dispositional matter, then his account looks more like the practical theory of desire (§1.5).

20 THE EPISTEMOLOGY OF DESIRE AND THE PROBLEM OF NIHILISM

emerge in what follows, this similarity is merely superficial. The accuracy condition for desire, according to AD, is goodness, not prudential goodness (§2.6). The prospective theory of desire has more in common with the practical theory of desire (§1.5), on which desire is not a species of evaluation. The prospective theory of desire sits more comfortably with Hume's own position on the passions (§1.2) than with the idea that we desire things "under the guise of the good," as Railton (2012) emphasizes (pp. 43–4), especially when we are careful to distinguish Hume's own views from those associated with the Humean theory of practical rationality.[49]

1.10 AD Is Not a Theory of Desire

Recall Anscombe's idea that there is a conceptual connection between desire and goodness, analogous to the conceptual connection between belief and truth (§1.6). That the connection between belief and truth is conceptual entails that truth is the *constitutive* accuracy condition for belief: part of what it is to be a belief is to have truth as your accuracy condition. However, the claim that truth is the constitutive accuracy condition for belief is not a theory of belief, because the fact that truth is the accuracy condition for belief does not exhaust the nature of belief. Truth is also the constitutive accuracy condition for suspicion: a suspicion that p is accurate if and only if it is true that p and inaccurate if and only if it is false that p.[50] Part of what it is to be a belief is to have truth as your accuracy condition, but there is more to the nature of belief than that.

In the same way, that the analogous connection between desire and goodness is conceptual entails that goodness is the *constitutive* accuracy condition for desire: part of what it is to be a desire is to have goodness as your accuracy condition. However, AD is not a theory of desire, because the fact that goodness is the accuracy condition for desire does not exhaust the nature of desire. Given that truth is the constitutive accuracy condition for belief, goodness is also the constitutive accuracy condition for evaluative belief, which is distinct from desire, on my view (§1.7). Part of what it is to be a desire is to have goodness as your accuracy condition, but there is more to the nature of desire than that.

---

[49] Cf. Railton 2007, 2017, and Schroeder's (2017) description of his reward theory of desire as "neo-Humean."
[50] Cf. Velleman 2000, pp. 247–50.

INTRODUCTION   21

We have described several accounts of the nature of desire—the practical theory of desire (§1.5), the evaluative belief theory of desire (§1.7), the evaluative perception theory of desire (§1.8), and the prospective theory of desire (§1.9). The practical theory and the prospective theory are incompatible with AD. The evaluative belief theory and the evaluative perception theory are compatible with AD, but neither is entailed by AD. AD tells us that desire has a constitutive accuracy condition, and it tells us what that constitutive accuracy condition is, but it does not provide a complete answer to the question of what desire is. AD tells us something important about the nature of desire, but it does not tell us the whole story.

I will not provide a theory of desire in this book. However, because I think desire is neither a species of belief nor a species of perceptual experience, I think desire is a *sui generis* mental representation—at least relative to belief and perceptual experience. Although this is not a theory of desire— i.e. not an account of the nature of desire—it is a theoretical position distinct from the four theories of desire we have encountered.

1.11   Desire and the Emotions

Hobbes, Descartes, and Hume (cf. §1.2) all classify desire as a passion.[51] In one sense, to call something a "passion" is to say that we are passive with respect to it. Passions, in this sense, are to be distinguished from judgment, with respect to which we are not passive. Since I think desire, like belief, is susceptible to deliberation (§1.8), I do not think desire is a passion in this sense. However, in another sense, to call something a "passion" is to say that it is an emotion or some kind of affective phenomenon. Is desire an emotion? And, more broadly, what is the relationship between desire and emotion? And how do these questions bear on my arguments in this book?

Many philosophers (among others) argue that emotions are evaluations.[52] If desires are evaluations, as I maintain (§1.6), then emotion and desire are at least species of the same genus. There are in-house disagreements

---

[51] See *Leviathan* 1.6, *Passions of the Soul* §57, *Treatise of Human Nature* 2.1.1, *Dissertation on the Passions* 1.6.

[52] See Broad 1954, Peters 1970, Solomon 1973, 1993, 2004, 2007, Taylor 1975, Lyons 1980, Marks 1982, De Sousa 1987, Greenspan 1988, 2004, Roberts 1988, 2003, Goldie 2000, 2004, Helm 2001, chapter 3, 2009, Döring 2003, 2007, Nussbaum 2001, Zagzebski 2012, chapter 4, Audi 2013, Brady 2013, Price 2015, Tappolet 2016, Magalotti and Kriegel 2021; see also Kenny 1963.

22 THE EPISTEMOLOGY OF DESIRE AND THE PROBLEM OF NIHILISM

between those who argue that emotions are evaluations, including disagreements about whether emotions are species of belief or judgment and about whether emotions can be accurate or inaccurate. I am not going to discuss any of those disagreements here.

Some philosophers identify particular emotions with particular desires. So, for example, Hobbes defines covetousness as a desire for wealth and Spinoza defines anger as a desire to inflict injury on someone you hate.[53] Aquinas suggests that emotions are species of desire,[54] and Anthony Kenny (1963) argues that "one emotion differs from another because of the different sort of things it makes one want to do" (p. 100). However, all these philosophers seem to be assuming the practical theory of desire (§1.5). This, at least, is clear when it comes to the practical theory of emotion—described by some defenders as a "conative" theory[55]—on which emotions are action tendencies.[56] Indeed, the practical theory of desire is widely assumed in the philosophical literature on emotion, where many argue that at least some emotions are not species of desire on the grounds that at least some emotions do not entail any practical dispositions or on the grounds that desires are not evaluations.[57]

Assuming the practical theory of desire is false, how plausible is it that emotions are species of desire? At least with some emotions this seems quite plausible. Fear plausibly incorporates a desire to escape from or avoid its object.[58] You are not afraid of spiders if you have no desire at all to stay away from them or to be rid of them. I don't mean that fear requires taking action. You might conquer or repress your fear and take a close look at a big spider or abide a small one living in your bathroom.[59] My point is that you would do these things despite wanting to do otherwise. Contrast a fearless arachnologist handling a venomous spider, who knows that the spider is dangerous, but is utterly unafraid. Both the arachnologist and the arachnophobe might remain calm around dangerous spiders, but only the arachnophobe does so in spite of a desire to freak out and run away. However, the case of

---

[53] *Leviathan* 1.6, *Ethics* 3.36.

[54] *Summa Theologica* I-II, Q22; see also Peters 1970, pp. 193–4, Marks, 1982, pp. 231–2, Solomon 1993, pp. 220, 2004, 2007, p. 147. For further discussion, see Taylor 1975, pp. 217–18, Lyons 1980, pp. 17–25, pp. 36–7.

[55] Frijda 1986, p. 5.   [56] See Frijda 1986, Deonna and Teroni 2012, Scarantino 2014.

[57] See e.g. De Sousa 1987, p. 168, Greenspan 1988, p. 33, p. 51, Goldie 2000, p. 36, pp. 78–9, Nussbaum 2001, p. 48, Döring 2003, pp. 219–20, Deonna and Teroni 2012, p. 30, Tappolet 2012, 2016, p. 11, p. 36, Brady 2013, p. 32, Price 2015, p. 98.

[58] Kenny 1963, p. 99, Lyons 1980, p. 94, Marks 1982, pp. 231–2, Solomon 1993, p. 254.

[59] Kenny 1963, p. 68.

INTRODUCTION   23

fear involves a desire to perform some action. Given our assumption that the practical theory of desire is false, we need to consider cases that do not involve a desire to perform some action, such as grief and pride. Could you grieve without wishing, at least to some degree, that things had been otherwise?[60] Could you be proud without being glad, at least to some extent, that things happened as they did? However, there are harder cases. Does contentment[61] or awe[62] require any desire? Perhaps merely a desire to continue doing what you are doing.[63] For my purposes in this book, we can leave open whether emotions are species of desire.

Consider, again, the question of whether desire is an emotion. There are various reasons you might have for thinking that desire is not an emotion. You might think desire is not an emotion because emotions, unlike desires (cf. §1.5), are essentially practical, incorporating dispositions to act in particular ways. You might think that desire is not an emotion because emotions, unlike desires (cf. §1.7), have a phenomenal character or a distinctive phenomenology, i.e. a way that they feel. You might think that desire is not an emotion because emotions, unlike desires (cf. §1.9), are essentially self-involving or prudential. You might think that desire is not an emotion because emotions, unlike desires, are essentially embodied or concerned with the body. Finally, you might think that desire is not an emotion because emotions, unlike desires (cf. §1.8), are not susceptible to deliberation.

It seems to me that, although both desires and emotions are evaluations, they are fundamentally different kinds of evaluation. Consider, again, the case of fear, and assume that fear incorporates a desire to escape from or avoid its object. Imagine that you are afraid of ordinary isopods, i.e. "roly-polys" or "pillbugs." Given the present assumption, your fear incorporates a desire to escape from or avoid isopods. According to AD, that desire is accurate if and only if it would be good were you to escape from or avoid isopods and inaccurate if and only if it would be bad were you to escape from or avoid isopods. In that sense, your desire represents your escaping from or avoiding isopods as good. That is the sense in which, given AD, your desire is an evaluation. However, according to the aforementioned contemporary defenders of the view that emotions are evaluations, fear represents its object as dangerous.[64] Your fear of isopods is accurate if and only if isopods are dangerous and inaccurate if and only if isopods are not dangerous. That is the sense in which, according to them, your fear is an

---

[60] Cf. Lyons 1980, p. 96.   [61] Solomon 1993, pp. 235–6.
[62] Lyons 1980, p. 58.   [63] Taylor 1986, p. 226.   [64] Or threatening, fearsome, etc.

24 THE EPISTEMOLOGY OF DESIRE AND THE PROBLEM OF NIHILISM

evaluation. We have here two evaluations: the evaluation of escaping from or avoiding isopods as good and the evaluation of isopods as dangerous. Fear may well incorporate both. But the evaluation that is distinctive of fear, according to contemporary defenders of the view that emotions are evaluations, is not an evaluation of escaping from or avoiding the object of fear as good. How these two evaluations are related is an important topic that I do not address in this book.[65]

1.12 The Epistemology of Desire

My primary aim in this book is to motivate and solve the problem of nihilism. Central to this task will be an articulation and defense of AD. However, I got interested in AD not because of the problem of nihilism, but because of its implications in epistemology. For this reason, I have a secondary aim here: to explore those implications. Moreover, my solution to the problem of nihilism requires understanding it as an epistemological problem. Thus, issues in epistemology will be central in what follows.

What is epistemology? Like most questions about disciplinary and sub-disciplinary boundaries, the answer to this question is not obvious. When it comes to contemporary epistemology, the question is especially difficult to answer. It might have done once to define epistemology as the theory of knowledge, but recent developments in epistemology—developments that are obviously and uncontroversially *in epistemology*—make that answer unacceptable. For one thing, many contemporary epistemologists defend theories of knowledge on which justification is not necessary for knowledge.[66] And yet the nature and scope of justification is surely a topic in epistemology. For another thing, many contemporary epistemologists argue that understanding is not a species of knowledge.[67] And yet the nature and scope of understanding is surely a topic in epistemology.[68] Contemporary epistemology seems in various ways preoccupied with the nature of epistemology—consider recent debates about the nature and scope of

---

[65] Cf. Lyons 1980, pp. 93–5, Marks 1982, p. 232.

[66] E.g. Goldman 1967, Nozick 1981, chapter 3, Foley 1993, pp. 85–8, Zagzebski 1996, Part III, chapter 2, Greco 2010, chapter 5.

[67] E.g. Zagzebski 2001, Kvanvig 2003, Pritchard 2010.

[68] This is not even to mention a number of trending topics in contemporary epistemology, including epistemic injustice, moral encroachment, and intellectual virtue, that are not in any straightforward way questions about knowledge. Could a case be made that these topics are not part of epistemology proper? Perhaps.

INTRODUCTION   25

"epistemic value,"[69] the nature and source of "epistemic normativity,"[70] the role of intuitions and the viability of conceptual analysis in epistemology,[71] the relationship between moral and epistemic virtues,[72] and sub-epistemological distinctions between "epistemic" and "theoretical" rationality, "gnoseology" and "intellectual ethics," and "epistemic" and "zetetic" norms.[73]

One familiar way of thinking about epistemology posits an essential connection between epistemology and *belief*. Although this way of thinking is not often made explicit, I think it is fairly widespread. It is suggested by the way that many of us are inclined to characterize epistemology when we introduce the subject. For example, Richard Fumerton (2006) describes "epistemological questions" as those that "involve the concepts of knowledge, evidence, reasons for believing, justification, probability, what one ought to believe, and any other concepts that can only be understood through one or more of the above" (p. 1). For another example, Linda Zagzebski (2008) describes epistemology as "the philosophical study of knowing and other desirable ways of believing and attempting to find the truth" (p. 1). And, for a final example, Richard Feldman (2003) writes that "[e]pistemologists are primarily interested in questions about the nature of knowledge and the principles governing rational belief" (p. 1). Each of these characterizations suggest an essential connection between epistemology and belief, to the effect that epistemology is essentially and distinctively concerned with questions about the nature and scope of rational or justified belief or with questions about what you ought to believe. Even philosophers who suggest broader conceptions of epistemology retain an essential connection between epistemology and the intellect. So, for example, elsewhere Zagzebski (1996) argues that the intellectual virtues are "all forms of the motivation to have cognitive contact with reality" (p. 167) and, for another, Matthias Steup and Ram Neta (2020) define epistemology as concerned with "cognitive" success and failure.

I think this is wrong. Given AD, because desire, like belief, has an accuracy condition, it is an appropriate target of epistemological inquiry, in the same way that belief is an appropriate target of epistemological inquiry.

---

[69] E.g. Zagzebski 2003, Haddock et al. 2009, Ahlstrom-Vij and Grimm 2013.
[70] E.g. Kelly 2003, Sosa 2007, chapter 4, Hazlett 2013, Littlejohn and Turri 2014, Henderson and Greco 2015, Maguirre and Woods 2020.
[71] E.g. Weinberg et al. 2001, Nichols et al. 2003, Goldman 2007, Sosa 2007, chapter 3, 2009a, Cappelen 2012, Nagel 2012.
[72] E.g. Zagzebski 1996, Part II, chapter 3, Driver 2003, Baehr 2011, Appendix, Wilson 2017.
[73] See, respectively, Kelly 2003, pp. 636–7, Sosa 2007, pp. 88–91, 2021, chapter 2, Friedman 2020.

26 THE EPISTEMOLOGY OF DESIRE AND THE PROBLEM OF NIHILISM

"Epistemology" is the right word here, because accuracy is the fundamental explanatory concept. If I am right, epistemology has no essential connection to belief—at least, no essential connection that it does not also have to desire. Just as there is an "epistemology of belief," there is an "epistemology of desire."

1.13 Synopsis

Here is the plan for the book.

Chapters 2, 3, and 4 constitute my defense of AD. In Chapter 2, I articulate and clarify AD. In Chapter 3, I argue that AD provides the best explanation of why it makes sense to criticize a desire on the grounds that its object is bad. In Chapter 4, I argue that the fact that desires can amount to knowledge is an appealing consequence of AD.

Chapters 5, 6, and 7 are concerned with the problem of nihilism. In Chapter 5, in defense of the view that desires can be irrational, I argue that desire is susceptible to deliberation, which turns out to be essential for the problem of nihilism. In Chapter 6, I articulate the problem of nihilism and discuss some more or less unsuccessful solutions to it. In Chapter 7, I argue that it can be rationally permissible to desire something you believe is not good, which, I maintain, solves the problem of nihilism.

If you were primarily interested in the problem of nihilism, you could skip Chapter 4 without losing too much. If you were primarily interested in the epistemology of desire, and were prepared to grant AD, you could focus on Chapters 4 and 5. If you were primarily interested in the idea that goodness is the accuracy condition for desire, and more broadly with the idea that desires are evaluations, you could focus on Chapters 2 and 3. Of course, I hope you will read everything, carefully and twice.

I am a fan of cross-referencing and my aim has been to ensure that you can find your way around when implicit or explicit reference is made to other parts of the book. However, there are two named principles that are invoked so frequently that I have chosen never to provide cross-references to the sections in which they are introduced. One is AD, which is given its official statement in §1.6 and then restated in §2.2. The other is AB—on which truth is the accuracy condition for belief—which is given its official statement in §2.1.

The Epistemology of Desire and the Problem of Nihilism. Allan Hazlett, Oxford University Press.
© Allan Hazlett 2024. DOI: 10.1093/9780191995583.003.0001

2

Accurate Desire

Hume maintained that desire has no accuracy condition; I maintain that goodness is the accuracy condition for desire (§1.6). However, there are many ways in which this claim might be misunderstood. We need to get clear on exactly what this means. That is the goal of this chapter.

Recall Anscombe's idea (§1.6): the conceptual connection between desire and goodness is the same as the conceptual connection between belief and truth. If this is our leading idea, we need to begin by asking: what exactly is the conceptual connection between belief and truth?

2.1 Truth as the Accuracy Condition for Belief

I propose that the following captures the conceptual connection between belief and truth:

> AB   A belief that p is accurate if and only if (and because) it is true that p and inaccurate if and only if (and because) it is false that p.

AB tells us the conditions under which a belief, whose content is the proposition that p, is accurate or inaccurate.[1] And what it says is: the truth of the proposition that p is the accuracy condition, and the falsehood of the proposition that p the inaccuracy condition, for belief.[2]

AB presupposes that belief is a propositional attitude, which takes the form of believing that p. I will sometimes have occasion to speak of beliefs as having "objects," e.g. when I say (below) that there is a sense in which belief represents its object as true. However, I do not mean to imply the

---

[1] Here, and in what follows, I'll use "a belief that p" in such a way that it does not presuppose that anyone actually believes that p. For example, if it is true that p, then a belief that p is accurate—i.e. if p and you believe that p, then your belief is accurate.

[2] In what follows, I'll use "truth is the accuracy condition for belief" to mean both that truth is the accuracy condition for belief and that falsehood is the inaccuracy condition for belief, i.e. to express what AB says.

28 THE EPISTEMOLOGY OF DESIRE AND THE PROBLEM OF NIHILISM

assumption of any substantive metaphysical claims about propositions, e.g. that propositions are objects to which we are related when we have propositional attitudes. To say that a belief has a particular object is just to say that it is a belief that p, for some proposition that p.

The concepts of accuracy and inaccuracy are reasonably familiar concepts and I think it is unlikely that they admit of explication or definition in terms of more familiar concepts. I mentioned, above, the view that perceptual experiences can be accurate or inaccurate (§1.8). Speech acts can be accurate or inaccurate: assertions, for example, are accurate if and only if they are true and inaccurate if and only if they are false. Pictures, it seems to me, can be accurate or inaccurate: they are accurate if and only if they are veridical, i.e. faithful or true to their subjects, and inaccurate if and only if they are falsidical, i.e. unfaithful or false to their subjects. Although the concepts of accuracy and inaccuracy are reasonably familiar, that is not to say that we would not like a metaphysical account of them, such as would be provided by, for example, a naturalistic account of representation. I neither assume nor provide such an account here.

AB says that belief has an accuracy condition. Imagination, by contrast, does not have an accuracy condition.[3] Suppose you daydream that you are eating lunch at a seaside café while not eating lunch at a seaside café. You imagine that you are eating lunch at a seaside café, and yet it is false that you are eating lunch at a seaside café. But your daydream is not inaccurate, in the way that a false belief or a false assertion is inaccurate. Truth, at least, is not the accuracy condition for imagination. However, you might think that (non-epistemic) possibility is the accuracy condition for imagination, such that an episode of imagining that p is accurate if and only if it is possible that p and inaccurate if and only if it is impossible that p.[4] If so, your daydream is accurate, because it is possible that you are eating lunch at a seaside café. However, it seems to me that possibility is not the accuracy condition for imagination. Imagine that you daydream, instead, about doing something impossible, like visiting the barber who shaves all and only those who do not shave themselves. Your daydream is not inaccurate, in the way that a false belief or a false assertion is inaccurate.[5]

---

[3] At least not essentially; there may be species of imagination that have an accuracy condition (cf. Hazlett 2017a).
[4] Cf. Yablo 1993, Hart 1988, chapter 2.
[5] You might object that you cannot really *imagine* something that isn't possible, in the same way that you cannot really *perceive* something that isn't actual (cf. Hart 1988). However, in that case, just as we sometimes seem to perceive unreal things in virtue of having inaccurate perceptual experiences—assuming, again, that perceptual experience has an accuracy condition

ACCURATE DESIRE   29

Note that AB represents an account of accurate belief, on which accurate beliefs are accurate in virtue of being true and inaccurate beliefs are inaccurate in virtue of being false (and on which a true belief is thereby an accurate belief and a false belief is thereby an inaccurate belief).

Given AB there is a sense in which to believe something is to represent it as true. In this sense, belief represents its object as good. But there is also a sense in which believing something does not require representing it as true, because believing does not require deploying the concept of truth, and there is a sense in which to represent x as F requires deploying the concept of being F. Consider believing that a is F, which requires deploying the concept of being F, but does not require deploying the concept of truth.

AB says that truth is the accuracy condition for belief. We could have said that truth is the formal object of belief (cf. §1.7). We could have said that truth is the "aim of belief" or "norm of belief," but those formulations are obscure and open to multiple interpretations.[6] We could have said that truth is the correctness condition for belief or that truth is the fittingness condition for belief, but both "correct" and "fitting" are ambiguous in this context. These ambiguities deserve comment. First, there is a sense in which to say that an attitude is correct or fitting is to say that it is rational. However, not all true beliefs are rational and some false beliefs are rational. Second, there is a sense in which to say that an attitude is correct or fitting is to say that it makes sense given the circumstances. However, not all true beliefs make sense given the circumstances and some false beliefs make sense given the circumstances. Third, there is a sense in which to say that something is correct or fitting is to say that it is prudent relative to some aim. Given the rules of chess and its constitutive aim of checkmating your opponent, it is generally correct or fitting to exchange a pawn for a queen.[7] Now, perhaps it could be argued that believing the truth is always prudent relative to some aim—the "aim of belief," presumably. But that is not what AB says. Fourth, there is a sense in which to say that something is correct or fitting is to say that it is proper relative to some norm. Given certain conventional norms of etiquette, it is only correct to set the salad fork to the left of the dinner fork.

(§1.8)—there is plausibly some mental state in virtue of which we sometimes seem to imagine impossible things. If possibility were the accuracy condition for imagination, that mental state would presumably be inaccurate in the relevant cases. But there is intuitively no inaccuracy involved when you daydream about visiting the barber who shaves all and only those who do not shave themselves.

[6] Cf. Wedgwood 2002, Boghossian 2003, 2005, Owens 2003, Shah 2003, Steglich-Petersen 2006, 2009, Sosa 2009b, McHugh 2011, Chan 2013.

[7] Cf. Maguirre and Woods 2020.

30   THE EPISTEMOLOGY OF DESIRE AND THE PROBLEM OF NIHILISM

There is a sense in which the salad fork ought only be set to the left of the dinner fork. Perhaps truth is the "norm of belief" in a related sense, such that you ought to believe only what is true. But that is not what AB says. "Correct" and "fitting" admit of these various interpretations; "accurate" doesn't.

Accuracy is not a prescriptive or deontic concept. AB entails neither that, if it is true that p, then you ought to believe that p, nor that, if you ought to believe that p, then it is true that p. If the normative is equivalent to the prescriptive or the deontic, then accuracy is not a normative concept. That "correct" and "fitting" admit of prescriptive or deontic readings is clear from the fact that it sounds fine to ask of someone whether it is correct or fitting for them to believe that p. It sounds weird, by contrast, to ask of someone whether it is accurate for them to believe that p. What you can ask, without weirdness, is whether their belief that p is accurate or if such a belief, were they to form it, would be accurate.

Accuracy and inaccuracy are properties of attitudes, rather than properties of the people who have them. To say that a belief is accurate or inaccurate is not to say anything about the believer apart from that they have an accurate or an inaccurate belief. There is an obvious sense in which attributions of accuracy and inaccuracy involve evaluation, but they involve evaluation of beliefs and not of believers. And there is an obvious sense in which to say that a belief is accurate is to commend it and to say that a belief is inaccurate is to criticize it, but to say that a belief is accurate is not to commend the believer and to say that a belief is inaccurate is not to criticize the believer (cf. §3.1). As Tom Kelly (2003) points out, "aim" is ambiguous in this connection: both beliefs and believers can be said to have aims, but that a belief aims at something—truth, say— does not entail that the believer aims at the same (p. 631). We have no such problem with "accurate," however. There is no temptation to conclude, from the fact that your belief that p is accurate, that *you* are accurate.

2.2 Goodness as the Accuracy Condition for Desire

AB captures the conceptual connection between belief and truth (§2.1). If the conceptual connection between desire and goodness is the same as the conceptual connection between belief and truth (§1.6), then the following captures the conceptual connection between desire and goodness:

ACCURATE DESIRE 31

AD   A desire that p is accurate if and only if (and because) it is good
that p and inaccurate if and only if (and because) it is bad that p.

AD tells us the conditions under which a desire, whose content is the proposition that p, is accurate or inaccurate.[8] And what it says is: the goodness of
the proposition that p is the accuracy condition, and the badness of the
proposition that p the inaccuracy condition, for desire.

In ordinary English, "it is good that p" and "it is bad that p" presuppose
that p. However, we often and in the paradigm case desire that p when it is
not the case that p. Thus, I use "it is good that p" and "it is bad that p" here
as terms of art, in place of "it is good that p or would be good if it were the
case that p" and "it is bad that p or would be bad if it were the case that p."

AD is designed to capture the idea that the conceptual connection
between desire and goodness is the same as the conceptual connection
between belief and truth. That is the substantial claim that AD makes. The
terms "accurate" and "inaccurate" are not essential for understanding or
expressing this claim (cf. §2.1). We could have said that, just as truth is the
formal object of belief, goodness is the formal object of desire. We could
have said that, just as truth is the "aim of belief" or "norm of belief," goodness is the "aim of desire" or "norm of desire." We could have said that, just
as truth is the correctness condition for belief, goodness is the correctness
condition for desire, or that, just as truth is the fittingness condition for
belief, goodness is the fittingness condition for desire. I think AD is the
clearest way to capture a particular idea—the idea that the conceptual connection between desire and goodness is the same as the conceptual connection between belief and truth—but the idea is what is important here, not
the words we use to formulate it.

AD presupposes that desire, like belief, is a propositional attitude, which
takes the form of desiring that p. I will have more to say about this presupposition in the next section (§2.3). And, as in the case of belief, I will sometimes have occasion to speak of desires as having "objects," but I assume no
substantive metaphysical claims about propositions. To say that a desire has
a particular object is just to say that it is a desire that p, for some proposition that p.

---

[8] Here, and in what follows, I'll use "a desire that p" in such a way that it does not presuppose that anyone actually desires that p. For example, if it is good that p, then a desire that p is
accurate—i.e. if it is good that p and you desire that p, then your desire is accurate.

32 THE EPISTEMOLOGY OF DESIRE AND THE PROBLEM OF NIHILISM

Just as AB represents an account of accurate belief (§2.1), AD represents an account of accurate desire, on which accurate desires are accurate in virtue of being for the good and inaccurate desires are inaccurate in virtue of being for the bad (and on which a desire for the good is thereby an accurate desire and a desire for the bad is thereby an inaccurate desire).[9]

Just as AB implies that there is a sense in which to believe something is to represent it as true, AD implies that there is a sense in which to desire something is to represent it as good, such that desire represents its object as good—but not in any sense that would entail deploying the concept of goodness.[10] Contrast believing that something is good, which does require deploying the concept of goodness (§1.7)

Recall our assumption that all desires are non-instrumental (§1.4). Given this assumption, it is clear that "good" and "bad," as they appear in AD, refer to non-instrumental goodness and badness. A desire that p is accurate if and only if it is non-instrumentally good that p and inaccurate if and only if it is non-instrumentally bad that p. AD says that non-instrumental goodness is the accuracy condition for (non-instrumental) desire. (For this reason, in what follows "good" and "bad," without qualification, always refer to non-instrumental goodness and badness.)

AD says that goodness is the accuracy condition for desire. But it does not entail that it is good to have accurate desires and bad to have inaccurate desires. Whether a propositional attitude is accurate or inaccurate is orthogonal to whether it is good or bad to have that attitude. This is obvious in the case of belief, and only slightly less obvious in the case of desire. A mind-reading villain might make it bad to believe something true (by threatening to do something awful if you do) and a mind-reading eccentric might make it good to believe something false (by promising to do something nice if you do). Likewise, a mind-reading villain might make it bad to desire something good (by threatening to do something awful if you do) and a mind-reading

---

[9] A case of "desire for the good," in the present sense, is just a case in which you desire that p and it is good that p, just as a case of "true belief" is a case in which you believe that p and it is true that p, and a case of "desire for the bad," in the present sense, is just a case in which you desire that p and it is bad that p, just as a case of "false belief" is a case in which you believe that p and it is false that p. We are not here concerned with cases in which you desire something bad "under that description" (§2.10). It would be nice if we could use "good desire" and "bad desire" in a way analogous to our use of "true belief" and "false belief," but "good desire" and "bad desire" are too easily understood as indicating, respectively, a desire that is good to have and a desire that is bad to have. Note that "true belief" is ambiguous—it can be used (as it is here) to describe a case in which you believe that p and it is true that p, but it can also be used to describe a case in which you believe with great conviction, in the manner of a "true believer."
[10] See Tenenbaum 2008, Schafer 2013, Friedrich 2017, Oddie 2017, pp. 50–2; cf. Hawkins 2008.

eccentric might make it good to desire something bad (by promising to do something nice if you do). Moreover, just as there are more familiar cases in which it is painful to believe the truth and pleasant to believe something false, there are cases in which it is painful to desire something good and pleasant to desire something bad.

We encountered, above (§1.5), the idea that belief and desire differ in their "direction of fit." Are AB and AD compatible with that idea? AD is not compatible with the idea that the nature of desire is exhausted by its functional role or dispositional profile. AD says that goodness is the constitutive accuracy condition for desire, so that is at least an additional fact about the nature of desire. If having the "mind-to-world" direction of fit is equivalent to having an accuracy condition and having the "world-to-mind" direction of fit is equivalent to not having an accuracy condition, then AD entails that both belief and desire have the "mind-to-world" direction of fit.

However, AB and AD are compatible with the idea that belief and desire differ in functional role or dispositional profile. And they are compatible with the idea that a desire that p, unlike a belief that p, is not mistaken when it is false that p. And they are compatible with the idea that desires are like the shopper's list and beliefs are like the detective's list (§1.5), if we are allowed to add that the shopper's list is explicitly or implicitly titled "things it would be good to buy" or "things worth buying." In as much as the shopper's list is analogous to desire, we need to conceive of it not merely as a causal factor that disposes the shopper to buy certain things, but as a representation of those things as having some property, and thus as a representation that is accurate depending on whether they indeed have that property.[11]

We need not conceive of AB and AD as providing an account of the difference between belief and desire. However, AB and AD naturally suggest the following account of the difference between belief and desire: truth is the accuracy condition for belief and goodness is the accuracy condition for desire.

I said that AD is the most plausible version of the idea that we desire things "under the guise of the good" (§1.6). However, AD is not threatened

---

[11] David Charles (1982/3) argues that "belief aims at the truth, and is constrained by evidence of what will occur," while "desire...aims at its satisfaction and is constrained only by evidence about the likelihood or ease of gaining satisfaction" (p. 207). This is false, at least if the way in which desire is constrained by evidence of likelihood is meant to be analogous to the way in which belief is constrained by evidence of actuality. Evidence that it is unlikely that p does not tend to cause us to not desire that p and evidence that it is likely that p does not tend to cause us to desire that p.

34 THE EPISTEMOLOGY OF DESIRE AND THE PROBLEM OF NIHILISM

by two standard objections to the idea that we desire things "under the guise of the good": that you can desire something without believing that it is good and that you can believe that something is good without desiring it.[12] AD suggests no such connections between desire and evaluative belief (cf. §1.7). AD is not the implausible claim that desires are necessarily accompanied by or caused by a distinct representation of the goodness of their objects; it is rather the claim that desires are themselves representations of the goodness of their objects.

2.3 Desire as Propositional

I assume that desire, like belief, is a propositional attitude, which takes the form of desiring that p, for some proposition that p. I assume, in other words, that desire is essentially propositional. Propositions, for our purposes here, are equivalent to states of affairs; true propositions are equivalent to facts; and events correspond to facts, in the sense that for every event that occurs, there is a corresponding fact, namely, the fact that it occurred. We have several ways of describing instances of desiring that p: we say that someone wants it to be the case that p, that they hope that p, that they are glad that p, that they wish it were the case that p, that they want the proposition that p to be true, and so on. What I assume is that every desire can be described in some such way.

However, there is also *objectual desire*, which takes the form of desiring *x*, where *x* is an individual thing (in a broad sense), and *practical* desire, which takes the form of desiring to φ, where φing is an action (in a broad sense).[13] If desire is essentially propositional, I need to show that objectual desire and practical desire are species of propositional desire. In defense of this, I offer three claims.

First, objectual desire is a species of practical desire. As several philosophers have observed, when we say that someone wants some individual thing, what we mean is that they want to do something to or with that thing.[14]

---

[12] See Watson 1975, pp. 209–12, Stocker 1979, Velleman 1992, Railton 1997, p. 66, Brink 2008, pp. 30–1, Setiya 2010, Gregory 2013, pp. 64–8, Döring and Eker 2017, pp. 91–5; see also Scanlon 1998, p. 35, Setiya 2007, pp. 33–8.

[13] In what follows, I'll use the variable <to φ> to indicate this restriction to actions; I'll use <to χ> when no such restriction is intended.

[14] Quine 1956/1966, p. 184, Kenny 1963, pp. 112–18, Searle 1983, p. 30, Scanlon 1998, p. 379, Parfit 2011, p. 21.

ACCURATE DESIRE   35

Someone who wants a sloop (presumably) wants to own a sloop, someone who wants the last dumpling (presumably) wants to eat it, someone who wants a holiday in Spain (presumably) wants to take a vacation there, someone who wants an encore (presumably) wants to hear the orchestra play something more. We could perhaps say that to want some individual thing is to want to get it, if "get" were understood in a suitably broad sense.[15] But we understand what it is for someone to want some individual thing, in particular cases, only by understanding what "getting" it would involve, which may or may not involve owning the thing you want and may or may not involve consuming the thing you want. If all you know is that someone wants a violin concerto, you do not yet know what they want—do they want to hear one performed, to own one as intellectual property, to have one performed for an audience in their theater, or what? This suggests that wanting some individual thing is always wanting to φ, where φing is some action that involves that thing in some way.

Second, practical desire can be plausibly understood as a species of propositional desire. Although I doubt a case could be made that practical desire *must* be understood in this way, I follow several other philosophers in treating practical desire as a species of *de se* propositional desire.[16] On the account I propose, to want to φ is to want *de se* that you φ. The object of a practical desire, in other words, is a species of proposition centered on the desiring subject. Someone who wants to take a walk is someone who wants *de se* that they take a walk; someone who wants to dance is someone who wants *de se* that they dance; someone who wants to own a sloop is someone who wants *de se* that they own a sloop.

Third, desire is not essentially practical. Note that there are two different senses in which an attitude could be said to be practical. In a substantive sense, to say that an attitude is practical is to say that it entails dispositions to act. In this sense, the practical theory of desire (§1.5) entails that desire is essentially practical. I argued that desire is not essentially substantively practical by appeal to counterexamples, including the case of wanting the Celtics to win the NBA Championship. In the formal sense, to say that an attitude is practical is to say that its object is an action, which we represent using the variable <to φ>, rather than a proposition, which we represent

---

[15] The idea that "the primitive sign of wanting is trying to get" (§1.5) suggests that all desire is objectual, but this is strained in many cases of practical desire, e.g. wanting to dance.
[16] Kenny 1963, p. 124, Lewis 1979, pp. 531–3, 1986, pp. 28–30, 1989, pp. 117–19, Oddie 2017, p. 31, 2018, pp. 249–51.

using the variable <that p>. The practical theory of desire does not imply that desire is essentially formally practical; on the practical theory of desire, desiring *that p* is understood as a disposition to act in certain ways. What I now want to consider is the idea that desire is essentially formally practical. Our counterexample to the idea that desire is essentially substantively practical will serve just as well as a counterexample to the idea that desire is essentially formally practical. Wanting the Celtics to win the NBA Championship is not desiring to φ; it is desiring that the Celtics win the NBA Championship, i.e. it is an instance of desiring that p.[17]

Intention, by contrast with desire, seems like it is essentially practical, both substantively and formally.[18] Intention, at least in the paradigm case and in a wide range of cases, takes the form of intending to φ.[19] And it is hard to imagine someone intending to φ without being at least somewhat disposed to φ.

If intention is, indeed, essentially practical, then I think we need to give desire and intention separate treatment, given that the former is not essentially practical. Our account of intention should reflect the fact that intention is essentially practical.[20] If intention has an accuracy condition, its accuracy condition should reflect the fact that intention is essentially practical. For example, we could say that S's intention to φ is accurate if and only if S ought to φ and inaccurate otherwise.[21] For another example, we could say that S's intention to φ is accurate if and only if S has most reason to φ and inaccurate otherwise. For a final example, we could say that S's intention to φ is accurate if and only if φing is the best of S's options and inaccurate otherwise.[22] In each case, the accuracy condition for intention is said to be the action of φing having some property. Notice, as well, that in each case we must mention the person who has the intention to state its accuracy condition. This, too, reflects the fact that intention is essentially practical. We need to know who we are talking about to ask whether they ought to φ, whether they have most reason to φ, or whether φing is the best of their

---

[17] Note also that not all cases involving "desiring to" are cases of practical desire: the person who wants to be rich does not want to perform some action "being rich"; they want it to be the case that they are rich.

[18] See Marks 1986, pp. 139–41, Schroeder 2004, pp. 16–20, Strawson 2010, chapter 9, Railton 2012, p. 33, Arpaly and Schroeder 2014, pp. 111–16; cf. Anscombe 1963, §36.

[19] However, we must say something about cases like this: making catering arrangements for a party, you intend the champagne to be served before the canapés and that the guests be seated at 9pm.

[20] Cf. Velleman 1996, p. 719, Hieronymi 2005, p. 45, Shah 2008, p. 8, Bratman 2009a, p. 25, 2009b, pp. 49–55, Schafer 2013.

[21] Cf. Shah 2008.   [22] Cf. Davidson 1978/2001, p. 101, Piller 2006, p. 162.

options. There is no such thing as "what ought to be done" or "the best option" without reference to a particular person in a particular situation. By contrast, we can ask whether it is true that p or whether it is good that p without any such reference.

2.4 Propositional Goodness

AD says that whether a desire that p is accurate depends on whether it is good that p and that whether a desire that p is inaccurate depends on whether it is bad that p. P.T. Geach (1956) argues that "we cannot sensibly speak of a good or bad event, a good or bad thing to happen" (p. 41; see also Foot 1961, Kraut 2011). I am assuming otherwise. I am assuming that we can make sense of the idea of its being good or bad that p, which seems equivalent to the idea of a good or bad event or a good or bad thing to happen (cf. §2.3). In making this assumption, I side with W.D. Ross (1930/2002), who argues that "what is good or bad is always something properly expressed by a that-clause, i.e. . . . a *fact*" (p. 137).

My aim here is to articulate and explain the idea that goodness is the accuracy condition for desire, so I won't attempt to refute Geach's arguments against propositional goodness here. AD says that whether a desire that p is accurate depends on whether it is good that p, and the question of whether it is good that p must be distinguished from questions about whether particular individuals are good instances of their kind (cf. §1.1). Imagine that a new luxury hotel has opened in Chicago and you want to stay there. AD says that your desire is accurate if and only if it would be good were you to stay there. It does not say that your desire is accurate if and only if the hotel at which you want to stay is a good hotel.[23]

Moreover, that an individual is a good instance of its kind does not entail that it is good *that* it is a good instance of its kind. It is not good that Bashar al-Assad is a good—because brutal and merciless—dictator. There is no such straightforward connection between the goodness of an individual *qua* member of its kind and propositional goodness.

Again, I'm not going to try to make a case that it makes sense to speak of its being good or bad that p. But I do want to note that there is no *grammatical* difficulty with propositional goodness. It's not good, and indeed quite

---

[23] Cf. Williams, 1985/2006, pp. 138–9; see also Geach 1956, pp. 36–7, Foot 1961, pp. 57–60.

38 THE EPISTEMOLOGY OF DESIRE AND THE PROBLEM OF NIHILISM

bad, that Assad is so brutal and merciless, but it's good that his tyranny is confined to Syria. Whether or not that makes sense ethically, I expressed it with a perfectly grammatical sentence.

AD is silent on the nature of goodness; it does not tell us what goodness is. Is this a liability? I don't think so. AB is likewise silent on the nature of truth (cf. §2.1), and my argument for AD won't make any controversial assumptions about the nature of goodness. AD is consistent both with the view that goodness is a non-natural property[24] and with the view that goodness is a natural property.[25] It is consistent with the view that good things are good in virtue of the fact that we are disposed to desire them under certain conditions.[26] It is consistent with the view that good things are good in virtue of there being a reason to desire them, which we will consider later (§3.10). And, as I shall have occasion to argue, AD is even consistent with the view that good things are good in virtue of desires for them being accurate (§3.8).

Recall the idea that desire represents its object as good (§2.2). This suggests that goodness is a property. However, propositional goodness functions logically as an operator: AD says that a desire that p is accurate if and only if it is good that p. Propositional goodness is like truth in this respect: AB says that a belief that p is accurate if and only if it is true that p. We can speak loosely of both truth and goodness as properties, as when we say that belief represents its object as true (§2.1) and desire represents its object as good. We likewise speak loosely of goodness as a property when we consider the question of whether goodness is a natural or a non-natural property or when we say that goodness is the property that makes things worthy of desire (§6.3). This does not commit us to the substantive metaphysical claim that truth and goodness are properties.

2.5 Aversion

AD says that goodness is the accuracy condition for desire. Is there something analogous when it comes to badness, i.e. something such that badness is its accuracy condition? Is there, for example, an attitude whose instances are accurate if and only if they are for the bad, in the same way that, per AD, instances of desire are accurate if and only if they are for the good?

---

[24] Cf. Moore 1903, Shafer-Landau 2003, Enoch 2011.
[25] Cf. Railton 1986, Boyd 1988, Brink 1989.   [26] Cf. Lewis 1989, Smith 1994.

It seems plausible that, in as much as goodness is the accuracy condition for desire, badness is the accuracy condition for *aversion*. However, I am going to assume that aversion is a species of desire. Aversion that p is simply desire that not-p. I am also going to assume that it is bad that p if and only if it is good that not-p. As Descartes argues, "there is no good whose privation is not an evil, and no evil…whose privation is not a good."[27] Thus, per AD, a desire that not-p—i.e. aversion that p—is accurate if and only if it is good that not-p—i.e. bad that p—and inaccurate if and only if it is bad that not-p—i.e. good that p. Thus, given our two assumptions, badness is the accuracy condition for aversion. But aversion is not an attitude distinct from desire.

Suppose that I am wrong and that aversion is not a species of desire.[28] That would complicate the discussion that follows, but nothing is going to depend on the assumption that aversion is a species of desire.

2.6 "Good" vs. "Good For"

There is a familiar sense of "good for," on which to say that something is good for someone is to say that it benefits them or that it contributes to their welfare, well-being, or flourishing. Adopting that sense of "good for" (and the corresponding sense of "bad for"), compare AD and the following account of accurate desire:

> BA1   S's desire that p is accurate if and only if it is good for S that p and inaccurate if and only if it is bad for S that p.

Are AD and BA1 equivalent? There is at least a conceptual distinction to be drawn between something's being good for you and it's being good, full stop. You can coherently think something is good but not good for you. AD and BA1 are not equivalent.

Now consider an ethical claim: something is good if and only if it is good for you (and bad if and only if it is bad for you). That is implausible. You, dear reader, are not that important. The claim that something is good if it is good for you (and bad if it is bad for you), however, is intuitively plausible. But it is intuitively plausible because it follows from the following intuitively

---

[27] *Passions of the Soul*, Part Two, §87 (trans. Robert Stoothoff).
[28] See e.g. Schroeder 2004, pp. 25–7.

40 THE EPISTEMOLOGY OF DESIRE AND THE PROBLEM OF NIHILISM

plausible ethical claim: something is good if it is good for someone (and bad if it is bad for someone).

Now consider the converse: something is good only if it is good for someone (and bad only if it is bad for someone). On a suitably broad reading of "someone," this has some intuitive appeal. Putting these two claims together, you might arrive at the following ethical claim: something is good if and only if it is good for someone (and bad if and only if it is bad for someone). If so, we can derive the following from AD:

> BA2 S's desire that p is accurate if and only if it is good for someone that p and inaccurate if and only if it is bad for someone that p.

However, these are matters of substantive ethics. The defender of AD is committed to neither BA1 nor BA2. To put this another way, AD says that goodness is the accuracy condition for desire. It does not say that *prudential* goodness is the accuracy condition for desire. The latter claim is compatible with AD, via the substantive ethical claim that something is good if and only if it is good for someone. But it is not entailed by AD.

2.7 Degrees of Goodness and Strength of Desire

Truth is the accuracy condition for belief and goodness is the accuracy condition for desire. However, there is a fundamental difference between truth and goodness: goodness, unlike truth, comes in degrees. It can be more or less good that p and it can be better that p than that q. By contrast, it cannot be more or less true that p and it cannot be truer that p than that q. Thus, the defender of AD faces a question: what degree of goodness is necessary and sufficient for accurate desire? Just how good does it have to be that p for a desire that p to be accurate?[29]

I answer: any degree of goodness. A desire that p is accurate if and only if it is to some degree good that p, i.e. if it is *at all* good that p or *to some extent* good that p. For the purposes of interpreting AD, I assume that it is good that p if and only if it is good to some degree that p. "Good," without qualification, refers to goodness of any degree.

---

[29] I focus on goodness and accurate desire here for the sake of simplicity; the extension to badness and inaccurate desire is straightforward.

ACCURATE DESIRE 41

Now, in something like the same way that goodness comes in degrees, desire comes in different strengths: you can desire something more or less strongly and you can desire one thing more or less than another.[30] Sometimes, we think of ourselves as having particularly strong desires—you might really, really want to visit the Dalmatian coast or have an incredible desire for a glass of cold rosé. And sometimes we have occasion to think of our desires as noticeably weak—your desire for a snack might not even be enough to get you off the couch to fetch one. Often, strength of desire is a comparative matter. We sometimes think of one of our desires as being stronger than another or that we want one thing more than another. (I assume that these are just two ways of describing the same situation, that there is no difference between desiring x more strongly than y and wanting x more than y. If not, things are even more complicated.) Finally, we are inclined to think of comparative strength of desire as a matter of degree: I want to have lunch outside more than I want to visit the art museum, but only a little bit more, whereas I want to avoid being tortured to death more than I want to visit the art museum, and not just a little bit more, but a whole lot more. In any event, given that desire comes in different strengths, the defender of AD faces a question: what strength of desire is necessary and sufficient for someone to count as have a desire?

I answer: any strength at all. To desire something is to desire it *at all*; if you want something at all, even if only a very little bit, then you desire it. For the purposes of interpreting AD, I assume that you desire that p if and only if you have some degree of desire that p. "Desire" refers to any desire, of any strength. (There are uses of the word "want" that do not jibe with this stipulation: to say that you want something is sometimes to indicate that you prefer it to the alternatives or to choose it. But there are uses of "want" that do jibe with this stipulation, as when we say that we want something, but not very much, or that we want something, but want some other thing more.)

Given that desire comes in different strengths, it is natural for those sympathetic to AD to wonder whether strength of desire has an accuracy condition. Let's assume that we can represent strength of desire as a real number between 0 and 1, where "0" represents no desire at all and "1" represents maximum-strength desire. Under what conditions is a desire that p with strength n accurate? Here is a natural thought: degree of goodness is the

---

[30] Cf. Watson 1975, pp. 209–10, Armstrong 1993, p. 153, Scanlon 1998, p. 50, Schroeder 2004, p. 13.

42 THE EPISTEMOLOGY OF DESIRE AND THE PROBLEM OF NIHILISM

accuracy condition for strength of desire. An accurate strength of desire is one that corresponds to how good the object of desire is. Let's assume, further, that we can represent degree of goodness as a real number between 0 and 1, where "0" represents no goodness at all and "1" represents the maximum degree of goodness. Consider:

ASD   A desire that p with strength n is accurate if and only if it is n good that p.

I am going to make it my task to defend AD. However, it seems clear that, if AD is true, something like ASD is also true.

Recall that it can be better that p than that q. Given this, a natural thought, for anyone sympathetic to AD, is that betterness is the accuracy condition for preference. I will have more to say about this, below (§7.7). Now, you might think that strength of desire can be explained in terms of preference, e.g. that you desire that p more than you desire that q if and only if you prefer that p rather than that q. However, it seems like strength of desire and preference can come apart. After eating a dinner of steak and fried potatoes, accompanied by a bottle of full-bodied wine, the sensible thing to do is to drink a small coffee, and that is what I prefer. But I really, really want to drink some Scotch. I want the Scotch more than I want the coffee, but I prefer the coffee to the Scotch. If that is possible, then the relationship between strength of desire and preference is, at best, complicated. (Moreover, recall the idea that comparative strength of desire is a matter of degree. Is preference likewise a matter of degree? If not, the relationship between strength of desire and preference is, again, complicated.)

At first glance, strength of desire seems like the analogue of credence (degree of belief). However, this is mere appearance. There are two main ways of thinking about the accuracy condition for credence. First, some argue that credences are estimates of truth, such that credence accuracy is a measure of how close a credence is to the truth.[31] If it is true that p, credence 1 that p is maximally accurate, credence .9 is relatively accurate, credence .8 is more accurate than credence .7, and so on. A middling credence, on this approach, cannot be highly accurate. By contrast, given ASD, a weak desire might be perfectly accurate, if it is a desire for something that is good to a correspondingly low degree. Second, some argue that credences are beliefs about likelihood, such that credence n that p is accurate if and only if

---

[31] See Konek 2016, Pettigrew 2016; cf. Moss 2018, pp. 105–6.

it is n likely that p.[32] By contrast, on my view, desire is distinct from evaluative belief (§1.7), so desiring that p with strength n is not a matter of believing that it is n good that p. Goodness comes in degrees; truth does not. For this reason, there may be nothing like strength of desire in the realm of belief, and nothing like credence in the realm of desire.

2.8 Axial Gaps

Truth is the accuracy condition for belief and goodness it the accuracy condition for desire. There is another fundamental difference between truth and goodness, and this one will be important in what follows: while it cannot be neither true nor false that p, it can be neither good nor bad that p. For example, there are an even number of paperclips in this dish on my desk, but it is neither good nor bad that there are an even number of paperclips in this dish on my desk. Although there cannot be alethic gaps, there can be axial gaps.

Given AB and AD, it follows that, although a belief cannot be neither accurate nor inaccurate, a desire can be neither accurate nor inaccurate. If you were to be glad that there are an even number of paperclips in this dish, your desire would be neither accurate nor inaccurate. Moreover, given the assumption that it is bad that p if and only if it is good that not-p (§2.5) and the assumption that it is false that p if and only if it is true that not-p, given AB and AD, either a belief that p or a belief that not-p must be accurate, but it is not the case that either a desire that p or a desire that not-p must be accurate. If you were to wish that there were not an even number of paperclips in this dish, that desire would also be neither accurate nor inaccurate.[33]

---

[32] See Moss 2018, p. 88, pp. 120–2.

[33] Selim Berker (2022) argues that that attitudes cannot be neither fitting nor unfitting, on the grounds that "unfitting" simply means "not fitting" (p. 46), and specifically that desires for the neutral are unfitting (p. 46n). He presents two arguments that desires for the neutral are unfitting, which I am going to adapt to yield arguments that desires for the neutral are inaccurate. First, you might think that if desires for the neutral are not inaccurate, then incredibly strong desires for the neutral are not inaccurate. It seems to me that we should accept this implication of the view that desires for the neutral are not inaccurate, and explain what is wrong with incredibly strong desires for the neutral by appeal to their abnormality (cf. §3.4). Second, you might think that the view that desires for the neutral are not inaccurate implies that attitudes in general (e.g. blame, admiration, amusement) are not inaccurate when their objects are neutral. It seems to me that we should reject this implication. Badness, I maintain, is the inaccuracy condition for desire (§2.2), but that does not imply, e.g. that praiseworthiness is the inaccuracy condition for blame, such that blaming someone for doing something that is neither blameworthy nor praiseworthy is not inaccurate.

44   THE EPISTEMOLOGY OF DESIRE AND THE PROBLEM OF NIHILISM

Brentano seems to be the first to have appreciated this difference between belief and desire. In *The Origin of Our Knowledge of Right and Wrong* (1889/1969), he says:

> Of the two opposing types of feeling – loving and hating, inclination and disinclination, being pleased and being displeased – in every instance one of them is correct [*richtig*] and the other incorrect [*unrichtig*]. (pp. 17–18)

However, in his posthumous *Doctrine of Correct Judgment* (1956), he posits a "law of excluded middle for emotions" according to which:

> It is impossible to incorrectly love what someone incorrectly hates and to incorrectly hate what someone incorrectly loves. (p. 175)

As Roderick Chisholm (1986) explains, Brentano chooses not to formulate the law of excluded middle for emotions by saying, as he had previously, that everything is "such that either it is correct to love it or it is correct to hate it" (p. 55). That previous formulation seems more natural as a "law of excluded middle," mirroring its plausible analogue in the case of judgment, i.e. the principle that every proposition is such that it is either correct to affirm it or correct to deny it (cf. pp. 54–5). Brentano also chooses not to say that everything is such that it is either correct to love it or incorrect to love it and such that it is either correct to hate it or incorrect to hate it. The reason, Chisholm argues, is that Brentano wanted to make room for things that were neither good nor bad. For Brentano, something is good just in case it is correct to love it (1889/1969, p. 18)—and, by implication, something is bad just in case it is correct to hate it. If something is neither good nor bad, therefore, it is neither correct to love it nor correct to hate it. On Brentano's mature view, Chisholm argues:

> One's emotive [attitude] toward a thing O is incorrect if and only if, the contrary emotion toward O is correct. That is to say, love of O is incorrect if and only if hatred of O is correct; and hatred of O is incorrect if and only if love of O is correct. (p. 56)

All this is just to say that, as Oskar Kraus (1937) explains, for Brentano, "the law of excluded middle has no analogue when it comes to value, because some things are indifferent" (p. 174). Every proposition is either true or false, but some things are neither good nor bad—some are (as I will say here) *neutral*.[34] And when it is neutral that p, both love and hatred are neither correct nor incorrect.[35]

Is there any reason to be skeptical of the existence of axial gaps? You might think that everything is to some extent instrumentally good (§1.4), given the ubiquity of causal connections, bearing positively in some way or other on the satisfaction of your antecedent desires. From my perspective, it is probably instrumentally good that there are an even number of paperclips in this dish, in as much as there being some paperclips in this dish is conducive to the satisfaction of desires I often have to hold pieces of paper together. However, AD says that non-instrumental goodness is the accuracy condition for desire (§2.2). You also might think that it might turn out to be non-instrumentally good that there are an even number of paperclips in this dish. Maybe it turns out that there is something beautiful or sublime about it. I agree, but I assume—quite reasonably, it seems to me—that there being an even number of paperclips in this dish is, in fact, in no way non-instrumentally good.

2.9 Axial Gluts?

At least at first glance, there is another fundamental difference between truth and goodness: it seems that, while it cannot be both true and false that p, it can be both good and bad that p. For example, imagine that you see one of your colleagues, whom you dislike and with whom you have a minor professional rivalry, stumble and fall over as he crosses the quad, which causes you to giggle with delight. Your *schadenfreude*, in this case, seems both in one respect good and in another respect bad. It seems both good that you were pleased by your colleague's fall, because you were after all pleased, but also bad that you were pleased by your colleague's fall, because your pleasure manifested vicious pettiness. It seems that, while there cannot be alethic gluts, there can be axial gluts.[36]

If so, given AB and AD, although a belief cannot be both accurate and inaccurate, a desire can be both accurate and inaccurate. If I were to be

---

[34] I prefer "neutral" to "indifferent" only because I use "indifference" as the name for neither desiring that p nor desiring that not-p (§6.1).

[35] Cf. Parfit 1984, p. 123.

[36] It is obvious that it can be both instrumentally good (§1.4) that p and instrumentally good that not-p, and in that sense instrumentally bad for you that p. But we are concerned here with non-instrumental goodness and badness (§2.2).

glad that you were pleased by your colleague's fall, my desire would be both accurate and inaccurate. Moreover, given the assumption that it is bad that p if and only if it is good that not-p (§2.5) and the assumption that it is false that p if and only if it is true that not-p, given AB and AD, although a belief that p and a belief that not-p cannot both be accurate, a desire that p and a desire that not-p can both be accurate. If I were to both be glad that you were pleased by your colleague's fall and wish that you had not been pleased by your colleague's fall, both of my desires would be accurate.

To understand the present case as a case in which it is both good and bad that p, I think we must assume something like that there are a plurality of goods, or forms of goodness, or aspects of the good. (We might also appeal, in defense of the possibility of its being both good and bad that p, to the idea that there are several species or domains of value, e.g. moral, aesthetic, epistemic.) Pleasure is good and manifesting vice is bad, and in the present case these two values come into conflict, because we have a case in which pleasure manifests vice.

You might object that what is really going on in the present case is that it is good that you were pleased and bad that you manifested vice. Thus, we do not really have a case in which it is both good and bad that p, but rather a case in which it is good that p and bad that q. We do not really have one fact that is both good and bad, but rather two facts, one good and one bad. However, what about the fact that you were pleased by your colleague's fall? That is a fact. On the present proposal, is it good or bad (or neither) that you were pleased by your colleague's fall? I think the answer, on the present proposal, has to be that it is *not* good that you were pleased by your colleague's fall. That is what Ross (1930/2002) says about such a case:

> [W]hen a moral being is feeling a pleasure or pain that is deserved or undeserved, or a pleasure or pain that implies a good or bad disposition, the total fact is quite inadequately described if we say 'a sentient being is feeling pleasure, or pain'. The total fact may be that 'a sentient and moral being is feeling a pleasure that is undeserved, or that is the realization of a vicious disposition', and though the fact included in this, that 'a sentient being is feeling pleasure' would be good if it stood alone, that creates only a presumption that the total fact is good, and a presumption that is outweighed by the other element in the total fact. (p. 137)

Your *schadenfreude*, in other words, is not in any respect good. It appears good, when we bracket or ignore the fact that it manifests vice, but once we take that fact into consideration, we can see that it is not actually good.

If this is right, given AD, if I were to be glad that you were pleased by your colleague's fall, my desire would not be accurate, and were I to wish that you had not been pleased by your colleague's fall, my desire would be accurate. It is for something like this reason that Brentano (1956) defends a "law of antagonism" on which "it is impossible to correctly love what someone incorrectly hates" (p. 175).[37]

It seems to me that this ignores something important about cases like the present case. Ambivalence, it seems to me, is the appropriate response to value conflicts.[38] Accuracy, in the present case, requires both being glad that you were pleased by your colleague's fall and wishing you had not been pleased by your colleague's fall. Merely being glad that you were pleased and wishing you had not manifested vice would not do justice to the idea that in the present case there is a genuine *conflict* between the goodness of pleasure and the badness of manifesting vice. Accuracy, it seems to me, requires that that conflict be mirrored with a pair of *inconsistent* desires. However, because it will not make a difference in what follows, I will leave the matter open. It seems to me that there are axial gluts. But perhaps there aren't.

2.10 Desiring the Bad

You cannot believe something because it is false. However, some philosophers argue that you can desire something because it is bad.[39] If so, the defender of AD owes an explanation of this difference between desire and belief. However, as I shall argue, you cannot desire something because it is bad.

We are not looking for a case in which you want to get a bad instance of some kind (§2.4)—it is no threat to AD that some people like to stay at bad hotels or, more familiarly, like to watch bad movies. Nor are we looking for a

---

[37] Cf. Chisholm 1986, p. 55; see also Greenspan 1980, Jackson 1985.

[38] See Feldman and Hazlett 2021.

[39] Watson 1975, p. 210, Stocker 1979, pp. 746–9, Velleman 1992, pp. 17–19; see also Velleman 1996, p. 716, Sussman 2009. You might also think that you can desire something because it is worthless, i.e. not good. What I say here about desiring the bad applies, mutatis mutandis, to desiring the worthless.

48 THE EPISTEMOLOGY OF DESIRE AND THE PROBLEM OF NIHILISM

case in which you want something that is both good and bad (§2.9) because it is good—it is no threat to AD that we desire things that are in one respect good, but which are in another respect bad, because they are in one respect good. Nor are we looking for a case in which you want something because it is bad for someone (§2.6)—it is no threat to AD that some people are malevolent. Nor are we looking for a case in which you merely want something that you believe is bad—AD is compatible with cases like that (§2.2). What would threaten AD would be a case in which you desire that p because it is bad that p. Is that possible?

Augustine claims to have stolen some pears because it was wrong.[40] If Augustine stole because it was wrong to steal, it is easy to imagine him wanting something to happen because it would be a bad were it to happen. But did he steal because it was wrong? I was also a juvenile delinquent, and I certainly did many things because they were rude, illegal, dangerous, annoying, and rebellious. And I certainly would have said that I was doing things that were wrong and that I did not care that they were wrong and indeed that I was doing them because they were wrong. But it now seems clear that I was doing those things because they were considered wrong by those against whom I was rebelling. Consider, again, the person who likes bad movies. Although I do think it is possible to want to watch a movie because it is, by your lights, a bad movie, there are two more familiar (and compatible) possibilities to consider here. One possibility is that the fan of bad movies really does think that the movies in question are bad, but likes them because of their good aspects, and not because of their bad aspects. Another possibility is that the fan of bad movies likes them because they considered bad according to some social norm or established aesthetic principle. Both of these have analogues in the case of the delinquent Augustine.[41] One possibility is that Augustine really does think that stealing is wrong, but chooses to steal because it is thrilling or because it demonstrates his independence. Another (compatible) possibility is that he chooses to steal because stealing is considered wrong according to prevailing moral or religious norms. Rebellion can be motivated by the perceived value of rebellion itself, rather than (as the rebel might have it) the perceived value of wrongdoing, vice, or sin. The rebel may indeed want things that they believe are bad, but they do not want them *because* they are bad.

---

[40] *Confessions*, Book II.
[41] Cf. Anscombe 1963, p. 75, Raz 1999, p. 32, Tenenbaum 2007, pp. 251–6.

ACCURATE DESIRE   49

Consider, alternatively, the case of someone who is in a silly or playful mood.[42] Let's grant that this may involve desiring things that you believe are bad. But it does not involve desiring those things *because* they are bad. When you want to race to the end of the block or pretend to be a fish, you do not want to do so because it would be bad were you to do so, but because it would be *fun*.[43] A silly or playful mood may well involve being indifferent to the bad, such that you want to do things *despite* their being bad. It does not involve a perverse attraction to the bad, such that you want to do things *because* they are bad.

2.11 Conclusion

My aim in this chapter was to articulate the idea that goodness is the accuracy condition for desire. AD is our official formulation of this idea. I have made a number of clarificatory comments and discussed some differences between truth and goodness. I have responded to a few familiar objections to AD, but I haven't yet said anything in its favor. Defending AD is my next order of business.

The Epistemology of Desire and the Problem of Nihilism. Allan Hazlett, Oxford University Press.
© Allan Hazlett 2024. DOI: 10.1093/9780191995583.003.0002

---

[42] Velleman 1992, pp. 17–18.
[43] Raz 2010, p. 123; cf. p. 115; see also Raz 2016, p. 12. Note that this does not mean that your desire, in these cases, is instrumental (§1.4).

3
Why Criticize Desires for the Bad?

Anscombe says that the conceptual connection between desire and goodness is the same as the conceptual connection between belief and truth (§1.6). If so, I argued, goodness is the accuracy condition for desire (§2.2). But why think that Anscombe's claim is true? Why think that the conceptual connection between desire and goodness is, indeed, the same as the conceptual connection between belief and truth? To put this question another way, assuming that AB is true, why think that AD is true?

In this chapter I will argue that AD provides the best explanation of why it makes sense to criticize a desire on the grounds that its object is bad, i.e. why it makes sense to criticize a desire that p on the grounds that it is bad that p. Let's call criticism of a desire that p on the grounds that it is bad that p *axial criticism* of a desire. So, my argument is that AD provides the best explanation of why axial criticism of desires makes sense.

Some defenders of AD argue—and this is common enough that we might call it the standard argument for AD—that AD provides the best explanation of why desires provide normative reasons for action.[1] I have nothing bad to say about this argument here, except that it relies on a relatively controversial premise: that desires provide normative reasons for action. I say this premise is relatively controversial, by which I mean it is more controversial—or so it seems to me—than the premise on which my argument relies: that it makes sense to criticize a desire that p on the grounds that it is bad that p.[2]

On the account I am going to propose (§3.2), it makes sense to criticize a desire that p on the grounds that it is bad that p because desires for the bad are inaccurate, in the same way that it makes sense to criticize a belief that p on the grounds that it is false that p because false beliefs are inaccurate.

---

[1] Stampe 1986, 1987, Quinn 1993, Johnston 2001, Tenenbaum 2007, Gregory 2018, 2021; see also Schafer 2013.

[2] I would say the same, mutatis mutandis, about the idea that AD provides the best explanation of how justified evaluative judgment is possible (Oddie 2005, chapter 3, 2017, pp. 35–6, 2018, pp. 240–3).

3.1 Axial Criticism of Desires

I am going to argue that AD provides the best explanation of why axial criticism of desires makes sense. This presupposes that axial criticism of desires does, indeed, make sense. In this section I'm going to motivate and clarify that presupposition.

Anscombe (1963) invites us to imagine someone who says they want a saucer of mud, points out that they "are likely to be asked what for" and that if we wanted to understand this person we would "try to find out in what aspect the object desired is desirable," and argues that, if there were no answer, we would dismiss their claim to want a saucer of mud as "fair nonsense" (p. 71). That all seems about right, but it does not yet suggest anything about axial criticism of desires. Even if we imagine someone wanting a saucer of mud, it is not particularly intuitive that it would be *bad* were they to get a saucer of mud.

A better example, for our purposes, is Hume's example of preferring the destruction of the whole world to the scratching of his finger (§1.2). Since we are interested in desires for the bad, imagine simply that you want the world to be destroyed. Intuitively, it would be bad if the world were destroyed—not only instrumentally, but non-instrumentally as well. So, we have here an intuitive case of desire for the bad. Moreover, it would be natural to criticize your desire on the grounds that it would be bad if the world were destroyed. If you reported that you wanted the world to be destroyed, a natural response would be: "Why in the world would you want that? It would be awful if the world were destroyed." Even Hume, as I read him, would not deny that axial criticism would make sense in this case; he would only deny that such criticism can take the form of the allegation that your desire is "contrary to reason."

So, I think that it would make perfect sense to criticize your desire that the world be destroyed on the grounds that it would be bad if the world were destroyed, and that in general it makes sense to criticize a desire that p on the grounds that it is bad that p. In other words, axial criticism of desires makes sense.

What do I mean when I say that axial criticism of desires "makes sense"? By way of illustration and suggestion (§3.2), compare the sense in which it makes sense to criticize a belief that p on the grounds that it is false that p. Call this *alethic criticism* of a belief. My claim here is that axial criticism of desires makes sense, in the same way that alethic criticism of beliefs makes sense. Suppose you believe that Brazil won the 1998 World Cup. It would make sense for me to criticize your belief on the grounds that France won the 1998 World Cup. By contrast, it would not make sense for me to criticize your belief on the grounds that Brazil has many white sand beaches or on the grounds that your belief was formed on a Tuesday or on the grounds that you were born in Singapore.

We can draw the same kind of contrast in the case of axial criticism of desires. It would make sense for someone to criticize your desire that the world be destroyed on the grounds that it would be bad if the world were destroyed. By contrast, it would not make sense for someone to criticize your desire on the grounds that the universe is expanding or on the grounds that your desire was formed on a Thursday or on the grounds that you were born in Hong Kong.

That it makes sense to criticize an attitude on the grounds that p does not entail that p. Criticism can "make sense," in the present sense, even if it is mistaken. Suppose you believe that Brazil won the 2002 World Cup. It would make sense for me to criticize your belief on the grounds that Germany won the 2002 World Cup, even though you are right, and I am wrong, about who won the 2002 World Cup. You would understand what I was getting at, even if you knew I was wrong about who won the 2002 World Cup. By contrast, if I appealed to the fact that Germany has the largest economy in Europe or the fact that you formed your belief on a Saturday or the fact that you were born in Missouri, you would not understand what I was getting at.

This has an important corollary: the assumption that axial criticism of desires makes sense does not entail that anything is bad. In the context of our discussion of the problem of nihilism (cf. 1.1), I want to leave open the possibility that nothing is bad. I am leaving open the possibility that, for any proposition that p, it is neither good nor bad that p, and, thus, the possibility that, for any proposition that p, is it not bad that p. However, because criticism can make sense even if it is mistaken, my claim that axial criticism makes sense does not entail that anything is bad.

I want to make three further clarifications of the idea that a species of criticism "makes sense." First, that it makes sense to criticize an attitude does not entail that you ought to do so. Such criticism might make sense, and yet be inappropriate, insensitive, or pointless. Imagine that your sweet old uncle believes with dogmatic conviction that all cats go to heaven. Alethic criticism of his belief would make sense (in the present sense of "make sense"), but it would be gratuitous and futile; all it would do is make your sweet old uncle upset and annoyed. In this case, facts about the circumstances speak against criticizing an attitude. There are also cases—and these are worth keeping in mind as we proceed (cf. §3.2)—in which facts about the content of an attitude speak against criticizing it. When it is insignificant whether p, it is often a waste of time to criticize someone's belief that p on the grounds that it is false that p. And when someone believes something that is close enough to the truth, it is likewise often a waste of time to criticize their belief that p on the grounds that it is false that p. Imagine that your companion on an extremely low-key and structureless beach vacation looks at the clock, which you know is 45 minutes slow, on the wall of the bar and says, "It's noon. Let's order lunch." Alethic criticism of their belief would make sense (in the present sense of "make sense"), but it would be silly and useless, since at this resort there are no business hours or scheduled events.

Second, criticizing an attitude does not entail criticizing the person who has said attitude.[3] Imagine that your sweet little niece believes that whales are fish. It might be reasonable to criticize her belief on the grounds that it is false—by pointing out that whales are mammals—and yet unreasonable to criticize *her* for believing that whales are fish. It might not be her fault; imagine that she just didn't get into the good preschool.

Third, criticizing an attitude does not imply that it is irrational. Of course, it makes sense to criticize an attitude on the grounds that it is irrational. Irrationality is always a sufficient basis for criticism that makes sense. But it is not the only possible basis. It makes sense to criticize a belief on the grounds that it is false while acknowledging that said belief is not irrational. And, of course, there might be several distinct sufficient bases for criticism of an attitude that makes sense. If your belief that p is both false and formed on the basis of insufficient evidence, it would make sense for me to criticize your belief both on the grounds that it is false and on the grounds that it is unjustified. That axial criticism of desires makes sense is consistent with there being other species of desire criticism that make sense, e.g. criticism of desires as irrational.

3.2 Desires for the Bad Are Inaccurate

Why does alethic criticism of beliefs (§3.1) make sense? AB provides a compelling explanation: false beliefs are inaccurate. Thus, to criticize a belief

---

[3] This is related to the fact that accuracy and inaccuracy are properties of attitudes, rather than properties of the people who have them (§2.1).

54　THE EPISTEMOLOGY OF DESIRE AND THE PROBLEM OF NIHILISM

that p on the grounds that it is false that p is plausibly to criticize it as inaccurate, and we easily understand what someone is doing when they criticize an attitude as inaccurate. Since it makes sense to criticize an attitude as inaccurate, and since false beliefs are inaccurate, it makes sense to criticize a belief that p on the grounds that it is false that p, which is just to say that alethic criticism of beliefs makes sense.

I submit that AD provides a likewise compelling explanation of why axial criticism of desires makes sense. Given AD, desires for the bad are inaccurate. Thus, to criticize a desire that p on the grounds that it is bad that p is plausibly to criticize it as inaccurate, and we easily understand what someone is doing when they criticize an attitude as inaccurate. Since it makes sense to criticize an attitude as inaccurate, and since desires for the bad are inaccurate, it makes sense to criticize a desire that p on the grounds that it is bad that p, which is just to say that axial criticism of desires makes sense.

Consider your desire that the world be destroyed (§3.1). If it would be bad if the world were destroyed, then, per AD, your desire is inaccurate. That is why it makes sense to criticize your desire on the grounds that it would be bad if the world were destroyed. Such criticism would amount to criticism of your desire as inaccurate.

In this way, AD provides an elegant explanation of why axial criticism of desires makes sense, analogous to our explanation of why alethic criticism of beliefs makes sense: desires for the bad are inaccurate, such that it makes sense to criticize a desire that p on the grounds that it is bad that p, in the same way that false beliefs are inaccurate, such that it makes sense to criticize a belief that p on the grounds that it is false that p.

It is important to keep in mind: that it makes sense to criticize an attitude does not entail that you ought to do so (§3.1). Thus, the present explanation does not entail that you ought always criticize inaccurate desires. It might make sense to criticize a desire as inaccurate, and yet it would be inappropriate, insensitive, or pointless to do so. It is worth highlighting two kinds of cases in which facts about the content of an intuitively inaccurate desire speak against criticizing it.

First, consider a desire for something that is only a little bit bad (cf. §2.7). Suppose that, instead of wanting the world to be destroyed, you want to eat a few blades of grass from my lawn. Intuitively, that would be bad, because it would ever-so-slightly detract from the overall health of my lawn. (We can imagine, to simplify matters, that you would not get anything out of eating this grass; your desire is of the inexplicable, "saucer of mud" type.) Given AD, if it would be bad were you to eat a few blades of grass from my lawn, then your desire is inaccurate. However, the apparent inaccuracy of your desire intuitively does not matter enough to make criticism worthwhile; the apparent badness of what you want is too insignificant to warrant calling you out for wanting it. Thus, it is permissible not to criticize your desire, despite its apparent inaccuracy.

Second, suppose that there are axial gluts (§2.9), and consider a desire for something whose badness is outweighed by its goodness. Above, we considered a case of vicious pleasure; let us now consider a case of virtuous pain. Imagine that your most hated enemy has suffered some undeserved misfortune, and that, despite the bitterness of your feelings towards them, you manage to feel sympathy for their plight, and are thereby pained by their suffering. Your pain seems in one respect bad and in another respect good, but it seems quite a bit more good than it is bad. Nevertheless, given AD, if it was to some extent bad that you were pained by your enemy's suffering, if I were to be glad that you were pained by your enemy's suffering, my desire would be inaccurate. However, the apparent inaccuracy of my desire seems irrelevant, given how intuitively good it was that you were pained by your enemy's suffering. The apparent badness of your being pained by your enemy's suffering is insignificant compared to the apparent goodness of your being pained by your enemy's suffering. Thus, it is permissible not to criticize your desire, despite its apparent inaccuracy.

On the present account, if a desire is inaccurate, then it makes sense to criticize it as such. It follows that it makes sense to criticize a desire if it is inaccurate. But it does not follow that it makes sense to criticize a desire only if it is inaccurate. It might make sense to criticize desires that are not inaccurate, e.g. on the grounds that they are irrational (cf. §3.1). That axial criticism of desires makes sense is orthogonal to the scope of other species of desire criticism that makes sense. Compare, again, belief. That alethic criticism of beliefs makes sense is orthogonal to the scope of other species of belief criticism that makes sense.

I maintain that AD provides the best explanation of why it makes sense to criticize your desire that the world be destroyed on the grounds that it would be bad if the world were destroyed, and in general the best explanation of why axial criticism of desires makes sense. This is an inference to the best explanation argument. We must therefore consider alternative explanations of why axial criticism of desires makes sense.

However, as we will see, several plausible explanations of why axial criticism of desires makes sense are plausible only if AD is true. Since my aim is to defend AD, I am happy with alternative explanations that in this way imply AD. Thus, my aim in what follows will be to show that alternative explanations of why axial criticism of desires makes sense are either

56 THE EPISTEMOLOGY OF DESIRE AND THE PROBLEM OF NIHILISM

implausible *or* plausible only if AD is true. What we are looking for, which would make trouble for my argument, is a plausible explanation of why axial criticism of desires makes sense that does not imply AD.

3.3 Desires for the Bad Depend on False Beliefs

I said that, according to Hume, passions cannot be rational or irrational (§1.2). But that is not exactly right. Hume concedes that passions can be called irrational (although not "properly speaking") when they depend on false beliefs.[4] If my instrumental desire to drink from this glass depends on my mistaken belief that it contains gin, my desire can be called irrational, although properly speaking it is my belief that the glass contains gin that is the culprit. We are here interested in non-instrumental desire (§1.4). But non-instrumental desires can depend on false beliefs as well. If my desire to take a walk depends on my mistaken belief that the sun is shining, it can therefore be called irrational, per Hume's concession.

You might argue that, assuming it would be bad if the world were destroyed, your desire that the world be destroyed (§3.1) must depend on some false belief, which explains why axial criticism in this case makes sense, and that in general axial criticism of desires makes sense because desires for the bad depend on false beliefs. However, there is no reason why we have to imagine the case in that way. Granted, we can imagine a case like that. We can imagine someone whose desire that the world be destroyed depends on their mistaken belief that the destruction of the world would be fun and enjoyable and beneficial for everyone. But we can also imagine someone without any false beliefs about what it would be like if the world were destroyed wanting the world to be destroyed. It would nevertheless make sense to criticize their desire on the grounds that it would be bad if the world were destroyed. Thus, we cannot explain why axial criticism of desires makes sense by appeal to the idea that desires for the bad depend on false beliefs.

3.4 Desires for the Bad Are Abnormal

You might argue that, assuming it would be bad if the world were destroyed, your desire that the world be destroyed (§3.1) is abnormal, which explains

---

[4] *Treatise* 2.3.3.6.

why axial criticism in this case makes sense, and that in general axial criticism of desires makes sense because desires for the bad are abnormal. R.M. Hare (1963a), responding to a case from Philippa Foot (1961), argues that it would be odd if someone had great moral admiration for those who clasp and unclasp their hands, but they would not be making a mistake (pp. 129–32). The same could be said of your desire that the world be destroyed. As Hare argues, there are desires that require no explanation when had by human beings, such as desires for food and warmth, and there are desires that do require an explanation when had by human beings, and among these there are desires so bizarre that no explanation seems possible. A desire that the world be destroyed, you might think, is one of these. If wanting a saucer of mud for no reason at all would make you a "dull babbling loon" (Anscombe 1963, §37), wanting the world to be destroyed would surely make you something much worse. If desires for the bad are abnormal, then to criticize a desire that p on the grounds that it is bad that p is plausibly to criticize it as abnormal. Since it plausibly makes sense to criticize an attitude as abnormal, axial criticism of desires makes sense.

However, we can imagine desires for the bad that are not abnormal. Indeed, we need not imagine that your desire that the world be destroyed is abnormal. We can imagine a community or species of world-haters who all want the world to be destroyed. Criticism of their desires on the grounds that it would be bad if the world were destroyed would still make sense, even though their desires are completely normal. Thus, we cannot explain why axial criticism of desires makes sense by appeal to the idea that desires for the bad are abnormal.

Perhaps we could say that "normal" and "abnormal" are indexical, such that what is normal and abnormal is fixed by what human beings are actually like. There is, let us grant, a sense in which an eight-limbed octopus is abnormal, relative to our human perspective, on account of the fact that human beings normally have four limbs. The eight-limbed octopus is, at least, a little weird and unfamiliar to us normally four-limbed creatures. This, however, puts pressure on a presupposition that it makes sense to criticize an attitude as abnormal. If "abnormal" is indexical in the way suggested, criticism that appeals in this way to abnormality would at best make sense when confined to members of your own species. We would never think to criticize the eight-limbed octopus on the grounds that it has eight limbs, which is abnormal (for human beings). But, as we saw, it would make sense to criticize a desire that the world be destroyed, on the grounds that it would be bad if the world were destroyed, even if said desire were had by someone for whom such a desire was normal. If "abnormal" is indexical,

58   THE EPISTEMOLOGY OF DESIRE AND THE PROBLEM OF NIHILISM

the fact that desires for the bad are abnormal cannot explain why axial criticism of desires makes sense.

3.5 Desires for the Bad Are Vicious

You might argue that, assuming it would be bad if the world were destroyed, your desire that the world be destroyed (§3.1) is vicious, which explains why axial criticism in this case makes sense, and that in general axial criticism of desires makes sense because desires for the bad are vicious. Your desire plausibly manifests malevolence, callousness, unkindness, or some such vice. If desires for the bad are vicious, then to criticize a desire that p on the grounds that it is bad that p is plausibly to criticize it as vicious. Since it plausibly makes sense to criticize an attitude as vicious, axial criticism of desires makes sense.

However, consider the question of *why* your desire that the world be destroyed is vicious. The intuitive answer, perhaps even the obvious answer, is that it would be bad if the world were destroyed. If it wouldn't be bad if the world were destroyed, it is unclear that your desire would be vicious. The status of attitudes as virtuous or vicious depends on their responsiveness or unresponsiveness to various values. For example, a malevolent person is unresponsive to the badness of harm to others, and what makes malevolent desires intuitively vicious is the fact that harm to others is intuitively bad. If such harm were not bad, it is unclear that malevolent desires would be vicious.

But now consider the question of *why* desires for the bad are vicious. The answer, if not the obvious answer, is that they are inaccurate. Given AD and the assumption that it would be bad if the world were destroyed, your desire that the world be destroyed is an inaccurate representation of the value of the world's being destroyed. The inaccuracy of your desire—as explained by AD—is what ultimately explains its intuitive viciousness.

So, the present account is plausible only if AD is true. Our inference to the best explanation defense of AD is not threatened by the idea that desires for the bad are vicious (cf. §3.2).

You might object that your desire that the world be destroyed is vicious, not because it is inaccurate, but because it might have bad consequences.[5] I'll consider that idea in the next section (§3.6). Alternatively, you might

---

[5] Cf. Hume, *Enquiry concerning Human Understanding*, Driver 2001.

WHY CRITICIZE DESIRES FOR THE BAD? 59

object that your desire that the world be destroyed is vicious, not because it is inaccurate, but because it is bad to desire the bad.[6] I'll consider that idea in the following section (§3.7). Finally, you might object that your desire that the world be destroyed is vicious, not because it is inaccurate, but because it is an unfitting response to the badness of the world being destroyed.[7] I'll consider that idea in the section after that (§3.8).

I have assumed that something explains why your desire that the world be destroyed is vicious. Some virtue ethicists might deny this. For example, Michael Slote (2001) defends an "agent-based" virtue theory, on which the virtuousness and viciousness of motives is ethically fundamental. If this means that the virtuousness and viciousness of desires is inexplicable, then it follows that the viciousness of your desire that the world be destroyed is inexplicable. For another example, Linda Zagzebski (1996, pp. 78–84, 2010, 2017) defends an "exemplarist" virtue theory, on which the virtuousness of particular persons is ethically fundamental. And while Slote (2001) is primarily concerned to show that "the moral or ethical status of *acts* is derivative from independent and fundamental aretaic...ethical characterizations of motives, character traits, and individuals" (p. 5, my emphasis), Zagzebski (2017) is explicit in defining a "good motive" as "a motive we admire in an exemplar," i.e. a supremely admirable or virtuous person, and in defining a "good state of affairs" as "a state of affairs that exemplars aim to bring about" (p. 21; see also 2010, p. 55). However these ideas are extended to cover bad motives and bad states of affairs, they are surely incompatible with the idea that your desire that the world be destroyed is vicious because it is inaccurate, and inaccurate because it would be bad if the world were destroyed. For Zagzesbki, the order of explanation would have to run in the opposite direction: it would be bad if the world were destroyed bad because it is vicious to desire that the world be destroyed, or because it is virtuous to desire the opposite, or some such explanation, with the viciousness of the desire explanatorily prior to the badness of its object (cf. §3.8).

It is beyond the scope of this book to engage in a comprehensive discussion of agent-based and exemplarist virtue theories. However, there are two reasons I think we should be suspicious of the idea that the viciousness of your desire that the world be destroyed is inexplicable. First, consider some of the motives that Slote (2001) considers as candidates for fundamentally virtuous motives (cf. Zagzebski 1996, p. 83): compassion or universal

---

[6] Cf. Hurka 2001. [7] Cf. Adams 2006, Arpaly and Schroeder 2014.

60 THE EPISTEMOLOGY OF DESIRE AND THE PROBLEM OF NIHILISM

benevolence (pp. 24–9), understood as impartial concern for "human or sentient happiness" (pp. 24–5) or a "general humane concern for human beings, a general humanitarianism" (p. 36), and care for particular individual people (pp. 29–32). It seems obvious that the intuitive *goodness* of human flourishing—the idea that it is at least generally a good thing for human beings to flourish—has something to do with why these are plausible candidates for being fundamentally virtuous motives. Virtuous people care about human flourishing because it is a good thing—and not the other way around.[8] Second, we should distinguish the idea that the virtuousness and viciousness of desires is *metaphysically* prior to the goodness and badness of their objects from the idea that the virtuousness and viciousness of desires is *epistemologically* prior to the goodness and badness of their objects. The former claim is what I deny; perhaps the latter claim is true. Perhaps we only know what states of affairs are good and bad on the basis of our antecedent knowledge of what desires are virtuous and vicious, which is grounded in our admiration of exemplars. That is compatible with the explanation of why axial criticism of desires makes sense provided by AD.

3.6 Desires for the Bad Might Have Bad Consequences

You might argue that, assuming it would be bad if the world were destroyed, your desire that the world be destroyed (§3.1) might have bad consequences, which explains why axial criticism in this case makes sense, and that in general axial criticism of desires makes sense because desires for the bad might have bad consequences. There is some plausibility to the idea that someone who wanted the world to be destroyed would be a dangerous person—we can, at least, imagine situations in which such a person would be dangerous, e.g. if they had access to weapons of mass destruction. If desires for the bad might have bad consequences, then to criticize a desire that p on the grounds that it is bad that p is plausibly to criticize it as potentially having bad consequences. Since it plausibly makes sense to criticize an attitude as potentially having bad consequences, axial criticism of desires makes sense.

However, not all desires for the bad might have bad consequences, and yet even in such cases axial criticism makes sense. This has to do with the

---

[8] Slote (2001) seems to agree: "agent-based moralities *do* take consequences into account because they insist on or recommend an overall state of motivation that worries about and tries to produce good consequences" (p. 34).

WHY CRITICIZE DESIRES FOR THE BAD? 61

fact that desiring that p does not always dispose you to bring it about that p (§1.5). Consider, first, desires directed towards the past. Imagine someone delighted that Pompeii was destroyed by the eruption of Mount Vesuvius in 79 CE or someone who wishes that Cahokia had been destroyed by an earthquake in 1225 CE. Such desires hardly tend to dispose their subjects to bring it about that Pompeii or Cahokia was destroyed. Do they perhaps tend to dispose their subjects to bring other awful things about? That is hardly clear. We can, of course, imagine such cases—a supervillain who tries to get other volcanoes to erupt or a maniac who attempts to blow up the remains of Cahokia. But we can also imagine cases in which these desires are more or less practically inert, manifested only in pleasant viewings of Pompeii documentaries or frustrated drives past the extant remains of Cahokia. Nevertheless, it would make sense to criticize these desires on the grounds, respectively, that it was bad that Pompeii was destroyed and that it would have been bad had Cahokia been destroyed.

In defense of the practical theory of desire (§1.5), some philosophers argue that when someone desires something they cannot possibly bring about, they would be disposed to bring it about if they believed it was in their power to do so.[9] The question, for our purposes here, is whether such a conditional disposition—the property of being such that you would be disposed to bring it about that p, if you believed it was in your power—is a plausible basis for criticism. Let's focus on the person who wishes that Cahokia had been destroyed by an earthquake. Let's grant that this person would, if they believed it was in their power—e.g. if they believed it was 1224 and that they had a magic spell that could create earthquakes in particular places—be disposed to bring it about that Cahokia was destroyed by an earthquake in 1225. Given this premise, another counterfactual conditional seems true: if it were indeed in their power to bring it about that Cahokia was destroyed by an earthquake (and they knew that it was), their desire for that outcome would be one that might have bad consequences, such as the destruction of Cahokia. If conditions were right, as it were, their desire would be one that might have bad consequences. The problem is that this is true of any desire whatsoever. Any desire is such that, under certain conditions, it might have bad consequences. There is a possible world in which your desire to take a walk (§1.4) might have bad consequences; imagine a world inhabited by demons who wreak havoc whenever anyone desires

[9] Armstrong 1993, pp. 154–6, Döring and Eker 2017, pp. 84–5.

62   THE EPISTEMOLOGY OF DESIRE AND THE PROBLEM OF NIHILISM

to take a walk. It makes sense to criticize a desire as potentially having bad consequences. But it does not make sense to criticize a desire as being such that it *would* potentially have bad consequences under certain counterfactual conditions.

Consider, second, idle wishes (§1.5). This category includes familiar cases such as a baseball fan who wants the Cardinals to win a game—just one lousy game!—or a foreign observer who wants Donald Trump to lose the US Presidential election. We can easily imagine that your desire that the world be destroyed is an idle wish, and thus does not dispose you to bring it about that the world be destroyed. You hope the world will be destroyed, but you are not disposed to take any action that might bring this about or have any other bad consequences. We can even imagine that you positively want not to be involved, that what you relish is the thought of the world being destroyed without your having to lift a finger. Nevertheless, it would make sense to criticize your desire on the grounds that it would be bad if the world were destroyed.

Thus, given that desiring that p does not always dispose you to bring it about that p, we cannot explain why axial criticism of desires makes sense by appeal to the idea that desires for the bad might have bad consequences.

3.7 Desires for the Bad Are Bad

Consider the idea that it is good to desire the good and bad to desire the bad.[10] Call this the *axial recursion principle*. You might argue that, assuming it would be bad if the world were destroyed, your desire that the world be destroyed (§3.1) is bad, because it is a desire for something bad, which explains why axial criticism in this case makes sense, and that in general axial criticism of desires makes sense because desires for the bad are bad. If desires for the bad are bad, then to criticize a desire that p on the grounds that it is bad that p is plausibly to criticize it as bad. Since it plausibly makes sense to criticize an attitude as bad, axial criticism of desires makes sense.

The question we must ask is: why, and in what sense, is it good to desire the good and bad to desire the bad? Recall that it can be bad to desire the good and good to desire the bad (§2.2). The alleged goodness of desiring the good must be present even when desiring the good would have bad

---

[10] Cf. Moore 1903, chapter VI, Hurka 2001.

consequences (e.g. the mind-reading villain's threatened mayhem) and the alleged badness of desiring the bad must be present even when desiring the bad would have good consequences (e.g. the mind-reading eccentric's promised reward). The goodness of desiring the good and badness of desiring the bad must somehow be *intrinsic* to desiring the good and desiring the bad, respectively.

Now, AD says that desires for the good are accurate and desires for the bad are inaccurate, and the accuracy of desires for the good and the inaccuracy of desires for the bad, given AD, are plausibly intrinsic to desiring the good and desiring the bad, respectively. You might think—although I implied otherwise, above (§2.2)—that accurate attitudes are thereby good and inaccurate attitudes are thereby bad. Putting this idea and AD together gets us the claim that desires for the good are good and desires for the bad are bad. However, if this is what explains why desires for the good are good and desires for the bad are bad, then the present account is plausible only if AD is true, and our inference to the best explanation defense of AD is not threatened by the idea that desires for the bad are bad (cf. §3.2).

Perhaps the intrinsic goodness of desiring the good and the intrinsic badness of desiring the bad cannot be explained. Is that a problem for the present account? Compare the explanation provided by AD (§2.2). I have not attempted to explain why desires for the good are accurate and desires for the bad are inaccurate; I have not attempted to explain *why* goodness is the accuracy condition for desire. Suppose that the intrinsic goodness of desiring the good and intrinsic badness of desiring the bad is inexplicable. And let us grant for the sake of argument that the fact that goodness is the accuracy condition for desire is likewise inexplicable. Why prefer the explanation of why axial criticism of desires makes sense provided by AD to the explanation provided by the axial recursion principle?

Compare two explanations of why alethic criticism of beliefs (§3.1) makes sense. The explanation provided by AB is that false beliefs are inaccurate (§3.2). Consider an alternative explanation that appeals to an inexplicable axiological principle: that it is good to believe the true and bad to believe the false. It seems obvious that the former explanation is better than the latter explanation. But why is that? The answer, it seems to me, is that AB explains what is wrong with false beliefs, by telling us that they are inaccurate. Given AB, when we criticize a belief on the grounds that it is false, we know what we are criticizing it for: for being inaccurate. The alternative explanation, by contrast, does not explain what is wrong with false beliefs. Given the principle that it is good to believe the true and bad to believe the

64 THE EPISTEMOLOGY OF DESIRE AND THE PROBLEM OF NIHILISM

false, when we criticize a belief on the grounds that it is false, although we can say that we are criticizing the belief on account of its being bad, we cannot say *what* is bad about it—we cannot explain *why* it is bad. AB, by contrast, provides a much more specific and determinate charge to level against allegedly false beliefs: that they are inaccurate.

However, the same reasoning applies when it comes to our two explanations of why axial criticism of desires makes sense. The explanation provided by AD is a better explanation, because AD explains what is wrong with desires for the bad, by telling us that they are inaccurate. Given AD, when we criticize a desire that p on the grounds that it is bad that p, we know what we are criticizing it for: for being inaccurate. The explanation that appeals to the axial recursion principle, by contrast, does not explain what is wrong with desires for the bad. Given that explanation, when we criticize a desire on the basis of its being for the bad, although we can say that we are criticizing the desire on account of its being bad, we cannot say *what* is bad about it—we cannot explain *why* it is bad. AD, by contrast, provides a much more specific and determinate charge to level against desires for the bad: that they are inaccurate.

For this reason, it seems to me that AD provides a better explanation of why axial criticism of desires makes sense, compared to the explanation provided by the axial recursion principle.

3.8 Desires for the Bad Are Unfitting

Consider the following "fitting desire" account of value, which is an instance of what is known as a "fitting attitudes" account of value, on which good things are good in virtue of its being fitting to desire them and bad things are bad in virtue of its being unfitting to desire them:[11]

> FD It is good that p if and only if (and because) it is fitting to desire that p and bad that p if and only if (and because) it is unfitting to desire that p.

---

[11] See Brentano 1889/1969, p. 18, Sidgwick 1907, p. 112, Broad 1930, p. 283, Brandt 1946, 1979, Ewing 1947, 1959, chapter III, Gibbard 1990, Mulligan 1998, McHugh and Way 2016, Cullity 2018; see also McDowell 1985/1998, Wiggins 1987/1998. Alternatively, we might understand the "fitting desire" account as saying that good things are good in virtue of its being fitting to desire them and bad things are bad in virtue of its being fitting to desire their negation. If there are axial gluts, these two formulations are not equivalent. If there are no axial gluts (§2.9), then it is plausibly fitting to desire that p if and only if it is unfitting to desire that not-p. (This is Brentano's "law of antagonism.")

Given FD, if it would be bad if the world were destroyed, then it is unfitting to desire that the world be destroyed. You might argue that, if it would be bad if the world were destroyed, then, per UD, your desire that the world be destroyed is unfitting, which explains why axial criticism in this case makes sense, and that in general axial criticism of desires makes sense because desires for the bad are unfitting. If desires for the bad are unfitting, then to criticize a desire that p on the grounds that it is bad that p is plausibly to criticize it as unfitting. Since it plausibly makes sense to criticize an attitude as unfitting, axial criticism of desires makes sense.

Is this account of why axial criticism of desires makes sense plausible? As Richard Brandt (1946) remarks in a similar context, "fitting" is a word "crying aloud for further discussion" (p. 113). With the proposed explanation in mind, what does it mean to say that it is "fitting" or "unfitting" to desire that p? I will consider three interpretations of "fitting" and "unfitting." In this section, I'll consider the possibility that to say that an attitude is fitting is to say that it is accurate and to say that an attitude is unfitting is to say that it is inaccurate. Then, in the following sections, I'll consider the possibility that to say that an attitude is fitting is to say that it is reasonable and to say that an attitude is unfitting is to say that it is unreasonable (§3.9) and the possibility that to say that an attitude is fitting is to say that there is a reason to have it and to say that an attitude is unfitting is to say that there is a reason not to have it (§3.10).

Note well that, in asking what it means to say that it is "fitting" or "unfitting" to desire that p, I am not asking for an account of fittingness and unfittingness. We must allow for the possibility that fittingness and unfittingness are ethically fundamental, such that the concepts of fittingness and unfittingness cannot be defined.[12] However, "fitting" and "unfitting" are ambiguous, admitting of multiple possible interpretations—as the present discussion will illustrate. Thus, even if fittingness and unfittingness are ethically fundamental, we must indicate the intended interpretation of "fitting" and "unfitting" to make any sense of FD.

You might think that to say that an attitude is fitting is to say that it is accurate,[13] which suggests that to say that an attitude is unfitting is to say that it is inaccurate. On this interpretation, we use "fit" in something like the way we would be using it if we were to say that beliefs have the

---

[12] Cf. McHugh and Way 2016, Cullity 2018.
[13] See D'Arms and Jacobson 2000a, Piller 2006, p. 162; see also Brentano 1889/1969, McDowell 1985/1998, Wiggins 1987/1998.

66 THE EPISTEMOLOGY OF DESIRE AND THE PROBLEM OF NIHILISM

mind-to-world "direction of fit" (cf. §1.5) or that it is fitting to be afraid of something only if it is dangerous (cf. §1.11). We can thus reformulate FD:

FD-ACCURACY   It is good that p if and only if (and because) a desire that p is accurate and bad that p if and only if (and because) a desire that p is inaccurate.

Our fittingness-based account thus becomes: if it would be bad if the world were destroyed, then, per FD-ACCURACY, your desire that the world be destroyed is inaccurate, which explains why axial criticism in this case makes sense, and in general axial criticism of desires makes sense because desires for the bad are inaccurate.

However, we seek an explanation of why axial criticism of desires makes sense that does not imply AD (§3.2). Isn't the fittingness-based account, given FD-ACCURACY, identical to the account provided by AD?

There is an important difference between AD and FD-ACCURACY. AD says that accurate desires are accurate in virtue of being for the good and inaccurate desires are inaccurate in virtue of being for the bad (§2.2), whereas FD-ACCURACY says that good things are good in virtue of desires for them being accurate and bad things are bad in virtue of desires for them being inaccurate. It thus appears that AD and FD-ACCURACY are incompatible.

However, it is possible to understand FD-ACCURACY in such a way that it is compatible with AD. Recall FD, on which good things are good in virtue of its being fitting to desire them and bad things are bad in virtue of its being unfitting to desire them. This is consistent with the theoretical identi-fication of goodness with the property of making desire fitting and badness with the property of making desire unfitting. On this view, goodness just is the property of making desire fitting and badness just is the property of making desire unfitting. Thus, we could say both that good things are good in virtue of its being fitting to desire them and bad things are bad in virtue of its being unfitting to desire them (since that is simply what it is to be good and bad, respectively) and that fitting desires are fitting in virtue of being for the good and unfitting desires are unfitting in virtue of being for the bad (since goodness makes desire fitting and badness makes desire unfitting).

Similarly, FD-ACCURACY is consistent with the theoretical identification of goodness with the property of making desire accurate and badness with the property of making desire inaccurate. Thus, consistent with FD-ACCURACY,

WHY CRITICIZE DESIRES FOR THE BAD? 67

we could say both that good things are good in virtue of desires for them being accurate and bad things are bad in virtue of desires for them being inaccurate (since that is simply what it is to be good and bad, respectively) and that accurate desires are accurate in virtue of being for the good and inaccurate desires are inaccurate in virtue of being for the bad (since goodness makes desire accurate and badness makes desire inaccurate). FD-ACCURACY is, therefore, compatible with AD.

However, FD-ACCURACY is not only compatible with AD; FD-ACCURACY is plausible only if AD is true. Consider something intuitively good, like the survival of the snow leopard, and suppose that you want it, i.e. that you hope the snow leopard survives. Assuming it would be good were the snow leopard to survive, given FD-ACCURACY, it would be good were the snow leopard to survive because your desire is accurate. Now, why is your desire accurate? AD would say: because it would be good were the snow leopard to survive. Suppose AD is false. Why, then, is your desire that the snow leopard survive accurate? I think we have to say, at this point, that there is no explanation—that it is a brute fact that your desire that the snow leopard survive is accurate.

But that is implausible. Compare the analogous idea in the case of belief. We could with some plausibility identify truth with the property of making belief accurate, such that it is true that p if and only if (and because) a belief that p is accurate. However, this is plausible only if AB is true. There is a desk in my office. Suppose that you believe that there is a desk in my office. Given the present view, it is true that there is a desk in my office because your belief is accurate. But why is your belief accurate? AB would say: because it is true that there is a desk in my office. If we reject AB, we have to say that there is no explanation—that it is a brute fact that your belief that there is a desk is my office is accurate. But that is absurd. The accuracy of your belief must depend, in some way, on the situation in my office—on the fact that there is a desk in there. The accuracy of particular beliefs is not brute and inexplicable. Neither, I conclude, is the accuracy of particular desires. (Perhaps the fittingness of particular attitudes is brute and inexplicable, but in that case we should reject the present idea, that to say that an attitude is fitting is to say that it is accurate.)

The same, mutatis mutandis, when it comes to inaccuracy. Assuming it would be bad if the world were destroyed, given FD-ACCURACY, it would be bad if the world were destroyed because your desire that the world be destroyed is inaccurate. Why is your desire inaccurate? AD would say: because it would be bad if the world were destroyed. If we reject AD,

68   THE EPISTEMOLOGY OF DESIRE AND THE PROBLEM OF NIHILISM

we have to say that there is no explanation—that it is a brute fact that your desire that the world be destroyed is inaccurate. But that is implausible.

Thus, we have failed to find an explanation of why axial criticism of desires makes sense that does not imply AD.

3.9 Desires for the Bad Are Unreasonable

Recall FD and the question of what "fitting" and "unfitting" mean (§3.8). You might think that to say that an attitude is fitting is to say that it is reasonable and to say that an attitude is unfitting is to say that it is unreasonable. We can thus reformulate FD:

> FD-REASONABLE   It is good that p if and only if (and because) it is reasonable to desire that p and bad that p if and only if (and because) it is unreasonable to desire that p.

Our fittingness-based account thus becomes: if it would be bad if the world were destroyed, then, per FD-REASONABLE, it is unreasonable to desire that the world be destroyed, which explains why axial criticism in this case makes sense, and in general axial criticism of desires makes sense because desires for the bad are unreasonable.

However, FD-REASONABLE is implausible. The reasonableness and unreasonableness of attitudes is relative to a given body of possessed evidence.[14] When we ask whether it is reasonable or unreasonable to have an attitude, we always presuppose some subject who has such-and-such evidence, such that our question is more perspicuously rendered as the question of whether it is reasonable or unreasonable *for that subject* to have said attitude. Whether it is reasonable or unreasonable for you to desire something depends on your evidence. Suppose your cactus is thirsty, but you have compelling but misleading evidence that your cactus has been over-watered. Intuitively, it would be good were your cactus watered, but it is not reasonable for you to want your cactus to be watered. Now suppose your cactus has been over-watered, but you have compelling but misleading evidence that your cactus is thirsty. Intuitively, it would be bad if your cactus were watered, but it is not unreasonable for you to want your cactus to be watered.

---

[14] D'Arms and Jacobson 2000b, p. 745.

Thus, on the present interpretation of "fitting" and "unfitting," "fit" is used in something like the way it is used when we say that justified beliefs must fit the evidence or that it is fitting to be afraid of something if you have reason to think it is dangerous. However, on this interpretation, FD is implausible.

We would encounter the same problem if we appealed to the idea that to say that an attitude is fitting is to say that it is rational or justified and to say that an attitude is unfitting is to say that it is irrational or unjustified. Just as whether it is reasonable or unreasonable for you to desire something depends on your evidence, whether it is rational or irrational for you to desire something and whether you are justified or unjustified in desiring something depends on your evidence. Likewise, we would encounter this problem if we appealed to the idea that to say that an attitude is fitting is to say that you subjectively ought to have it and to say that an attitude is unfitting is to say that you subjectively ought not have it. Just as whether it is reasonable or unreasonable for you to desire something depends on your evidence, whether you subjectively ought or ought not desire something depends on your evidence. FD cannot plausibly be formulated using any of these (as it were) evidence-relative concepts.[15]

3.10 Desires for the Bad Are Desires There Is a Reason Not to Have

Derek Parfit (2011) argues that:

> Our desires are rational...when we want events whose features give us reasons to want them. Our desires are not rational, and are in the old phrase *contrary to reason*, when we want some event that we have reasons *not* to want, and no reasons, or only weaker reasons, to want. (p. 56)

Recall FD and the question of what "fitting" and "unfitting" mean (§3.8). Perhaps to say that an attitude is unfitting is to say that it is contrary to reason, in Parfit's sense. Might we argue that your desire that the world be destroyed is, in this sense, contrary to reason? Let us grant that there is a reason not to want the world to be destroyed—presumably, something

---

[15] Cf. Berker 2022, pp. 35–45, for further reasons not to understand "fitting" and "unfitting" in deontic terms.

70 THE EPISTEMOLOGY OF DESIRE AND THE PROBLEM OF NIHILISM

having to do with what it would be like if the world were destroyed. However, we need not imagine that your desire is contrary to reason, in Parfit's sense, because we need not imagine that you *have* the aforementioned reason not to want the world to be destroyed. For example, we can imagine that your desire that the world be destroyed depends on your mistaken belief that the destruction of the world would be fun and enjoyable and beneficial for everyone (§3.3; cf. §3.9). There is a fact of the matter, unknown to you, about what it would be like if the world were destroyed, and that fact is a reason not to want the world to be destroyed. But you do not know that fact, and, therefore, you do not have that reason. Your desire is not contrary to reason. Nevertheless, it would make sense to criticize your desire that the world be destroyed on the grounds that it would be bad if the world were destroyed.

However, Parfit's invocation of reasons suggests an alternative account of why axial criticism of desires makes sense. You might think that to say that an attitude is fitting is to say that there is a reason to have it and so to say that an attitude is unfitting is to say that there is a reason not to have it. If so, we might reformulate FD:

> FD-REASONS It is good that p if and only if (and because) there is a reason to desire that p and bad that p if and only if (and because) there is a reason not to desire that p.

This is what is known as a "buck-passing" account of value, on which good things are good in virtue of there being a reason to desire them and bad things are bad in virtue of there being a reason not to desire them.[16] This account sits most comfortably with the idea that reasons—rather than values—are ethically fundamental.[17] Our fittingness-based account thus becomes: if it would be bad if the world were destroyed, then, per FD-REASONS, there is a reason not to desire that the world be destroyed, which explains why axial criticism in this case makes sense, and in general

---

[16] See Scanlon 1998, pp. 95–100, Parfit 2001, pp. 18–20, 2011, pp. 38–9, Olson 2004, Rabinowicz and Rønnow-Rasmussen 2004, Suikkanen 2004. It seems to me that those who say that good things are good because one ought to desire them (Sidgwick 1907, Ewing 1947, 1959, Gibbard 1990) have something like this in mind. They mean that good things are good because one objectively ought to desire them, just as those who say that one ought to believe that p only if p mean that one objectively ought to believe that p only if p (cf. Boghossian 2003, 2005).

[17] Cf. Scanlon 1998, Parfit 2001, 2011, Lord 2018, Schroeder 2021.

WHY CRITICIZE DESIRES FOR THE BAD? 71

axial criticism of desires makes sense because desires for the bad are desires there is a reason not to have.

However, FD-REASONS needs to be amended to avoid a version of the "wrong kind of reasons" problem that afflicts "buck-passing" accounts of value.[18] Imagine that you want to take a walk, but a mind-reading villain threatens to do something awful unless you abandon your desire. (They will leave you alone otherwise, even if you end up taking a walk.) Does this give you a reason not to want to take a walk? If it does, then, per FD-REASONS, it would be bad were you to take a walk. However, intuitively, given the story we told, it would not be bad were you to take a walk.

I think the villain's threat does not give you a reason not to want to take a walk.[19] (If you prefer to say that it gives you the "wrong kind" of reason, you could replace "reason" with "right kind of reason" in what follows, and what I say should remain plausible.) The reason I think this is that I accept the following necessary condition on reasons:

The fact that p is a reason to χ only if it is possible to χ because p – i.e. for the reason that p or on the basis of the fact that p.

Following Nishi Shah (2006), I'll call this the "deliberative constraint on reasons."[20] Given the deliberative constraint on reasons, not all facts that speak in favor of χing are reasons to χ. Only those facts that speak in favor of χing on the basis of which it is possible to χ are reasons to χ. However, it is not possible for you to abandon your desire to take a walk because—i.e. for the reason that or on the basis of the fact that—the villain threatened to do something awful unless you do. You might, the basis of the villain's threat, wish that your desire would go away, or undertake a course of therapy to extinguish your desire, but you could not, on the basis of the villain's threat, stop wanting to take a walk. Therefore, the fact that the villain threatened to do something awful unless you abandon your desire is not a reason not to want to take a walk.

---

[18] See Crisp 2000, p. 459, D'Arms and Jacobson 2000b, Rabinowicz and Rønnow-Rasmussen 2004.

[19] Cf. Parfit 2011, pp. 420–32, Gibbard 1990, pp. 36–7.

[20] See esp. pp. 484–8; see also Williams 1980/1981, p. 102, 1989/1995, p. 39, Kolodny 2005, pp. 548–51, Parfit 1997, p. 114n. Note well (cf. Parfit, 1997, p. 114n.; see also Parfit 2006, 334–7) that the deliberative constraint on reasons is not equivalent to "internalism" about reasons, on which there is a reason for you to χ only if you have some motive that would be served or furthered by your χing (cf. Williams 1980/1981, p. 101).

72 THE EPISTEMOLOGY OF DESIRE AND THE PROBLEM OF NIHILISM

However, to solve the "wrong kind of reasons" problem, we need to do more. We need to provide a *substantive* account of what distinguishes reasons for having or not having an attitude from mere considerations that speak in favor of having or not having an attitude. Granted, mere facts that speak in favor of having or not having an attitude violate the deliberative constraint on reasons, whereas genuine reasons do not. But we need to know: what do the latter facts have in common, that distinguishes them from the former?

AD suggests an elegant answer. Consider the intuitive idea that reasons for having or not having an attitude are facts about the *content* or *object* of the attitude, rather than facts about the having of the attitude.[21] The villain's threat is intuitively a fact about your wanting to take a walk, rather than a fact about your taking a walk, e.g. that you would enjoy taking a walk. This is on the right track, but the distinction between "facts about" the content or object of an attitude and "facts about" the attitude itself is obscure.[22] Given the villain's threat, it is a fact about your taking a walk that a villain has threatened to do something awful if you want to do it. What this shows is that reasons for having or not having an attitude will involve some narrower or more specific set of facts about the content or object of the attitude. Consider the following account: reasons for having or not having an attitude are facts that bear on its accuracy or inaccuracy.[23] Consider the case of belief: reasons for believing or not believing that p are facts that bear on the accuracy or inaccuracy of believing that p, i.e. given AB, evidence relevant to whether it is true or false that p, i.e. evidence relevant to whether p. And we can say the same about desire: reasons for desiring or not desiring that p are facts that bear on the accuracy or inaccuracy of desiring that p, i.e. given AD, evidence relevant to whether it is good or bad that p. The villain's threat is not such a fact, because it does not bear on whether it would good or bad were you to take a walk. By contrast, the fact that you would enjoy taking a walk is intuitively evidence that it would be good were you to take a walk.

Note the essential role that AD plays in this account. Reasons for desiring or not desiring that p must be facts that bear on whether it is good or bad

---

[21] Parfit 2001, pp. 21–2, 2011, pp. 50–1, Piller 2006.

[22] See Rabinowicz and Rønnow-Rasmussen 2004, p. 406, Olson 2004, p. 299, Piller 2006, pp. 156–8.

[23] Note that we need to distinguish between reasons for not having an attitude with a particular content and reasons for not forming an attitude of a particular kind, e.g. between reasons for not believing that p and reasons for not forming a belief about whether p (McGrath 2021a, 2021b). Reasons for not forming an attitude of a particular kind need not be facts that bear on accuracy or inaccuracy (e.g. undercutting defeaters).

that p. This is what enables us to rule out cases in which there is a reason to desire something that is not good or in which there is a reason not to desire something that is not bad.

We have arrived at a solution to the "wrong kind of reasons" problem for FD-REASONS that implies AD. Several contributors to the literature on the "wrong kind of reasons" problem have arrived at something like this solution.[24] However, we seek an explanation of why axial criticism of desires makes sense that does not imply AD (§3.2). Perhaps the "wrong kind of reasons" problem can be solved in some other way, one that does not involve AD. However, in the absence of such a solution, we have failed to find an alternative to AD.

You might think the "wrong kind of reasons" problem can be avoided by abandoning FD-REASONS in favor of a more modest principle, which merely says that goodness and badness entail reasons:

> VER   If it is good that p, then there is a reason to desire that p, and, if it is bad that p, then there is a reason to desire that not-p.

VER gives up on giving an account of value, and settles for a necessary connection between value and reasons to desire. VER is not threatened by any "wrong kind of reasons" problem. So, consider an account of why axial criticism of desires makes sense: if it would be bad if the world were destroyed, then, per VER, there is a reason not to desire that the world be destroyed, which explains why axial criticism in this case makes sense, and in general axial criticism of desires makes sense because desires for the bad are desires there is a reason not to have.

Recall that AD plausibly implies that, if it is good that p, then there is a reason to desire that p and that, if it is bad that p, then there is a reason not to desire that p. AD is not only compatible with VER, but suggests an explanation of why VER is true. Note, as well, that VER is entailed by FD-REASONS, and that FD-REASONS suggests an explanation of why VER is true: good things are good because there is a reason to desire them and bad things are bad because there is a reason not to desire them, so, trivially, if something is good, there is a reason to desire it and, if something is bad, there is a reason not to desire it. However, in the present context, we cannot appeal to FD-REASONS to explain why VER is true, nor can we appeal to

---

[24] See Rabinowicz and Rønnow-Rasmussen 2004, pp. 420–2, McHugh and Way 2016, Oddie 2017, pp. 37–41, Cullity 2018, pp. 35–6; see also Hieronymi 2005.

74 THE EPISTEMOLOGY OF DESIRE AND THE PROBLEM OF NIHILISM

AD, given that we seek an explanation of why axial criticism of desires makes sense that does not imply AD (§3.2). Why, then, is VER true? What explains the fact that there is a necessary connection between value and reasons to desire? There is no such necessary connection between truth and falsehood and reasons to desire—it might be true that p even if there is no reason to desire that p or false that p even if there is no reason not to desire that p—and there is no necessary connection between value and reasons to imagine—it might be good that p even if there is no reason to imagine that p or bad that p even if there is no reason not to imagine that p. Why is there this connection between value and reasons to desire? Even allowing that reasons are ethically fundamental, I think this question has to have an answer. However, if we can appeal neither to AD nor to FD-REASONS, it is obscure what that answer might be.

3.11 Conclusion

In this chapter, I argued that AD provides the best explanation of why it makes sense to criticize a desire that p on the grounds that it is bad that p. Desiring the bad is like believing the false: in both cases, your attitude is inaccurate. Belief and desire each have an accuracy condition: truth is the accuracy condition for belief and goodness is the accuracy condition for desire. This opens up the possibility of the epistemology of desire, to which we'll now turn. Later on, we'll see how AD gives rise to the problem of nihilism.

The Epistemology of Desire and the Problem of Nihilism. Allan Hazlett, Oxford University Press.
© Allan Hazlett 2024. DOI: 10.1093/9780191995583.003.0003

4
Desire That Amounts to Knowledge

That goodness is the accuracy condition for desire represents a striking point of analogy between belief and desire: both belief and desire have an accuracy condition. We are familiar with the idea that belief can amount to knowledge—i.e. that instances of belief can also be instances of knowledge. In this chapter, I'll defend an unfamiliar idea: that desire can amount to knowledge—i.e. that instances of desire can be instances of knowledge. I will call cases of desire that amounts to knowledge cases of *orectic knowledge*[1], by contrast with familiar cases of belief that amounts to knowledge, i.e. cases of propositional knowledge.

When we say that belief can amount to knowledge, we mean that there are conditions under which belief amounts to knowledge. We don't assume that those conditions are or ever could be met. A philosophical skeptic could agree that belief can amount to knowledge, in the intended sense. They might assume, for example, that knowledge is justified true belief, and go on to argue that it is impossible for a belief to be justified. In the same way, when I say that desire can amount to knowledge, I mean that there are conditions under which desire amounts to knowledge. I don't assume that those conditions are or ever could be met. A skeptic about orectic knowledge could agree that desire can amount to knowledge, in the intended sense. This is important, in the present context, because the nihilist about value (§1.1) turns out to be just such a skeptic (§4.4).

To put all this another way, to say that belief can amount to knowledge is just to say that there is such a thing as propositional knowledge and to say that desire can amount to knowledge is just to say that there is such a thing as orectic knowledge. My thesis, therefore, is that there is such a thing as orectic knowledge.

---

[1] "Orectic" mirrors "doxastic" and is based on ὄρεξις, "longing or yearning after a thing, desire for it" (Liddell and Scott's *Greek–English Lexicon*), which Aristotle uses as a generic term for desire.

76 THE EPISTEMOLOGY OF DESIRE AND THE PROBLEM OF NIHILISM

My argument that there is such a thing as orectic knowledge is relatively simple. Knowledge is apt mental representation. Given AD, desires can be apt. Therefore, desires can amount to knowledge, i.e. there is such a thing as orectic knowledge.

However, the conclusion that there is such a thing as orectic knowledge is independently appealing—as I will try to show—and, therefore, although AD is a premise of my argument in this chapter, the fact that AD leads us to the conclusion that there is such a thing as orectic knowledge provides further support for the idea that goodness is the accuracy condition for desire.

4.1 Orectic Knowledge as Knowledge of Goodness

Recall that, given AB and AD, there is a sense in which beliefs represent their objects as true (§2.1) and in which desires represent their objects as good (§2.2). Given the sense in which beliefs represent their objects as true, when a belief of yours amounts to knowledge, there is a corresponding sense in which you enjoy knowledge of truth. Now, suppose I am right and desire can amount to knowledge. Given the sense in which desires represent their objects as good, when a desire of yours amounts to knowledge, there is a corresponding sense in which you enjoy knowledge of goodness.

This point allows us to forestall a confusion. Belief and desire are both propositional attitudes (§2.3). When a belief of yours amounts to knowledge, your belief that p amounts to knowledge that p. However, again supposing that there is such a thing as orectic knowledge, when a desire of yours amounts to knowledge, your desire that p does not plausibly amount to knowledge that p. Rather, in the same way that a belief that p might amount to knowledge of the truth of the proposition that p, a desire that p might amount to knowledge of the goodness of the proposition that p.[2]

So, on my view, orectic knowledge is a species of knowledge of goodness. If your desire that p amounts to knowledge, you enjoy knowledge of the goodness of the proposition that p. Why do I say this, as opposed to saying that, if your desire that p amounts to knowledge, you enjoy knowledge that it is good that p? Because knowing that it is good that p, it seems to me, requires deploying the concept of goodness, but desiring that p does not (§1.7)—including, I assume, cases in which desire amounts to knowledge.

---

[2] Keep in mind that we speak loosely when we speak of truth and goodness as properties of propositions (§2.4).

On my view, there are two species of knowledge of goodness: a conceptually-unsophisticated species constituted by desire and a conceptually-sophisticated species constituted by evaluative belief.

4.2 The Ethical Importance of Orectic Knowledge

The history of philosophical ethics is often animated by a clash between two ideas. On the one hand, there is a Platonic insight that the good life requires knowledge of goodness—since you will not easily realize goodness in your life without such knowledge. Living a good life without knowledge of goodness would seem to require a great deal of luck—you would need to stumble upon the good life, like someone stumbling upon a trove of treasure without having known where it was to be found. On the other hand, there is a Pyrrhonian insight that the good life does not require beliefs about goodness—since people can easily live well while avoiding ethical theorizing altogether. The idea that the good life requires knowledge of goodness seems to over-intellectualize the good life. Debates between Stoics and skeptics, between rationalists and sentimentalists, and between cognitivists and non-cognitivists are all variants on this clash.

The idea that there is such a thing as orectic knowledge puts us in a position from which we can reconcile these ideas. Orectic knowledge is a species of knowledge of goodness (§4.1). The Platonic claim that the good life requires knowledge of goodness and the Pyrrhonian claim that the good life does not require beliefs about goodness are, therefore, compatible. Not all knowledge is constituted by belief—some knowledge is constituted by desire. And, indeed, this seems like the plausible thing to say about the kind of knowledge of goodness required for living well. This explains why sensible parents are more concerned that their children care about what really matters, i.e. that they desire the good, than they are concerned that their children have true beliefs about what really matters, i.e. that they believe of the good that it is good. And this explains why plausible accounts of virtue require an affective or motivational orientation towards the good, as opposed to propositional knowledge of it.[3]

Consider Smith, a prejudiced jailer. Smith holds an extremely negative view of the moral status of her prisoners, who belong to a marginalized

---

[3] See e.g. Zagzebski 1996, Slote 2001, Adams 2006.

78 THE EPISTEMOLOGY OF DESIRE AND THE PROBLEM OF NIHILISM

outgroup (class, caste, race, etc.), such that, specifically, she believes that their suffering is not intrinsically bad. Smith's job requires treating her prisoners very roughly. However, despite her prejudice, Smith finds her work distasteful. She does not like it. She finds herself wanting to go easy on her prisoners—i.e. to refrain from hitting them, to sneak them food, etc.—even though she believes that doing so would be in no way good. Smith is embarrassed by her desire to go easy on her prisoners, which she attributes to a lack of discipline, believing, as she does, that going easy on her prisoners would not be good. But she is wrong about the source of her feelings: her desire to go easy on her prisoners actually manifests compassion, a compassion which has survived despite her indoctrination. To put that another way, her desire is a response to her prisoners' needs, to which she is, in spite of her prejudice, sensitive. This responsiveness is evidenced by the fact that she is not generally tempted not to do her job—she doesn't mind passing out the prisoners' mail, sweeping the floors, etc. It is only when her job calls for rough treatment of the prisoners that she finds herself wanting to shirk her duties. Smith is not the undisciplined jailer she takes herself to be; she is actually a compassionate, if prejudiced, jailer.

I am going to argue that knowledge is apt mental representation, that desires can be apt, and that Smith's desire to go easy on her prisoners is intuitively apt. On my view, if Smith's desire is apt, then it amounts to knowledge of the goodness of her going easy on her prisoners. This is an appealing result, for at least two reasons.

First, suppose that Smith acts on her desire to go easy on her prisoners. In that case, if Smith knows the goodness of her going easy on her prisoners, that explains why it is virtuous for her to act as she does.[4] Acting on her desire to go easy on her prisoners is not a case of "giving in to temptation" or "letting her emotions get the better of her"—even though Smith is inclined to describe things that way. When Smith acts on her desire, she is wisely trusting her reliable feelings, despite their conflict with her bigoted ideology. If Smith did not know the goodness of her going easy on her prisoners, we could not easily make sense of her actions as virtuous. We might welcome her actions as fortuitous, but we could not plausibly praise Smith for her virtue. But that would miss something important about the

---

[4] Cf. Bennett 1974, Audi 1990, MacIntyre 1990, Arpaly 2000, 2004. Note that the present version of the case involves a clash between Smith's *evaluative* beliefs—her beliefs about what is *good*—and her desires, rather than a clash between her *deontic* beliefs—her beliefs about what she *ought* to do—and her intentions.

difference between Smith, as described, and her undisciplined counterpart. The undisciplined jailer who goes easy on her prisoners out of laziness enjoys a kind of moral luck—they end up doing the right thing, but do not deserve credit for it. Smith, by contrast, deserves credit for going easy on her prisoners. That is easily explained if her action is based on knowledge of the goodness of her going easy on her prisoners.[5]

Second, suppose that Smith does not act on her desire to go easy on her prisoners, and continues to treat them roughly. In that case, if Smith knows the goodness of her going easy on her prisoners, that explains why she is morally culpable for her actions. Smith's cognitive commitment to the worthlessness of her prisoners' lives does not excuse her conduct, given her orectic awareness of their lives' worth. There is an important moral difference between Smith and the wholehearted prejudiced jailer, whose desires are in line with their bigoted beliefs. Smith is blameworthy in a way that the wholehearted prejudiced jailer isn't. This is not to say that the wholehearted prejudiced jailer isn't blameworthy—perhaps they are, e.g. in virtue of the fact that they are responsible for their uncritical acceptance of their negative beliefs about the targeted outgroup. But they are not blameworthy in the way that Smith is blameworthy: Smith is *aware* of the badness of her prisoners' suffering. That she continues to treat her prisoners roughly despite such awareness betrays a kind of vice that is not present in the case of the wholehearted prejudiced jailer. All this sits well with the idea that Smith has knowledge of the goodness of her going easy on her prisoners.

Note well that I am not going to argue like this: Smith has knowledge of the goodness of her going easy on her prisoners; therefore, there is such a thing as orectic knowledge. That is an inference to the best explanation argument, and there is a salient alternative explanation of Smith's knowledge: that she aptly *believes*—perhaps "tacitly" or "implicitly" or "unconsciously"—that it would be good were she to go easy on her prisoners. Granted, she also believes that it would not be good were she to go easy on her prisoners; but you might think that such is the inconsistency that befalls the compassionate person whose beliefs are warped by ideology. We might say that it is counterintuitive that Smith believes that it would be good were she to go easy on her prisoners. But intuitions may differ, and philosophers

---

[5] On necessary connections between knowledge and rational action, see Hawthorne 2004, p. 30, Stanley 2005, p. 9, Fantl and McGrath 2007, p. 557, 2009, p. 59 and p. 66, Hawthorne and Stanley 2008, p. 578.

80 THE EPISTEMOLOGY OF DESIRE AND THE PROBLEM OF NIHILISM

may be committed to accounts of belief that imply that Smith believes that it would be good were she to go easy on her prisoners.

4.3 Knowledge as Apt Mental Representation

My argument that there is such a thing as orectic knowledge has two premises. The first premise is AD. The second premise is that knowledge is apt mental representation. Consider a familiar virtue-theoretic account of *propositional* knowledge, on which propositional knowledge is apt belief:

> VPK You know that p if and only if your belief that p is apt, where your belief that p is *apt* if and only if (i) it is true, (ii) your having it manifests one or more of your epistemic virtues, and (iii) its truth manifests one or more of your epistemic virtues, where *epistemic virtues* are reliable capacities to form true beliefs and to avoid forming false beliefs.[6]

For short, I'll say that a belief is apt if and only if it is true, it manifests epistemic virtue, and its truth manifests epistemic virtue.

Defenders of VPK are attracted to it for three reasons. First, VPK requires, for knowledge, the kind of link between the believer and the truth of their belief that is missing in cases of justified true belief that fall short of propositional knowledge, thereby improving on the tripartite analysis of knowledge. Second, VPK facilitates an elegant explanation of the value of knowledge, over and above the value of true belief, in terms of achievement. Third, VPK provides a naturalistically kosher account of knowledge in terms of reliable capacities, without the use of unanalyzed normative notions of justification and evidence.

In the theory of knowledge, we standardly begin by distinguishing between several species of knowledge. There is *propositional knowledge*, i.e. knowledge that p—VPK offers a theory of that. But there is also *explanatory knowledge*, i.e. knowledge why p; and there is also *individual knowledge*, as when you know some person, or place, or topic; and there is also *practical knowledge*, i.e. knowing how to φ. Moreover, we also standardly note at some point that there are other mind-world relations of interest to epistemologists, such as understanding—which itself seems to admit of several

---

[6] Cf. Sosa 1988, 2007, 2015, Zagzebski 1996, Greco 1999, 2003, 2010, Turri 2011, Miracchi 2015. The term "apt" comes from Sosa.

DESIRE THAT AMOUNTS TO KNOWLEDGE   81

species. All of these things—propositional knowledge, explanatory knowledge, individual knowledge, practical knowledge, understanding—seem to have something in common; they seem to be species of the same genus. I propose the following virtue-theoretic account of that genus, which is a generalization of VPK:

> VK   A mental representation of yours amounts to knowledge if and only if (i) it is accurate, (ii) your making it manifests one or more of your representational virtues, and (iii) its accuracy manifests one or more of your representational virtues, where a *representational virtue* is a reliable capacity to make accurate representations and to avoid making inaccurate representations.

For short, I'll say that a mental representation is apt if and only if it is accurate, it manifests representational virtue, and its accuracy manifests representational virtue. VK says that knowledge is apt mental representation.

VK amends VPK in two key ways. First, it replaces belief, in particular, with mental representation, in general. Second, it replaces truth, understood as a property of belief, with accuracy (cf. §2.1), understood as a property of mental representations. VPK thus leaves open the possibility of non-doxastic species of knowledge—instances of apt mental representation that are not instances of belief. At first glance, this seems like it goes against an epistemological platitude: that knowledge requires belief. But what is platitudinous is that *propositional* knowledge requires belief, and VK is consistent with that.

VK inherits the three aforementioned attractive features of VPK, mutatis mutandis. However, VK's most attractive feature is the fact that it provides a principled explanation of the unity of the various species of knowledge—in the present broad sense of "knowledge," which includes understanding. Compare the idea that these are all "epistemic goods"[7] or the idea that they are all species of "cognitive contact with reality,"[8] neither of which provides us with any principled way of determining what is included in and what is excluded from the proposed category.

---

[7] Indeed, I would suggest the other order of explanation: what makes something an "epistemic good" is the fact that it is a species of knowledge (per VK) (cf. Ahlstrom-Vij and Grimm 2013).

[8] Zagzebski 1996, p. 45 and passim.

82 THE EPISTEMOLOGY OF DESIRE AND THE PROBLEM OF NIHILISM

Note that the argument here is not about ordinary language. In English, "knowledge" and "knows" can be used to refer to carnal knowledge, but while the species of knowledge canvassed above all seem to have something in common, whatever this something is, it does not seem to be something that they have in common with carnal knowledge. Moreover, we have included understanding—which in English goes by the name "understanding"— in the group of things whose commonality we are attempting to capture. It is that apparent commonality to which VK answers, not to any linguistic data.

There is one possibility that would undermine this motivation for VK. If we were convinced that all knowledge—in the present broad sense—is propositional, then VPK would effectively provide the principled explanation of the unity of the various species of knowledge. Some philosophers argue about whether explanatory knowledge is a species of propositional knowledge.[9] Others argue about whether practical knowledge is a species of propositional knowledge.[10] And others argue about whether understanding is a species of propositional knowledge.[11] If all the various species of knowledge could be reduced to propositional knowledge, then there would be no need to speak in terms of mental representation and accuracy, as opposed to speaking in terms of belief and truth. However, here we should leave open the question of whether all knowledge is propositional knowledge— and thus it makes sense to assume VK, rather than that all knowledge is propositional knowledge. VK allows for a pluralistic understanding of the various species of knowledge. It allows us to say, for example, that in the same way that knowledge that p requires a representation of the fact that p, in the form of a belief that p, knowledge of how to φ requires a representation of how to φ, whether or not said representation is a belief, and understanding why p requires a representation of the explanation of the fact that p, whether or not said representation is a belief.[12]

The question of whether all knowledge is propositional is fraught with difficulty in virtue of the fact that it is not at all clear what we mean by "propositional" in this context. Some epistemologists associate propositions

---

[9] See Schaffer 2007, 2009, Brogaard 2009, Kallestrup 2009; cf. Stanley and Williamson 2001, pp. 420–4.

[10] See Ryle 1946, Roland 1958, Stanley and Williamson 2001, Stanley 2011; cf. Schiffer 2002, Hawley 2003, Rumfitt 2003, Snowdon 2003, Nöe 2005, Bengson and Moffett 2007, 2012, Brogaard 2009, 2012, Cath 2009, 2012, Devitt 2011, Glick 2011, 2012, 2015, Fantl 2012, Hornsby 2012.

[11] See Zagzebski 2001, Kvanvig 2003, 2009, Grimm 2006, 2014, Sliwa 2015.

[12] Cf. Hazlett 2018.

with sentences, such that the question of whether all knowledge is propositional is equivalent to the question of whether all knowledge has sentential structure or involves representing that which is known in a sentential way.[13] Others associate propositional knowledge with "that"-clauses.[14] That may or may not suggest that all propositional knowledge can be described with a sentence containing a "that"-clause. According to a different way of thinking about the propositional, the concept of a proposition is simply the concept of something that can be true or false, and thus has no essential connection to sentences or descriptions.

VK entails that all knowledge is mental. We do sometimes speak of knowledge that is not straightforwardly mental. Some books, for example, are filled with knowledge. However, I think what we are doing in cases like these is using "knowledge" to refer to propositions that are known by someone salient. Just as "observation" can be used both to refer to an instance of observing and to that which is observed and "belief" can be used both to refer to an instance of believing and to that which is believed, "knowledge" can be used both to refer to an instance of knowing and to that which is known.

Knowledge requires a knower. But that does not entail that all knowledge is mental. Is there a principled, theoretical reason for thinking that nonmental representations, such as assertions, cannot amount to knowledge? As above, set aside the sense in which an assertion can be knowledge when it is an assertion of something known. The question here is: might your asserting that p, itself, be an instance of your knowing that p? Alternatively, might there be non-sentient or non-intelligent knowers? There is obviously a sense in which morning glories open because they know it is day and cicadas emerge because they know it is time to mate. Are these instances of non-mental knowledge? Bernard Williams (1970/1973) describes a machine that "gathers information about the environment" that is "represented in the inner states of the machine" and which "produces messages that express propositions" (p. 145), and argues that "much of the point of the concept of knowledge could be preserved if it were applied to things such as our machine" (p. 147). His point is that knowledge may not require belief (which he argues the machine would lack), but if the case shows there can be knowledge without belief, it seems like it shows there can be non-mental knowledge as well. I will continue to assume that knowledge requires

---

[13] See e.g. Zagzebski 2001, pp. 241–2, 2008, p. 4.
[14] See e.g. Feldman 2003, p. 9, Fumerton 2006, p. 1.

84 THE EPISTEMOLOGY OF DESIRE AND THE PROBLEM OF NIHILISM

mental representation. However, this won't make a difference in what follows. If knowledge is simply apt representation, the case for orectic knowledge is just as strong as it is given VK.

VK has two implications that I welcome, although they are controversial. First, if perceptual experience has an accuracy condition (§1.8), perceptual experiences can plausibly be apt, and thus amount to knowledge, per VK.[15] Second, if credence has an accuracy condition (§2.7), credences can plausibly be apt, and thus amount to knowledge, per VK.[16]

You might object that VK does not count *acquaintance* as a species of knowledge, because acquaintance is not a species of mental representation, or at least not a species of mental representation that can be accurate or inaccurate.[17] Acquaintance is standardly characterized as direct awareness, with the implication that such awareness is not mediated by any representation. When you are acquainted with x, nothing mediates your awareness of x, and in particular no representation of x mediates your awareness of x. However, I think this is an appealing consequence of VK. Acquaintance, so understood, is not a species of knowledge. It makes sense to say that someone knows something only if they are in a kind of state such that we can conceive of states of that kind being inaccurate.[18]

4.4 An Account of Orectic Knowledge

AD tells us that desires can be accurate. If desires can be accurate, then they can be apt—in the sense provided by VK (§4.3). VK tells us that knowledge is apt mental representation. Given the assumption that desires are *mental* representations, we can conclude that apt desires amount to knowledge.

We can capture this conclusion by articulating an account of orectic knowledge, on which orectic knowledge is apt desire:

VCK   Your desire that p amounts to knowledge if and only if it is apt, where your desire that p is *apt* if and only if (i) it is accurate, (ii) your

---

[15] Cf. Byrne 2015, Jenkin 2020.   [16] Cf. Moss 2018.

[17] I have also said nothing about *phenomenal knowledge*, or knowledge of what it is like to χ. But I don't think VK implies that phenomenal knowledge isn't a species of knowledge. You can accurately or inaccurately represent what it is like to χ. Just as there is knowing what it is like to χ, there is being wrong about what it is like to χ, which implies that phenomenal knowledge is a species of mental representation that can be accurate or inaccurate.

[18] I think this is a principal lesson from Wittgenstein's *On Certainty* (1969): the concept of knowledge gets its application only where we can conceive of the possibility of a mistake.

having it manifests one or more of your orectic virtues, and (iii) its accuracy manifests one or more of your orectic virtues, where *orectic virtues* are reliable capacities to form accurate desires and to avoid forming inaccurate desires.

For short, I'll say that a desire is apt if and only if it is accurate, it manifests orectic virtue, and its accuracy manifests orectic virtue.

Consider Smith's desire to go easy on her prisoners (§4.2). Let's assume that it would be good were Smith to go easy on her prisoners. It follows, per AD, that her desire is accurate. We stipulated that Smith's having this desire manifests her compassion. Is compassion a orectic virtue? At least part of what it is to be compassionate is to be disposed to form desires in response to the needs of other creatures—specifically, desires to help and desires not to harm them. Someone who lacked such a disposition would not be a compassionate person. Moreover, typical manifestations of such a disposition are intuitively desires for the good, because intuitively it is good to help and not to harm other creatures. Thus, compassion seems to be, at least in part, a reliable capacity to form accurate desires, i.e. a orectic virtue. So, Smith's desiring as she does intuitively manifests orectic virtue. Finally, does the accuracy of her desire manifest orectic virtue? Yes. The reason she desires something good, in this case, is because she is compassionate. The three conditions for aptness are met. Given VCK, if Smith's desire is apt, it amounts to knowledge.

Recall that the claim that there is such a thing as orectic knowledge is consistent with skepticism about orectic knowledge. Just as the question of the nature of propositional knowledge is distinct from the question of the scope of propositional knowledge, the question of the nature of orectic knowledge is distinct from the question of the scope of orectic knowledge. We might accept VPK (§4.3), for example, and thus accept that there is such a thing as propositional knowledge, and yet be unsure whether anyone's beliefs are apt, and thus unsure whether anyone actually has any propositional knowledge. Likewise, we can accept VCK, and thus accept that there is such a thing as orectic knowledge, and yet be unsure whether anyone's desires are apt, and thus unsure whether anyone actually has any orectic knowledge.

There are at least three things you might worry about when it comes to the scope of propositional knowledge. First, you might wonder whether any of the things we believe really are true. Second, you might wonder, even if some of the things we believe are true, whether we actually have any epistemic virtues, i.e. reliable capacities to form true beliefs. Third, you might

86 THE EPISTEMOLOGY OF DESIRE AND THE PROBLEM OF NIHILISM

wonder, even if we have some epistemic virtues, whether our beliefs actually manifest said virtues. In the same way, there are at least three things you might worry about when it comes to the scope of orectic knowledge. First, you might wonder whether any of the things we desire really are good. Second, you might wonder, even if some of the things we desire are good, whether we actually have any orectic virtues, i.e. reliable capacities to form accurate desires. Third, you might wonder, even if we have some orectic virtues, whether our desires actually manifest said virtues.

The first of these worries is, of course, relevant in the context of the problem of nihilism (cf. §1.1).[19] If nothing is good or bad, then none of our desires are accurate, and, therefore, given VPK, none of our desires amount to knowledge. Given AD and VCK, the plausibility of the claim that Smith's desire to go easy on her prisoners amounts to knowledge depends on the assumption that it would be good were Smith to go easy on her prisoners. Nihilism about value is inconsistent with this assumption. That is why the nihilist about value must be a skeptic about orectic knowledge.

4.5 Sources of Orectic Knowledge

Epistemologists often describe a plurality of *sources* of knowledge, such as sense perception, memory, testimony, rational insight, and inference. A "source of knowledge," in this context, is something like a particular capacity to acquire knowledge or a particular method for acquiring knowledge. I have argued that there is such a thing as orectic knowledge. Are there sources of orectic knowledge, analogous to the sources of propositional knowledge, and, if so, what are they?

My treatment of the case of Smith (§4.4) suggests that compassion is a source of orectic knowledge, in something like the sense that epistemic virtues are sources of propositional knowledge, given VPK (§4.3). Assuming compassion is a moral virtue—or, more precisely, that there is a moral virtue of compassion, which incorporates a reliable capacity to form accurate desires—it is plausible that certain other moral virtues are sources of orectic knowledge, namely, those that incorporate a disposition to form desires. These include generosity, in as much as it incorporates a disposition to want

---

[19] So is the second, but I'll focus on the first.

to give to others, and truthfulness, in as much as it incorporates a disposition to want to tell the truth and nothing but the truth.

Our beliefs about what is true determine what candidates we find credible as sources of propositional knowledge. I included sense perception on my list, and excluded divine revelation, which tells you something about my conception of the world. In the same way, our beliefs about what is good will determine what candidates we find credible as sources of orectic knowledge. Compassion seems like a credible candidate only on the assumption that it is good to help and not to harm others.

Are sense perception, memory, testimony, rational insight, and inference sources of orectic knowledge? That list of sources of knowledge was developed with propositional knowledge in mind. There is no reason to think that the sources of propositional knowledge are necessarily also sources of other species of knowledge. Aristotle argues that sense perception is a source of propositional knowledge but not a source of understanding,[20] and many argue that testimony is a source of propositional knowledge but neither a source of practical knowledge nor a source of understanding.[21] In general, that something is a source of one species of knowledge does not suggest that it is a source of another species of knowledge.

However, there is something that needs explaining when that happens. There is going to be an explanation—perhaps conceptual, perhaps empirical—of why something that is a source of one species of knowledge is not a source of another species of knowledge.[22] Consider the debate about moral testimony.[23] If there is such a thing as moral knowledge, and if testimony is not a source of moral knowledge, then we want an explanation of why testimony is not a source of moral knowledge, given that testimony is a source of non-moral knowledge.

There are at least two broad categories of explanation of why something, which is a source of one species of knowledge, is not a source of another species of knowledge. First, there are explanations on which the would-be source is, in the relevant cases, insufficiently reliable to count as a source of knowledge. Think here, for example, of the idea that there are no moral experts, as an explanation of why testimony is not a source of moral

---

[20] *Metaphysics* I.1 981b 10–13.
[21] Zagzebski 2008, pp. 145–6, 2012, pp. 174–8, Hills 2009, 2016, 2020, Hawley 2010, Carter and Pritchard 2015, Poston 2016, Gordon 2017.
[22] Cf. Hazlett 2018, pp. 144–5.
[23] See e.g. Nickel 2001, Hopkins 2007, Hills 2009, McGrath 2011, Sliwa 2012, Howell 2014, Fletcher 2016, Hazlett 2017b, Callahan 2018.

88 THE EPISTEMOLOGY OF DESIRE AND THE PROBLEM OF NIHILISM

knowledge. (Of course, we still want to know: why are there no moral experts?) Second, there are explanations on which the kind of mental representation that constitutes the relevant species of knowledge cannot be transmitted through testimony. Think here, for example, of the idea that affective states, which are partly constitutive of moral knowledge, cannot be transmitted through testimony, as an explanation of why testimony is not a source of moral knowledge. (Of course, we still want to know: why can't affective states be transmitted through testimony?)

My account of desire formation through deliberation (§5.8) may suggest that desires can be inferential. Conceiving of inference as a source of orectic knowledge would, of course, require a liberal conception of inference, on which inference is not essentially a capacity to form beliefs or a method of belief formation, but rather a capacity to form attitudes or a method of attitude formation. In addition, we would need to ask whether inference, in cases of desire, is sufficiently reliable to count as a source of knowledge.

Again, there is no reason to think that the sources of propositional knowledge are necessarily also sources of orectic knowledge. The fact that we lack an explanation of why something that is a source of one species of knowledge is not a source of another species of knowledge is no reason to doubt that the latter is not really a species of knowledge after all. Someone who lacked an explanation of why sense perception is not a source of understanding—someone who did not know why the senses tell us that fire is hot, but not why it is hot, to borrow Aristotle's example—would have no reason to doubt that understanding is a species of knowledge, in the present sense. It would be no reason to doubt that understanding is a species of apt mental representation (cf. §4.3).

I emphasize this because it seems like desire cannot be transmitted through testimony. Our desires can be affected by other people's desires both directly, as in cases of associative sympathy or "emotional contagion," and indirectly, as when I draw some conclusion on the basis of facts about what you desire, which causes me to desire the same thing. However, we do not seem to find anything like the speaker-hearer structure we get in paradigm cases of belief transmission through testimony, in which there is someone who performs some speech act—variously described as asserting, telling, assuring, or testifying—in response to which someone else forms a belief. Granted, your desire that p might depend on your belief that q, and you might tell me that q, and I might believe you, thereby forming a belief that q, which might result in my coming to form a desire that p. But that would merely be a case in which belief is transmitted through testimony, not a case in which desire is transmitted through testimony. What seems lacking, in the case of desire, is both the requisite speech act—the orectic analogue of asserting, telling, assuring, or testifying—and the requisite response—the orectic analogue of believing someone. We do have ways of expressing desire linguistically—we can say things of the form <If only it were the case that p> or <Let it be the case that p> or <Would that it were the case that p>.[24] But there is something lacking here. When you linguistically express a desire that p, in any of these ways, you do not represent yourself as knowing something, in anything like the way that you plausibly represent yourself as knowing something when you assert that p.[25] Moreover, when you linguistically express a desire that p, in any of these ways, you do not invite your interlocutor to trust you, in anything like the way that you plausibly invite your interlocutor to trust you that p when you tell them that p.[26] In the case of belief there are things you can do—represent yourself as knowing that p, invite your interlocutor to trust you that p—that seem to have no analogue in the case of desire.[27]

Suppose that desire cannot be transmitted through testimony. If so, testimony is not a source of orectic knowledge. I have not attempted to explain why testimony is not a source of orectic knowledge. I have not attempted to explain why desire cannot be transmitted through testimony. However, neither the fact that testimony is not a source of orectic knowledge nor the fact that we lack an explanation of why testimony is not a source of orectic knowledge gives us any reason to doubt that there is such a thing as orectic knowledge. The same should be kept in mind should it turn out that other familiar sources of knowledge are not sources of orectic knowledge. Suppose that sense perception does not produce desires in anything like the way that it produces beliefs. We might conclude that sense perception is not a source of orectic knowledge, and have no idea why, because we have no idea why sense perception does not produce desires in anything like the way it produces beliefs, without having any reason to doubt that desire can amount to knowledge.

---

[24] Cf. Wittgenstein 1958, §544, Kenny 1963, p. 123, p. 207, Searle 1969, p. 22, Taylor 1986, p. 222, Humberstone 1987, pp. 50–1; see also Drucker 2022, pp. 11–13.

[25] Cf. Unger 1975, p. 253, Davidson 1979/1984, p. 112, Slote 1979, Owens 2006.

[26] Cf. Hinchman 2005, Moran 2005, Fricker 2006; see also Anscombe 1979, Ross 1986, Coady 1992, pp. 38–48, Graham 1997, Wanderer 2012.

[27] For further discussion of what is involved in something's being "transmitted through testimony," see Greco 2016, Hills 2020, Graham 2021.

4.6 Orectic Knowledge and Epistemic Luck

Above, I mentioned the idea that propositional knowledge requires some kind of link between the believer and the truth of their belief (§4.3). VPK requires such a link for propositional knowledge, by requiring for propositional knowledge that the truth of your belief manifest epistemic virtue. Consider the way this requirement is not met in cases of "epistemic luck." Suppose you see a dog in a field and reasonably mistake the dog for a sheep, while unbeknownst to you there is a sheep elsewhere in the field.[28] Your belief that there is a sheep in the field is true and plausibly manifests epistemic virtue, but you do not know there is a sheep in the field, because the *truth* of your belief does not manifest epistemic virtue. Instead, the truth of your belief is explained by the fortuitous presence of the sheep. You are lucky to have a true belief, rather than an false belief. Your belief is "epistemically lucky."

VCK (§4.4), in an analogous way, requires for orectic knowledge that the accuracy of your desire manifest orectic virtue. Are there likewise cases of epistemically lucky desire? Are there cases in which your desire is both accurate and manifests orectic virtue, but in which the *accuracy* of your desire does not manifest orectic virtue, but is instead explained by some fortuitous circumstance? Are there cases in which, in that way, you are lucky to have a desire for the good, rather than desire that is not for the good?[29]

A desire might depend on an epistemically lucky belief. Imagine that you hope the sheep in the field lives a long and happy life. Assume that your desire is accurate—i.e. that it would be good were the sheep to live a long and happy life—and manifests orectic virtue—e.g. that it manifest compassion (cf. §4.4). Are you lucky to have a desire for the good, rather than a desire that is not for the good? What seems clear is that you are lucky to have a desire that is about a real sheep. The accuracy of your belief that there is a sheep in the field is explained by the fortuitous presence of the sheep. But the accuracy of your desire is not exactly explained by the fortuitous goodness of the sheep's living a long and happy life. We might do better to search for a case involving a desire that does not depend on an epistemically lucky belief.

Two related insights from the literature on epistemic luck may be useful here. Linda Zagzebski (1996) argues that cases of epistemically lucky belief

---

[28] Chisholm 1977, p. 107; see also Gettier 1963, Goldman 1976.
[29] Note that we allow here for axial gaps (§2.8).

DESIRE THAT AMOUNTS TO KNOWLEDGE   91

involve "the combination of two accidental features," such that "an accident of bad luck is canceled out by an accident of good luck" (p. 285). In the case of the sheep in the field, it is your bad luck that the dog looks so much like a sheep (i.e. that your evidence is misleading) but it is your good luck that there is a sheep elsewhere in the field (i.e. that your belief turns out to be true). And Richard Foley (2012) argues that in cases of epistemically lucky belief there is always "important information" that the believer lacks (p. 3). In the case of the sheep in the field, the missing information is that the animal you see is a dog and that the sheep remains unseen by you. Can we find a case of desire that has analogues of these features—the combination of bad and good luck and the missing information?

The case of the sheep in the field relies on the fact that the proposition you believe can be true in two different ways. It can be true in virtue of the animal you see being a sheep or it can be true in virtue of there being a sheep elsewhere in the field. What makes the case a case of epistemically lucky belief is the fact that you are ignorant about the way in which what you believe is true. This suggests that a case of epistemically lucky desire will be a case in which the thing you desire can be good in two different ways. For this, we are going to need to assume that there are a plurality of goods (cf. §2.9). What will make our case a case of epistemically lucky desire will be the fact that you are ignorant about the way in which what you desire is good.

Here is a case. Admittedly, it is contrived, but perhaps not very much more contrived than other cases of epistemic luck. Imagine that you want to dance, and your desire to dance depends on your belief that you are a great dancer. In particular, it depends on your belief that, were you to dance, your dancing would be graceful and sublime. However—here is the accident of bad luck—your beliefs about your dancing abilities are mistaken. You have been getting bad advice from your sycophantic friends. You cannot dance at all, and were you to dance, your dancing would not be graceful and sublime. However—here is the accident of good luck—it turns out that you would very much enjoy dancing. Were you to dance, you would enjoy it very much. You don't realize this. You think dancing will be a thankless chore. Your desire to dance is not selfish, but aesthetically motivated. You want to create something beautiful, even if it means making a personal sacrifice.

Is this a case of epistemically lucky desire? Let's assume, first, that it would be good were you to dance, in virtue of the fact that you would very much enjoy it. Your desire is therefore accurate. Let's assume, second, that were your dancing graceful and sublime, it would be good were you to

92 THE EPISTEMOLOGY OF DESIRE AND THE PROBLEM OF NIHILISM

dance, in virtue of its being graceful and sublime. Your desire therefore plausibly manifests orectic virtue—it is plausibly a response to the goodness of graceful and sublime dancing. However, the accuracy of your desire does not manifest orectic virtue. Instead, the accuracy of your desire is explained by the fortuitous fact you would very much enjoy dancing. You are lucky to have a desire for the good, rather than a desire that is not for the good. Your desire, it seems, is epistemically lucky.

We have the accident of bad luck, in the form of your misleading evidence that you are a great dancer, and we have the accident of good luck, in the form of the fact that you would enjoy dancing. We have the missing information, in the form of the fact that you would enjoy dancing but would not dance well. We have the desired thing that can be good in two different ways: dancing can be aesthetically and hedonically valuable. And we have the ignorance about the way in which what you desire is good: you think your dancing would be aesthetically valuable, when in fact it would be hedonically valuable.[30]

However, suppose desires cannot be epistemically lucky, in a sense analogous to the sense in which beliefs can be epistemically lucky. That is no threat to VCK. The appeal of virtue-theoretic accounts of knowledge is not merely that they explain why cases of epistemic luck do not count as cases of knowledge. Even the idea that propositional knowledge requires some kind of link between the believer and the truth of their belief does not derive its appeal solely from the existence of cases of epistemically lucky belief: consider your belief that you will not win the lottery, which would not amount to knowledge even if it were true. VK would be a credible

---

[30] You might object that, in the case of the sheep in the field, the evidence on which your belief is based corresponds to the fact that makes your belief true, but that in the case of the bad dancer, the belief on which your desire depends does not correspond to the fact that makes your desire for the good. In the case of the bad dancer, you believe that were you to dance, your dancing would be graceful and sublime. Unbeknownst to you, what makes it the case that it would be good were you to dance is the fact that, were you to dance, you would enjoy it very much. The belief on which your desire depends does not correspond to the fact that makes your desire for the good. By contrast, in the case of the sheep in the field, it seems like your evidence is something like an appearance or seeming as of there being a sheep in the field. Moreover, what makes it the case that it is true that there is a sheep in the field is exactly what your evidence indicates: the presence of a sheep in the field. The evidence on which your belief is based corresponds to the fact that makes your belief true. However, I reject the idea that your evidence, in the case of the sheep in the field, is an appearance or seeming. I think your belief that there is a sheep in the field is inferred from a prior perceptual belief that *that* is a sheep— where "that" is a perceptual demonstrative that refers, in this case, to a dog. Your belief that there is a sheep in the field is therefore based on evidence that does not correspond to the fact that makes your belief true.

account of knowledge in general, even if there are species of knowledge that do admit of corresponding cases of epistemic luck. VCK derives its credibility from VK, not from considerations of epistemic luck.

4.7 Conclusion

I have argued that desire, like belief, can amount to knowledge. My argument appealed to AD and the premise that knowledge is apt mental representation. Desire that amounts to knowledge, or orectic knowledge, is a species of knowledge of the good. I argued that this conclusion is independently appealing, which lends further support to AD. That concludes my defense of AD. The conclusion that desire, like belief, can amount to knowledge, suggests another epistemological question: can desires be rational or irrational, in the same sense that beliefs can be rational or irrational? We turn to that question next.

The Epistemology of Desire and the Problem of Nihilism Allan Hazlett, Oxford University Press.
© Allan Hazlett 2024. DOI: 10.1093/9780191995583.003.0004

5
Irrational Desire

The epistemology of desire is taking shape: desires, like beliefs, can be accurate or inaccurate; and desires, like beliefs, can amount to knowledge. Can desires, like beliefs, be rational or irrational?

I am going to argue that a mental representation admits of irrationality only if it is susceptible to deliberation (§5.1), or what is sometimes called "rational control" or (in some contexts) "reasoning." When I say that a mental representation is susceptible to deliberation, I mean that instances of it can be formed through deliberation.[1] Belief, I assume, admits of irrationality, and I assume that it meets the proposed condition: belief is susceptible to deliberation, i.e. beliefs can be formed through deliberation. If desire is not susceptible to deliberation, i.e. if desires cannot be formed through deliberation, then desire does not admit of irrationality. Given AD, I think this is the main obstacle to maintaining that desire admits of irrationality. So, my main task in this chapter will be to argue that desire is susceptible to deliberation. A number of philosophers have observed, without elaboration, that desire is susceptible to deliberation.[2] But others say the opposite.[3] For example, T.M. Scanlon (1998) cites the "familiar idea that desires are unreflective elements in our practical thinking – that they 'assail us' unbidden" (p. 39).

I said that beliefs can be formed through deliberation. More precisely, I assume that beliefs can be formed through deliberation about what to believe, or what is known as "doxastic deliberation." On my view, desires can be formed through deliberation about what to desire, or what I will call "orectic deliberation." Thus, desire is susceptible to deliberation.

---

[1] I assume a broad conception of attitude formation here, which includes both cases in which you come to have an attitude you did not have before and cases in which you continue to have an attitude that you already had.

[2] Nagel 1970, p. 29, Davis 1986, p. 70, Schueler 1995, p. 13, Moran 2001, pp. 63–4; see also Byrne 2012, p. 175, Gregory 2017, pp. 202–3.

[3] Hulse et al. 2004, p. 77, Hawkins 2008, p. 246.

5.1 Irrationality and Deliberation

I am going to focus on what Scanlon (2007) calls "structural irrationality." I am going to focus on structural irrationality because the problem of nihilism presupposes that desires can be structurally irrational, as I will propose in the next chapter (§6.1). Claims of structural irrationality, Scanlon explains, "are structural because they are claims about the relations between an agent's attitudes that must hold insofar as he or she is not irrational, and the kind of irrationality involved is a matter of conflict between these attitudes" (pp. 84–5). In what follows, "irrational" and "irrationality" will always refer to structural irrationality.

Structural irrationality is a property of certain combinations of attitudes, rather than a property of attitudes considered in isolation. Thus, the question of whether a mental representation admits of irrationality is, more precisely, the question of whether there can be structurally irrational combinations of attitudes that include at least one instance of it. The question of whether desire admits of irrationality, for example, is, more precisely, the question of whether there can be structurally irrational combinations of attitudes that include at least one desire. However, for the sake of simplicity, I will continue to speak of mental representations as "admitting of irrationality," and of individual attitudes as "irrational" when they are part of an irrational combination of attitudes.

In focusing on the question of whether desires can be structurally irrational, I set aside the question of whether desires can be responsive to reasons.[4] However, recall (§3.10) that AD suggests an account of reasons for desire, on which reasons for desire are evidence relevant to whether it is good or bad that p, just as reasons for belief are evidence relevant to whether it is true or false that p. To put this another way, reasons for desire are evidence of goodness, just as reasons for belief are evidence of truth. Moreover, in defense of the claim that desire is susceptible to deliberation, I will describe a case of successful orectic deliberation (§5.7), which will strongly suggest that desires can be responsive to reasons. I suspect, but will not assume here, that a mental representation admits of reasons-responsiveness only if it is susceptible to deliberation.[5]

---

[4] On the relationship between structural rationality and reasons-responsiveness, see Broome 1999, 2007, 2013, Kolodny 2005, 2007, Scanlon 2007, Kieswetter 2017, Lord 2018.

[5] For further discussion of the reasons-responsiveness of desire, see Parfit 1984, pp. 120–6, 2001, pp. 25–7, 2011, pp. 43–57, Zagzebski 2012, pp. 76–7.

96   THE EPISTEMOLOGY OF DESIRE AND THE PROBLEM OF NIHILISM

I claim that a mental representation admits of irrationality only if it is susceptible to deliberation. Consider perceptual experience. Why isn't it irrational, when you know that the Müller-Lyre lines are equal in length, to have a visual experience of them as unequal in length? Why is that any different from believing something you know is false? The answer, I submit, is that perceptual experience is not susceptible to deliberation.

I assume that it is not irrational, even when you know that the Müller-Lyre lines are equal in length, to have a visual experience of them as unequal in length. This remains plausible even if we grant that a perceptual experience of a as F is accurate if and only if a is F and inaccurate otherwise (§1.8). Either your belief that the lines are equal in length or your visual experience of the lines as unequal in length, therefore, must be inaccurate (cf. §7.1). Nevertheless, it is not irrational for you to have that visual experience.[6] Moreover, the assumption that the present case is not a case of irrationality remains plausible even when we imagine that you are aware of the inaccuracy of your visual experience. The present case, so we can easily imagine, is not like the case of Lois Lane, who both knows that Superman can fly and believes that Clark Kent cannot fly, but who is unaware of the inaccuracy of her belief that Clark Kent cannot fly. In the present case, you know that your visual experience of the Müller-Lyre lines as unequal in length is inaccurate. Nevertheless, it is not irrational for you to have that visual experience.

It is not irrational, even when you know that the Müller-Lyre lines are equal in length, to have a visual experience of them as unequal in length. By contrast, it seems irrational, if you know isopods are harmless (cf. §1.11), to be afraid of isopods. This is why it makes sense to object to the view that emotion is a species of perception on the grounds that recalcitrant emotions are irrational.[7]

I assume that perceptual experiences cannot be formed through deliberation. You can deliberate about what to believe, but you cannot deliberate about what perceptual experiences to have. You can deliberate about whether to believe that there is a tree in the quad, but you cannot deliberate about whether to have a visual experience of the quad as containing a tree. You can deliberate about what to look at or what to listen to, but you cannot

---

[6] If perceptual experience does not have an accuracy condition, then it seems relatively easy to explain why the present case is not a case of irrationality: having a visual experience of the Müller-Lyre lines as unequal in length is no more irrational than imagining something you know is false (cf. §2.1).

[7] See e.g. Helm 2001, pp. 41–6.

deliberate about what to see or hear. Perceptual experience is passive in a way that precludes deliberation.

The claim that perceptual experience is not susceptible to deliberation is consistent with the fact that perception involves actively engaging with our environment—that perceiving is an action, rather than a passion.[8] It is consistent with the possibility of cases of "cognitive penetration" in which our beliefs affect what perceptual experiences we have.[9] It is consistent with the idea that what perceptual experiences we have can depend on our past experiences—i.e. with the possibility of "perceptual learning."[10] To say that perceptual experience is not susceptible to deliberation is neither to deny that our choices can affect what perceptual experiences we have nor to deny the possibility of so-called "top-down" effects on perceptual experience.

Some philosophers argue that perceptual experiences can be (in a sense, more on which in a moment) irrational because perceptual experience is at least sometimes inferential.[11] On their view, perceptual experiences can be inferred from other perceptual experiences and from other perceptual experiences and beliefs in combination. When such an inference is irrational, the resulting perceptual experience is thereby irrational. If Jill's visual experience of Jack as angry is inferred merely from her visual experience of Jack as having a blank stare, for example, then her visual experience is an instance of jumping to conclusions, and is therefore irrational (Siegel 2017, pp. 117–19). Although the alleged irrationality of Jill's visual experience is not of the structural sort that we are focusing on here, you might think that, if perceptual experiences can be in this way inferentially irrational, then they can be structurally irrational, too. And, if perceptual experiences can be structurally irrational, then perhaps it is irrational to have a visual experience of the Müller-Lyre lines as unequal in length, when you know they are equal in length.

I want to concede that there is an important sense in which perceptual experiences can be inferential, and consequently an important sense in which perceptual experiences can be irrational. However, there remains an important difference between the irrationality of belief and the irrationality of perceptual experience. We can be prescribed to avoid irrational belief in a way that we cannot be prescribed to avoid irrational perceptual experience. When you are aware that a belief of yours is irrational, you are under pressure to change something so as to resolve the irrationality, whereas no such

---

[8] Cf. Noë 2004.   [9] Cf. Stokes 2013.   [10] Cf. Connolly 2017.
[11] McGrath 2013, Siegel 2017, Jenkin 2022.

98 THE EPISTEMOLOGY OF DESIRE AND THE PROBLEM OF NIHILISM

pressure exists when you are aware that a perceptual experience of yours is irrational. And the reason such pressure exists in the one case, but not in the other, is that we have a way of responding to the irrationality of a belief, but no way of responding to the irrationality of a perceptual experience. We can change our beliefs so as to avoid irrationality, but we cannot change our perceptual experiences so as to avoid irrationality.[12]

For this reason, the irrationality of your beliefs can reflect badly on you, the believing subject, in a way that the irrationality (in the present sense) of your perceptual experiences cannot.[13] Perhaps the irrationality of your perceptual experiences reflects badly on the sub-personal systems (or mechanisms, modules, etc.) that produced them. Perhaps those systems can change your perceptual experiences so as to avoid irrationality, and perhaps they are subject to a kind of pressure or governed by a kind of prescription to do so. All this serves to illustrate the stark difference between belief and perceptual experience when it comes to irrationality. My argument (above) assumes that perceptual experience is not susceptible to deliberation. Given the concession that there is an important sense in which perceptual experiences can be inferential, let me be more careful: there is a kind of deliberation that is possible in the case of belief that is not possible in the case of perceptual experience. There is something you can do, in the cases of belief, that you cannot do in the case of perceptual experience. The kind of deliberation that is possible in the case of belief is, crucially, something done by you, the believing subject, as opposed to by a sub-personal system. For this reason, belief can be irrational in a way that perceptual experience can't.

To sum up: perceptual experience does not admit of irrationality because perceptual experience is not susceptible to deliberation. I conclude that a mental representation admits of irrationality only if it is susceptible to deliberation.

In characterizing irrationality, I said that it is a property of certain combinations of attitudes. There is a sense in which it follows from this that perceptual experience does not admit of irrationality, since perceptual experience is not a type of *attitude*, but a type of *experience*. But what exactly is the relevant distinction between "attitudes" and "experiences" here? Our discussion suggests an answer: attitudes are susceptible to deliberation; experiences are not susceptible to deliberation. This stipulation makes sense of the idea that perceptual experience does not admit of irrationality

---

[12] Cf. Siegel 2017, p. 36.
[13] Cf. Peacocke 2018, pp. 757–8, O'Callaghan 2019, pp. 129–30.

because irrationality is a property of combinations of attitudes. The question of whether desire is susceptible to deliberation could thus be understood as the question of whether it really is a propositional *attitude*, as opposed to a species of *experience*. In any event, I am going to assume, going forward, that attitudes, as such, are susceptible to deliberation.

5.2 Desire and Deliberation

I am going to argue that desire, like belief, is susceptible to deliberation, i.e. that desires, like beliefs, can be formed through deliberation. I am going to provide an account of orectic deliberation, i.e. deliberation about what to desire. My account of orectic deliberation is compatible with there being other ways in which desires can be formed as a result of reasoning or learning.[14] Susceptibility to deliberation, however, is required for irrationality (§5.1), so that is my focus here.

The view that desires cannot be formed through deliberation might be motivated by appeal to the idea that all our desires—i.e. all our non-instrumental desires (§1.4)—are innate, determined by our human, primate, or mammalian nature, and thus not subject to change or individual difference. We find this kind of view in Aristotle and in Spinoza, who each posit a single non-instrumental desire (for happiness and for survival, respectively); in Hume, who allows for a plurality of innate human passions (including self-interest and sympathy); and in much contemporary psychology, where lists of basic drives (e.g. for food and sex) are sometimes posited. It seems to me that this is mistaken, if it is meant to rule out the possibility of someone coming to desire something they did not desire before. Moreover, the example of non-instrumental desire that we began with—your desire to take a walk—was not a case of an innate desire. And it seems forced to insist that such cases must involve instrumental reasoning—that you must think that taking a walk is a means to some other thing, for which you have an innate desire.

The view that desires cannot be formed through deliberation might also be motivated by appeal to the idea that only a few things are non-instrumentally good or bad. For example, consider the view that only pleasure is non-instrumentally good and only pain is non-instrumentally bad.

---

[14] See Dretske 1988, pp. 125–6, Millgram 1997, Schroeder 2004, Railton 2012, 2017, Drucker 2022.

100 THE EPISTEMOLOGY OF DESIRE AND THE PROBLEM OF NIHILISM

For another, consider the view that only flourishing or *eudaimonia* is non-instrumentally good. For another, consider the view, suggested by G.E. Moore (1903), that "the pleasures of human intercourse and the enjoyment of beautiful objects" (p. 188) are the only things that are non-instrumentally good. It seems to me that these views are also mistaken. Just as the view that we have only a few basic drives oversimplifies our psychology, the view that there are only a few basic values oversimplifies the intuitive evaluative landscape. Consider some evaluative questions. Would it be good, in virtue of the non-instrumental value of biodiversity, if some microscopic freshwater bacterium, which is threatened with extinction, and whose survival would by definition contribute to biodiversity, survives? Would it be bad, because of the non-instrumental value of beauty, if a beautiful rock formation on a distant uninhabited planet were destroyed by an earthquake? Was it bad, because of the non-instrumental value of life, that we eradicated smallpox? I don't think the answer to any of these questions is obvious.

5.3 Doxastic Deliberation

Because we are interested in whether desire, like belief, is susceptible to deliberation, we need to examine doxastic deliberation. Doxastic deliberation is deliberation about what to believe. More precisely, I assume that *doxastic deliberation* is deliberation about whether to believe that p, for some proposition that p, with the aim of determining—in the sense of fixing or settling—whether you believe that p.

Doxastic deliberation can be associated with a characteristic question, namely, whether p.[15] What makes the question of whether p the "characteristic question" for doxastic deliberation is the fact that your answering this question in the affirmative, i.e. your concluding that p, can directly result in your forming a belief that p, along with the fact that this is the only question your affirmative answering of which can directly result in your forming a belief that p.[16] To put this another way, by answering the question of whether p in the affirmative, i.e. by concluding that p, you can thereby form

[15] See Williams 1970/1973, Shah 2003, Hieronymi 2005, 2006, Shah and Velleman 2005; cf. Moran 2001, chapter 2.
[16] Given our broad conception of attitude formation, this includes cases in which you come to believe something you did not believe before and cases in which you continue to believe something you already believed.

a belief that p, and the question of whether p is the only question such that by answering it in the affirmative you can thereby form a belief that p. Concluding that p can directly result in your forming a belief that p; by contrast, concluding that it would beneficial were you to believe that p cannot directly result in your forming a belief that p. Because of this, if you aim to determine whether you believe that p, you must attempt to answer the question of whether p. Thus, doxastic deliberation takes the form of attempting to answer the question of whether p. A consequence of this is that in doxastic deliberation you consider evidence relevant to whether p, which represents your means of attempting to answer the question of whether p.

Doxastic deliberation is *successful* if and only if you conclude that p and as a direct result form a belief that p.[17] In such cases, and only in such cases, beliefs are formed *through* deliberation. Beliefs are formed *through* deliberation, in the present sense, only when they are formed as a direct result of the believer affirmatively answering the characteristic question for doxastic deliberation, namely, whether p.

Three clarifications are in order. First, as I implied above, that belief is susceptible to deliberation is consistent with the claim that we lack direct control over what we believe. Second, that belief is susceptible to deliberation is silent on the extent to which our beliefs are formed through deliberation. It is consistent with the claim that the vast majority of our beliefs are formed in an automatic and non-deliberative way. Third, that belief is susceptible to deliberation is consistent with the fact that there are things you cannot help believing or that you cannot bring yourself to believe.[18] The claim is that belief is the kind of thing that can be formed through deliberation.

5.4 Attitude Formation through Deliberation

I said that your concluding that p can directly result in your forming a belief that p (§5.3). Pamela Hieronymi (2005) argues that "for certain attitudes, settling a question amounts to forming the attitude" (p. 447), and she argues that belief is one such attitude, where the relevant question is the question

---

[17] This includes the case in which you conclude that not-p. There is no distinction to be drawn between attempting to answer the question of whether p and attempting to answer the question of whether not-p. You answer the question of whether p in the negative if and only if you answer the question of whether not-p in the affirmative.

[18] Cf. Price 1954.

102 THE EPISTEMOLOGY OF DESIRE AND THE PROBLEM OF NIHILISM

of whether p.[19] This suggests that your concluding that p not only *can* directly result in your forming a belief that p, but that it *always* directly results in your forming a belief that p. Let's grant, for the sake of argument, that concluding that p amounts to forming a belief that p, and thus that your concluding that p always directly results in your forming a belief that p. Is something like this required for attitude formation through deliberation? Do you form an attitude through deliberation only when you answer some question the answering of which amounts to forming that attitude, such that your answering that question always directly results in your forming that attitude?

I shall argue that attitude formation through deliberation does not require answering such a question. Intention, I submit, provides a counter-example to the proposed requirement. Intention is susceptible to deliberation; intentions can be formed through deliberation. But there is no question the answering of which amounts to forming an intention, such that your answering it always results in your forming an intention.

Practical deliberation is deliberation about what to intend. More precisely, I assume that *practical deliberation* is deliberation about whether to intend to φ, with the aim of determining whether you intend to φ. Moreover, practical deliberation has a characteristic question: the question of whether you should φ, which I take to be equivalent to the question of whether φing is the best of your options. However, for my purposes here, it will not matter whether we take the characteristic question for practical deliberation to be the question of whether you should φ (in the present sense), the question of whether you are required to φ, the question of whether you have most reason to φ, or the question of whether φing is the thing for you to do. What I am assuming, here, is that practical deliberation takes the form of attempting to answer some such question.[20] Your answering the question of whether you should φ in the affirmative, i.e. your concluding that you should φ, can directly result in your forming an intention to φ, and the question of whether you should φ is the only question your affirmative answering of which can directly result in your forming an intention to φ. To put this another way, by answering the question of whether you should φ in

---

[19] Note well that Hieronymi's claim is not that concluding that p amounts to believing that p, but that concluding that p amounts to *forming* a belief that p. Concluding and believing belong to different ontological categories, such that the former cannot amount to—or constitute—the latter. For the same reason, I said that, by concluding that p, you can thereby *form* a belief that p (§5.3).

[20] Cf. Kavka 1983, Hieronymi 2005, 2006, Shah 2008; cf. Moran 2001, chapter 2.

the affirmative, i.e. by concluding that you should φ, you can thereby form an intention to φ, and the question of whether you should φ is the only question such that by answering it in the affirmative you can thereby form a intention to φ. Concluding that you should φ can directly result in your forming an intention to φ; by contrast, concluding that it would be beneficial were you to intend to φ cannot directly result in your forming an intention to φ. Because of this, if you aim to determine whether you intend to φ, you must attempt to answer the question of whether you should φ. Thus, practical deliberation necessarily takes the form of attempting to answer the question of whether you should φ. A consequence of this is that in practical deliberation you consider evidence relevant to whether you should φ, which represents your means of attempting to answer the question of whether you should φ. Finally, practical deliberation is successful if and only if you conclude that you should φ and as a direct result form an intention to φ. In such cases, and only in such cases, intentions are formed through deliberation.

However, concluding that you should φ does not amount to forming an intention to φ. Your concluding that you should φ does not always directly result in your intending to φ. There are familiar cases—cases of *akrasia*—in which you believe that you should φ and yet do not intend to φ. Should we say, then, that intentions cannot be formed through deliberation, and that intention, unlike belief, is not susceptible to deliberation? No. Forming an intention through deliberation requires merely that your affirmatively answering the characteristic question for practical deliberation, i.e. your concluding that you should φ, directly results in your intending to φ. It does not require that concluding that you should φ amounts to forming an intention to φ.

In general, forming an attitude through deliberation requires merely that your affirmatively answering the characteristic question for the relevant species of deliberation can directly result in your forming that attitude. It does not require that affirmatively answering the characteristic question for the relevant species of deliberation amounts to forming that attitude.

Hieronymi suggests (2005, p. 450) that affirmatively answering the question of whether to φ amounts to forming an intention to φ. However, to affirmatively answer the question of whether to φ is to conclude that φing has some property that makes it worthy of intention. This doesn't mean that you can't form an intention to φ, and in that sense decide to φ, without concluding that φing has some property that makes it worthy of intention. You can form an intention to do something for no reason, in the sense that there is nothing about what you intend that makes it worthy of intention, by your

104 THE EPISTEMOLOGY OF DESIRE AND THE PROBLEM OF NIHILISM

lights. But such an intention cannot be formed through deliberation. Practical deliberation—by contrast with intention formation in general, which can be arbitrary—must concern itself with whether an action is worthy of intention. Thus, the question of whether to φ must be understood, in the present context, as a question about whether φing has some property that makes it worthy of intention. And whatever that property is, given the possibility of akrasia, you can conclude that φing has that property without forming an intention to φ.

Can your concluding that you should φ directly result in your forming an intention to φ? As Nishi Shah (2008) argues:

> [O]ne can fail to intend to A, even though one has settled the question *whether A-ing is the thing to do*, but it does not follow that there is another step that one must perform between judging that A-ing is the thing to do and intending to A. (p. 13)

The absence of "another step" between concluding that you should φ and forming an intention to φ is crucial to the possibility of intentions formed through deliberation. If there were some additional "step" that you had to perform to form an intention to φ, having concluded that you should φ— some mental act of choosing or deciding to φ, say—then it is unclear that intention would be susceptible to deliberation. For, in that case, your concluding that you should φ would not directly result in your forming an intention to φ. In addition to your having concluded that you should φ, we would need to cite something more—your performance of the additional "step"—to explain your forming an intention to φ. However, there is no additional "step" that you have to perform, once you have concluded that you should φ, to form an intention to φ. When you non-akratically conclude that you should φ, you form an intention to φ straightaway, without doing anything else.

Suppose you conclude that you should mow the lawn, and as a direct result form an intention to mow the lawn. Why did you form an intention to mow the lawn? Because you concluded that you should mow the lawn, and nothing more. Once you drew that conclusion, straightaway you formed an intention to mow the lawn. That explanation is plausible on its face. We do not need to cite anything further to explain your forming that intention. For one thing, we need not cite your antecedently willing or choosing to mow the lawn—your intending to mow the lawn just is your willing or choosing to mow the lawn. For another, we need not cite your antecedently deciding to intend to mow the lawn—you decided to mow the lawn, not to intend to mow the lawn. Finally, we need not cite your desiring or planning to intend to do what you should—no such higher-order attitude is needed to explain your intending to mow the lawn. That you concluded that you should mow the lawn is explanation enough.

It is fine to say that you formed an intention to mow the lawn because you both concluded that you should do so and did not suffer from akrasia. But that is just to say that akrasia could have prevented you from forming an intention to mow the lawn. Your forming an intention to mow the lawn is fully explained by your concluding that you should mow the lawn, not by said conclusion along with the absence of anything that might have prevented you from intending to mow the lawn, including akrasia. Had you failed to form an intention to mow the lawn, the *presence* of akrasia might explain why, but the *absence* of akrasia does not explain why you formed an intention to mow the lawn.

It is natural to ask at this point: if your concluding that you should φ can directly result in your forming an intention to φ, what prevents this from happening in cases of akrasia? This question can only be an empirical one, about the causes of akrasia. We are familiar from our own experience with some of its common causes: fatigue or stress, our attention being captured by appealing but lesser goods, and bad habits can all result in our failing to intend to do what we conclude we should. Anything beyond that should be left to social psychology and cognitive science, whose job it is to fill in the details and provide a more accurate and complete account of akrasia.

The possibility of akrasia is consistent with the susceptibility of intention to deliberation. The upshot of this is that the susceptibility of an attitude to deliberation requires merely that your affirmatively answering the characteristic question for the relevant species of deliberation can directly result in your forming that attitude. It does not require that that affirmatively answering the characteristic question for the relevant species of deliberation amounts to forming that attitude.

I assume that beliefs can be formed through doxastic deliberation (§5.3). Can desires be formed through orectic deliberation, i.e. deliberation about what to desire? I want to describe a prima facie case of successful orectic deliberation, before providing an account of orectic deliberation. To do this, we need to set aside two kinds of case.

5.5 Orectic Deliberation Is Not Practical Deliberation

Suppose you are deliberating about whether to eat an éclair. You might ask yourself: do I want to eat this éclair? You might describe what you are doing by saying that you are trying to decide whether you want to eat an éclair. It sounds like orectic deliberation, but it's not. You already want to eat an éclair, and know that you want to eat an éclair, and are not reconsidering whether to want to eat an éclair. Your question is whether you will do it. That is not orectic deliberation. Your deliberation, in this case, is practical deliberation. Thus, our case of orectic deliberation must not appear merely to be a case of practical deliberation.

Above, I said that practical deliberation is deliberation about what to intend (§5.4), and I said that you were, in the present case, deliberating about whether to eat an éclair. I did not say you were deliberating about whether to intend to eat an éclair. However, you are deliberating about whether to φ if and only if you are deliberating about whether to intend to φ. Of course, you might φ without intending to φ and you might intend to φ without φing. But it is unclear what it would be mean for you to be deliberating about whether to φ but not deliberating about whether to intend to φ, and likewise unclear what it would mean for you to be deliberating about whether to intend to φ but not deliberating about whether to φ. You cannot deliberate about whether to eat an éclair without deliberating about whether to intend to eat an eclair. To deliberate about whether *to* eat an éclair—as opposed to deliberating about whether to believe that you *will* eat an éclair—requires the aim of determining whether you intend to eat an éclair. Nor can you deliberate about whether to intend to eat an éclair without deliberating about whether to eat an éclair. You cannot come down in favor of intending to eat an éclair without coming down in favor of eating an éclair. Thus, although practical deliberation is officially deliberation about what to intend, i.e. deliberation about whether to intend to φ, we can say, informally, that it is deliberation about what to do, in the sense of what action to perform, i.e. deliberation about whether to φ.

5.6 Orectic Deliberation Is Not Instrumental Doxastic Deliberation

Imagine that a new luxury hotel, the Continental Hotel, has opened in Chicago, and someone asks you whether you would like to stay there—in other words, whether you have any desire to stay there. You might ask yourself: do I want to stay at the Continental Hotel? (Your question is not whether to stay there, nor whether to intend or plan or resolve to stay there, but whether to want to stay there.) You might consider everything relevant that you know about the Continental Hotel in an attempt to figure out whether staying there would be to your liking, and conclude that it would be very pleasant indeed. It is easy to imagine all this resulting in your wanting to stay at the Continental Hotel. Have we not just described a case of orectic deliberation, and indeed a case in which you formed a desire through deliberation?

Recall that we are concerned here with non-instrumental desire (§1.4). Aristotle argues that:

> We deliberate not about ends but about what contributes to ends. For a doctor does not deliberate about whether he shall heal, nor an orator about whether he shall convince, nor a statesman about whether he shall produce law and order, nor does any one else deliberate about his end. Having set the end they consider how and by what means it is to be attained. (*Nicomachean Ethics* III.3 1112b13–17, trans. W.D. Ross)

This is unconvincing. It may be that a doctor, in as much as they are a doctor, in as much as they are occupying that role, or *qua* doctor, does not deliberate about whether to heal their patients. But a doctor can obviously deliberate about whether or not to heal a patient. A doctor who has been offered a substantial bribe not to heal their patient's warts can certainly deliberate about whether or not to heal their patient's warts. Occupations, roles, practices, and the like may be individuated by certain distinctive or characteristic ends. But that does not preclude individuals from deliberating about whether to pursue those ends.

However, Aristotle's argument suggests that there will be cases in which deliberation about what contributes to ends will superficially appear to be deliberation about ends. And the worry is that the case of the Continental Hotel is a case of that kind. There are certain things you want in a hotel—well-appointed rooms and a discreet lobby bar, perhaps—and you are attempting to figure out whether the Continental Hotel has those features. If so, what you are really deliberating about is not whether to desire to stay at the Continental Hotel, but about what to *believe* about the Continental Hotel, given your antecedent desires—for example, whether to believe that it has well-appointed rooms and a discreet lobby bar. If so, the present case

108 THE EPISTEMOLOGY OF DESIRE AND THE PROBLEM OF NIHILISM

merely shows that belief is susceptible to deliberation, not that desire is susceptible to deliberation.

Let's say that *instrumental doxastic deliberation* is deliberation about whether to believe that something is a means to something that you want. As the name implies, instrumental doxastic deliberation is a species of doxastic deliberation. The problem posed by instrumental doxastic deliberation is that would-be cases of orectic deliberation will turn out to be cases of instrumental doxastic deliberation. If you are attempting to answer the question of whether x is a means to something that you want, you are engaged in doxastic deliberation; specifically, you are engaged in deliberation about whether to believe that x is a means to something that you want. That is not orectic deliberation. Thus, our case of orectic deliberation must not appear merely to be a case of instrumental doxastic deliberation.

5.7 A Case

We want a case that looks neither like a case of practical deliberation (§5.5) nor like a case of instrumental doxastic deliberation (§5.6). In this section I am going to describe a case that I take to be a case of successful orectic deliberation.

Imagine that you have been listening to a credible and informative podcast about the smooth handfish (*Sympterichthys unipennis*), which was declared extinct in 2020. The podcast tells the story of the unsuccessful campaign to save the smooth handfish. It's compelling stuff, and you find yourself rooting for the environmental activists who are fighting to save the smooth handfish, and wishing it had not gone extinct. But then you ask yourself: do I really care about this fish? Does that really make sense? Do I really wish the smooth handfish had survived? And so, having thus called your desire into question, you ask yourself: was it really a bad thing that the smooth handfish went extinct? Would it have been good if the smooth handfish had survived? Would the survival of this particular fish have been a good thing?

Suppose that it is clear, given the facts presented, that there is absolutely nothing to be done. Your question is not whether to join the struggle, or write an elegy for the smooth handfish, or bring the smooth handfish back from extinction using genetic engineering. Nor is it whether to do something about other endangered species or whether to listen to a more cheerful podcast next time. Your question is not about what to do or intend. You are not engaged in practical deliberation.

Suppose that it is also clear, given the facts presented, that the survival of the smooth handfish would not have been instrumentally good. The podcast has been thorough in presenting the facts of the case: you now know the physiology, behavior, natural history, ecology, and life cycle of the smooth handfish. It is clear, given all this, that the survival of the smooth handfish would not have caused, or realized, or constituted anything else you want. The smooth handfish was neither a source of medicine, nor a tourist attraction, nor a keystone species essential to the health of its ecosystem. And you have no antecedent desire that species of fish, or of living things in general, survive. We can imagine that you have up to this point been more or less a humanist, although not a dogmatic one, on the premise that human beings are the sort of sentient, rational creatures that matter. Your question is not about whether the survival of the smooth handfish would have been a means to something that you want. You are not engaged in instrumental doxastic deliberation.

Your question is: would it have been non-instrumentally good if the smooth handfish had survived? How might you go about attempting to answer that question? We can easily imagine that you attempt to answer this question by thinking about what it would have been like if the smooth hand-fish had survived. In the present case, you are able to do this because you now know the relevant facts about the physiology, behavior, natural history, ecology, and life cycle of the smooth handfish. You know what it would have been like if the smooth handfish had survived. To answer the question of whether it would have been non-instrumentally good if the smooth handfish had survived, you attend to what it would have been like if the smooth hand-fish had survived, by attending to and considering those properties of the smooth handfish in virtue of which its survival might have been a good thing.

Imagine that, having done that, you conclude that the smooth handfish did matter, that it was worth saving, that its survival would have been non-instrumentally good. And imagine that your drawing this conclusion results in your continuing to wish that the smooth handfish had survived. You considered whether to desire that the smooth handfish had survived, and formed such a desire as a result.

5.8 Orectic Deliberation

I maintain that the case of the podcast about the smooth handfish (§5.7) represents a case of successful orectic deliberation. In this section, I want to begin to make good on that claim by providing an account of orectic deliberation.

110   THE EPISTEMOLOGY OF DESIRE AND THE PROBLEM OF NIHILISM

Orectic deliberation is deliberation about what to desire (§5.2). More precisely, I assume that *orectic deliberation* is deliberation about whether to desire that p, for some proposition that p, with the aim of determining whether you desire that p.

Just as the characteristic question for doxastic deliberation is the question of whether p (§5.3), the characteristic question for orectic deliberation is the question of whether it is good that p.[21] What this means is that your answering the question of whether it is good that p in the affirmative, i.e. your concluding that it is good that p, can directly result in your forming a desire that p, and the question of whether it is good that p is the only question your affirmative answering of which can directly result in your forming a desire that p.[22] To put this another way, by answering the question of whether it is good that p in the affirmative, i.e. by concluding that p, you can thereby form a desire that p, and the question of whether it is good that p is the only question such that by answering it in the affirmative you can thereby form a desire that p. Concluding that it is good that p can directly result in your forming a desire that p; by contrast, concluding that it would beneficial were you to desire that p cannot directly result in your forming a desire that p. Because of this, if you aim to determine whether you desire that p, you must attempt to answer the question of whether it is good that p. Thus, orectic deliberation takes the form of attempting to answer the question of whether it is good that p. A consequence of this is that in orectic deliberation you consider evidence relevant to whether it is good that p, which represents your means of attempting to answer the question of whether it is good that p.

Orectic deliberation is *successful* if and only if you conclude that it is good that p and as a direct result form a desire that p.[23] In such cases, and only in such cases, desires are formed *through* deliberation. Desires are formed *through* deliberation, in the present sense, only when they are formed as a direct result of the desirer affirmatively answering the characteristic question for orectic deliberation, namely, whether it is good that p.

---

[21] Again (§2.2), I use "it is good that p" to mean "it is good that p or would be good if it were the case that p."

[22] Given our broad conception of attitude formation, this includes cases in which you come to want something you did not want before and cases in which you continue to want something you already wanted.

[23] Given the existence of axial gaps (§2.8), this does not include the case in which you conclude that it is not good that p.

The question of whether it is good that p must be distinguished from several similar questions. First, the question of whether it is good that p must be distinguished from the question of whether it is good to desire that p (cf. §2.2). Second, the question of whether it is good that p must be distinguished from questions about whether particular individuals are good instances of their kind (cf. §2.4). Third, the question of whether it is good that p must be distinguished from the question of whether it is good for anyone that p (cf. §2.6). Finally, the question of whether it is good that p must be distinguished from questions about whether anyone ought to make it the case that p and in general from practical questions (cf. §5.5).

I said that in orectic deliberation you consider evidence relevant to whether it is good that p. Although there may be various theoretical accounts of evidence, we are more or less familiar with the idea of evidence relevant to whether p (cf. §5.3). However, the idea of evidence relevant to whether it is good that p is relatively unfamiliar. I am not going to provide an account of such evidence here, but I want to say something in defense of the assumption that there is such a thing as evidence relevant to whether it is good that p. Recall that non-instrumental desires depend on beliefs about what the desired thing is like (§1.4). Goodness supervenes on the non-evaluative: if it is good that p and not good that q, then there must be some non-evaluative difference between what it would be like if it were the case that p and what it would be like if it were the case that q, in virtue of which it is good that p and not good that q. I submit that non-evaluative facts in virtue of which it might be good that p are always evidence relevant to the question of whether it is good that p. This is why, when we think that someone does not appreciate something's value, we invite them to attend to its non-evaluative properties. Animal welfare charities urge us to think about what animal flourishing is like so that we might come to appreciate its goodness. The evidence relevant to whether animal flourishing is good includes the non-evaluative facts in virtue of which it might be good: animals' capacity for joy and suffering, their sentience and possession of a point of view, what things are like from their point of view, what sorts of thoughts and feelings they have, and so on. Those facts, in virtue of which animal flourishing might be good, constitute evidence relevant to whether animal flourishing is good.

Non-evaluative facts in virtue of which it might be good that p are always evidence relevant to the question of whether it is good that p. This is why, in the case of the podcast about the smooth handfish (§5.7), it is easy to imagine that you attempt to answer the question of whether it would have been

112 THE EPISTEMOLOGY OF DESIRE AND THE PROBLEM OF NIHILISM

good if the smooth handfish had survived by thinking about what it would have been like if the smooth handfish had survived. The evidence relevant to your evaluative question includes the relevant non-evaluative facts—the very facts that the podcast has made clear and to which it has drawn your attention.

Again, three clarifications are in order (cf. §5.3). First, the claim that desire is susceptible to deliberation is consistent with the fact that we lack direct control over what we desire.[24] Second, the claim that desire is susceptible to deliberation is silent on the extent to which our desires are formed through deliberation and is consistent with the claim that the vast majority of our desires are formed automatically and in a non-deliberative way.[25] Third, the claim that desire is susceptible to deliberation is consistent with the fact that there are things you cannot help desiring or that you cannot bring yourself to desire.[26]

That second clarification should be emphasized. I do not want to suggest that desire formation through deliberation is a familiar or common thing. In the case of the vast majority of things that we non-instrumentally desire, we rarely, if ever, have occasion to deliberate about whether to desire them. We have occasion for deliberation when there is controversy or doubt, and controversy and doubt about ends is far less common than controversy and doubt about means. Nevertheless, if I am right, desire is susceptible to deliberation.

5.9 Acedia

I maintain that your concluding that it is good that p can directly result in your forming a desire that p. However, just as your concluding that you

---

[24] Cf. Bennett 1990, pp. 97–100, Millgram 1997, chapter 2, Scanlon 1998, p. 40.

[25] It is consistent, for example, with Kurt Schafer's (2013) observation that "we often seem to be passive with respect to what we desire" (p. 267).

[26] Nomy Arpaly and Timothy Schroeder (2014) argue that deliberation about whether to non-instrumentally desire something is rarely successful. They argue that non-instrumental desires "rarely vanish in an instant and often linger despite changes in our relevant beliefs and other desires" and that "desires vanishing in response to reasoning" is "not the usual course of things" (p. 9). This is consistent with my position. However, their argument is unconvincing. They point out that someone might easily conclude that they ought not eat meat and yet continue to want to eat meat (p. 9). However, given my account of orectic deliberation, that does not suggest that orectic deliberation is rarely successful. Orectic deliberation takes the form of attempting to answer the question, not of whether you ought to φ, but of whether it is good that p, and is successful if and only if you conclude that it is good that p and as a direct result form a desire that p. Perhaps concluding that you ought to φ rarely results in your desiring to φ and concluding that you ought not φ rarely results in your not desiring to φ. That does not suggest that concluding that it would be good were you to φ rarely results in your desiring to φ.

should φ does not always directly result in your forming an intention to φ (§5.4), your concluding that it is good that p does not always directly result in your forming a desire that p. There are familiar cases—cases of *acedia*—in which you believe that it is good that p and yet do not desire that p (cf. §1.7).

However, just as the possibility of akrasia is consistent with the susceptibility of intention to deliberation (§5.4), the possibility of acedia is consistent with the susceptibility of desire to deliberation. Although concluding that it is good that p does not amount to forming a desire that p, there is no additional "step" you have to perform, once you have concluded that it is good that p, to form a desire that p. When you non-acedically conclude that it is good that p, you form a desire that p straightaway, without doing anything else.

This is what happens in the case of the podcast about the smooth handfish (§5.7). Why did you form a desire that the smooth handfish had survived? Because you concluded that it would have been good if the smooth handfish had survived, and nothing more. You did not choose or decide to desire that the smooth handfish had survived, nor is your desire dependent on an antecedent desire or plan to desire that which is good. That you concluded that it would have been good if the smooth handfish had survived is explanation enough. It is fine to say that you formed said desire because you concluded that it would have been good if the smooth handfish had survived and did not suffer from acedia, as that is just to say that the presence of acedia could have prevented you from forming your desire, not that the absence of acedia partially explains why you formed it. You concluded that it would have been good if the smooth handfish had survived, and straightaway you formed a desire that the smooth handfish had survived. No further explanation is needed. Granted: acedia could have interfered. Listening to depressing podcasts about extinctions during a global pandemic marked by periodic civil unrest is exhausting, and it is more than possible that someone could conclude it would have been good if the smooth handfish had survived and yet find themselves utterly unmoved. Nevertheless, we can imagine that acedia did not interfere: your concluding that it would have been good if the smooth handfish had survived directly resulted in your forming a desire that the smooth handfish had survived.

As with akrasia, it is natural ask an explanatory question: if your concluding that it is good that p can directly result in your forming a desire that p, what prevents this from happening in cases of acedia? But this can only be an empirical question about the causes of acedia, some of which we are

114 THE EPISTEMOLOGY OF DESIRE AND THE PROBLEM OF NIHILISM

familiar with from our own experience: temporary bad moods, deeper and more prolonged depressions, and resentment or anger can each leave us unmoved by our conclusions about what is good. Anything beyond that should be left to social psychology and cognitive science, whose job it is to fill in the details and provide a more accurate and complete account of acedia.

Akrasia is possible because the intellect and the will are separate: although our conclusions can determine—in the sense of fixing or settling—our intentions, our conclusions do not necessitate our intentions. You can conclude that you should φ without intending to φ. Acedia is possible because the intellect and the appetite (or conatus) are separate: although our conclusions can determine our desires, our conclusions do not necessitate our desires. You can conclude that it is good that p without desiring that p. By contrast, the self-identity of the intellect allows for at least the possibility of conclusions that necessitate belief, e.g. the possibility that concluding that p amounts to forming a belief that p (§5.4).

5.10 Is Acedia Irrational?

You might think that my account of orectic deliberation (§5.8) implies that acedia (§5.9) is irrational. I said that the problem of nihilism presupposes that desires can be irrational (§5.1), and I am going to assume that desires can be irrational in what follows. Moreover, I suggested that acedia interferes with orectic deliberation, by preventing your concluding that it is good that p from directly resulting in your forming a desire that p, in the same way that akrasia interferes with practical deliberation, by preventing your concluding that you should φ from directly resulting in your forming an intention to φ. Given the common assumption that akrasia is irrational, all this suggests that acedia is likewise irrational.

However, you might think that acedia, unlike akrasia, is not irrational. You might think that it is irrational to believe that you should φ without intending to φ, but not irrational to believe that it is good that p without desiring that p. You might think that, if my argument implies that acedia is irrational, then there is something wrong with my argument.

Let us grant, for the sake of argument, that akrasia is irrational.[27] I think it is no less plausible that acedia is irrational. This becomes clear when we

---

[27] Against this, see Audi 1990, Arpaly 2000, 2004.

set aside several phenomena that superficially resemble acedia. First, consider cases in which you believe that something is a good instance of its kind without wanting to get it (cf. §2.4). You might believe that *Midnights* is the best Taylor Swift album, but not want to listen to it, because you dislike Taylor Swift. That might be irrational, but it is not a case of acedia. It would be a case of acedia if you believed that it would be good were you to listen to *Midnights*, but did not want to. Second, consider cases in which you believe that something is beneficial—whether to you or others—without wanting it (cf. §2.6). You might believe that going to therapy would be good for you, but not want to go to therapy, because it is embarrassing to talk about your emotions. That might be irrational, but it is not a case of acedia. It would be a case of acedia if you believed that it would be good—not just good for you, but good, full stop—were you to go to therapy, but did not want to. Third, consider cases in which you believe that something is good without wanting to perform some salient action. You might think it is good that the Museum of Fine Arts maintains a collection of eighteenth-century porcelain miniatures, but not want to attend their upcoming exhibition of them, because they are boring. That might be irrational, but it is not a case of acedia. It would be a case of acedia if you believed that it would be good were you to visit the exhibition, but did not want to.

So, I am prepared to grant that my argument implies that acedia is irrational. That acedia is irrational is no less plausible than that akrasia is irrational.

5.11 Orectic Deliberation Is Not (the Same Thing as) Evaluative Doxastic Deliberation

Doxastic deliberation takes the form of attempting to answer the question of whether p (§5.3); orectic deliberation takes the form of attempting to answer the question of whether it is good that p (§5.8). Suppose you are attempting to answer the question of whether it is good that p. Are you engaged in orectic deliberation (specifically, deliberation about whether to desire that p) or doxastic deliberation (specifically, deliberation about whether to believe that it is good that p)? Or are you engaged in both? Let's say that *evaluative doxastic deliberation* is deliberation about whether to believe that it is good that p. Orectic deliberation deliberation and evaluative doxastic deliberation have the same characteristic question. What, then, distinguishes them?

116 THE EPISTEMOLOGY OF DESIRE AND THE PROBLEM OF NIHILISM

It is again instructive to compare orectic deliberation and practical deliberation (cf. §5.9). Practical deliberation has the same characteristic question as a species of doxastic deliberation, namely, deliberation about whether to believe that you should φ, which we can call *deontic doxastic deliberation*. Although practical deliberation and deontic doxastic deliberation have the same characteristic question, they have different aims. Recall that in doxastic deliberation you aim to determine whether you believe that p (§5.3) and in practical deliberation you aim to determine whether you intend to φ (§5.4). In practical deliberation, therefore, you aim to determine whether you intend to φ, whereas in deontic doxastic deliberation, you aim to determine whether you believe that you should φ. However, you might aim to do both of these things. A single episode of deliberation can realize two distinct kinds of deliberation. A single episode of deliberation might amount both to practical deliberation and deontic doxastic deliberation.

Indeed, it is hard to imagine engaging in practical deliberation without at the same time engaging in deontic doxastic deliberation. Let's grant, again, that concluding that p amounts to forming a belief that p (§5.4). Imagine that you are attempting to answer the question of whether you should mow the lawn. If you conclude that you should, you will form a belief that you should. It is hard to deny that you have the aim of determining whether you believe that you should mow the lawn. At a minimum, it seems you must be aware that affirmatively answering your question will constitute your forming a belief that you should mow the lawn.

However, the possibility of akrasia (§5.4) makes it possible to engage in deontic doxastic deliberation without at the same time engaging in practical deliberation. In particular, consider cases in which you know that, even if you were to conclude that you should φ, you would nevertheless not form an intention to φ. Suppose that you have recklessly promised to come to my birthday party, even though you know that you will not intend to go when the time comes, because of how dull you know the party will be, and that, even if you were to conclude that you should go, you would not form an intention to go. You are disposed to akrasia, and you know it. Might you deliberate about whether to intend to go to the party? Not really. What would be the point? You cannot sensibly aim to determine whether you intend to go, because you know in advance that you will not form such an intention, even if you conclude that you should go. However, you nevertheless might deliberate about whether to believe that you should go to the party. It might still make sense to ask whether you should go to the party, e.g. in the hopes of discovering that you have a good excuse for not going.

Does your promise oblige you to go? Does the dullness of the party perhaps trump or override your prima facie obligation to attend? Was it really a promise, after all, when you knew full well that you would not go to the party, on account of its dullness? You can sensibly aim to determine whether you believe that you should go to my birthday party, even if you cannot sensibly aim to determine whether you intend to go.

Just as practical deliberation and deontic doxastic deliberation are distinguished by their aims, orectic deliberation and evaluative doxastic deliberation are distinguished by their aims. In orectic deliberation you aim to determine whether you desire that p (§5.8), whereas in evaluative doxastic deliberation, you aim to determine whether you believe that it is good that p. However, a single episode of deliberation might amount both to orectic deliberation and evaluative doxastic deliberation.

Moreover, just as it is hard to imagine engaging in practical deliberation without at the same time engaging in deontic doxastic deliberation, it is hard to imagine engaging in orectic deliberation without at the same time engaging in evaluative doxastic deliberation. Assuming that concluding that p amounts to forming a belief that p (§5.4), if you are attempting to answer the question of whether it would have been good if the smooth handfish had survived (§5.7), it seems you at least must be aware that affirmatively answering your question will constitute your forming a belief that it would have been good if the smooth handfish had survived.

Finally, just as the possibility of akrasia makes it possible to engage in deontic doxastic deliberation without at the same time engaging in practical deliberation, the possibility of acedia (§5.9) makes it possible to engage in evaluative doxastic deliberation without at the same time engaging in orectic deliberation. Imagine that you are a government administrator who has become jaded and cynical after decades in politics, such that you no longer care about anyone or anything other than your own family.[28] You now face the question of whether to oppose the implementation of a new policy that will have considerable benefits, but which will swiftly lead to the extinction of an endangered lichen. Your indifference, of course, might lead you to shirk your responsibilities. But we can imagine that you summon the motivation to do your job. You know that, even were you to conclude that it would be good were the lichen to survive, you would not form a desire that the lichen survive. You cannot, therefore, deliberate about whether to desire

---

[28] Cf. Stocker 1979, pp. 741–2.

118 THE EPISTEMOLOGY OF DESIRE AND THE PROBLEM OF NIHILISM

that the lichen survive. However, you might nevertheless deliberate about whether to believe that it would be good were the lichen to survive. It might still make sense to ask whether the survival of the lichen would be good, because evaluating the proposed policy requires figuring out the costs and benefits of implementing it. You can sensibly aim to determine whether you believe that it would be good were the lichen to survive, even if you cannot sensibly aim to determine whether you desire that the lichen survive.

5.12 Why Is Desire Susceptible to Deliberation?

Recall the idea that concluding that p amounts to forming a belief that p (§5.4). If this is true, we have a kind of explanation of why belief is susceptible to deliberation. There is a question—namely, the question of whether p—the affirmative answering of which amounts to forming a belief. However, there is no question the affirmative answering of which amounts to forming a desire (§5.9). Instead, I have argued, your concluding that it is good that p can directly result in your forming a desire that p (§5.8). Desire is, in this way, susceptible to deliberation. But why is it? Why is it the case that your concluding that it is good that p can directly result in your forming a desire that p?

Our question is not why desire is susceptible to deliberation, as opposed to desire not being susceptible to deliberation, as it seems plausible that mental representations that are susceptible to deliberation are *essentially* susceptible to deliberation. To put this another way, it seems plausible that particular attitudes are essentially attitudes (cf. §5.1). Our question is why we have an attitude like desire at all. Why do we have an evaluative attitude, an attitude whose accuracy condition is goodness? Why do we have a mental representation, whose accuracy condition is goodness, that can be determined by our conclusions about what is good?

I am not going to try to answer this question here, but I will make a few comments about it. First, our lack of an explanation of why desire is susceptible to deliberation does not undermine the argument that desire is susceptible to deliberation. I argued that desire is susceptible to deliberation by describing a prima facie case of successful orectic deliberation (§5.7) and providing an account of orectic deliberation (§§5.8–5.11). Compare how things stand with intention. Just as we can ask why desire is susceptible to deliberation, we can ask why intention is susceptible to deliberation. Why do we have a mental representation that can be determined by our conclusions about what we should do? Even if we lack an answer to this question, we should not doubt that intention is susceptible to deliberation.[29]

Second, although we have considered a kind of explanation of why belief is susceptible to deliberation, we have said nothing about why we are capable of deliberation in the first place—about why, in other words, we are capable of attempting to answer questions and sometimes coming to conclusions about their answers. Even if it is obvious why your concluding that p can directly result in your believing that p, this does not suggest an explanation of why we have the capacity to conclude that p in the first place.

Third, we can distinguish the question of why we have an evaluative attitude, as opposed to merely having an evaluative type of experience, from the question of why we are capable of evaluative mental representation in the first place. We may struggle to answer the first question unless we are confident of the answer to the second.

Fourth, desire is not susceptible to deliberation because it has an accuracy condition. Even if perceptual experience has an accuracy condition (§1.8), it is not susceptible to deliberation (§5.1). Moreover, the fact that goodness is the accuracy condition for desire does not explain why your concluding that it is good that p can directly result in your forming a desire that p. Truth is the accuracy condition for assertion (§2.1): an assertion that p is accurate if and only if it is true that p and inaccurate if and only if it is false that p. But your concluding that p cannot directly result in your asserting that p. Deliberation about whether to assert that p is a species of practical deliberation, and thus takes the form of attempting to answer the question of whether you should assert that p (§5.4). And there are various considerations other than the truth of the proposition that p that go into whether you should assert that p, including considerations of rudeness, consequences, and conversational relevance. It is tempting to think that accuracy plays a special role in deliberation, such that the accuracy of χing provides a decisive reason to χ, but it doesn't: you might know that an assertion would be accurate and yet reasonably choose not to make it.[30]

Fifth, given that desire is susceptible to deliberation, any plausible account of desire should be consistent with the susceptibility of desire to

---

[29] Cf. Bennett 1990 on explaining why belief is involuntary.

[30] Cf. Williams 2002, pp. 84–8, Kelly 2003, p. 11. Note well that the same problem would arise if we formulated all this in terms of constitutive norms (cf. Steglich-Petersen 2006, McHugh 2011).

deliberation, but this does not mean that any plausible account of desire must explain why desire is susceptible to deliberation. Perhaps the fact that desire is susceptible to deliberation is not explained by the nature of desire. We should be open both to the possibility that the nature of desire partially or wholly explains why desire is susceptible to deliberation and to the possibility that the explanation lies elsewhere.

5.13 Conclusion

I argued that a mental representation admits of irrationality only if it is susceptible to deliberation. I then argued that desire is susceptible to deliberation. We now turn to the problem of nihilism, where this conclusion turns out to be important: nihilism puts rational pressure on us to become indifferent to everything only if desire admits of irrationality.

The Epistemology of Desire and the Problem of Nihilism. Allan Hazlett, Oxford University Press.
© Allan Hazlett 2024. DOI: 10.1093/9780191995583.003.0005

6

The Problem

Let us now return to the problem of nihilism. I want to begin by giving a more rigorous statement of the problem. This will enable us to discuss various solutions to the problem, in this chapter, and my own preferred solution, in the following chapter.

6.1 Statement of the Problem

Suppose you think that nothing matters, i.e. that for any proposition that p, it is neither good nor bad that p (§1.1). I said that thinking this seems to put rational pressure on you to become indifferent to everything—i.e. to neither desire that p nor desire that not-p, for any proposition that p. Thinking that nothing is good or bad seems to put rational pressure on you to desire nothing.

AD suggests something like this. I have been defending a version of Anscombe's idea that the conceptual connection between desire and goodness is the same as the conceptual connection between belief and truth (§1.6). I have argued that, just as truth is the accuracy condition for belief, goodness is the accuracy condition for desire. It is precisely this similarity that generates the problem of nihilism. Given AB, it seems obvious that:

BTP   It is irrational to both believe that p and believe that it is not true that p.

And, given AD, the analogous claim about desire seems irresistible:

DGP   It is irrational to both desire that p and believe that it is not good that p.

Given DGP, it is irrational to both desire something and believe that nothing is good or bad. It is irrational to think that, for any proposition that p, it is neither good nor bad that p, and yet desire that p, for some proposition

122 THE EPISTEMOLOGY OF DESIRE AND THE PROBLEM OF NIHILISM

that p. Given DGP, if you believe that nothing is good or bad, then it is irrational for you to desire anything. If it is irrational to desire something you believe is not good, nihilism about value—i.e. the thought that nothing is good or bad—makes it irrational to desire anything.

Note well that BTP and DGP are claims of structural rationality (§5.1), and keep this in mind when I say that DGP says that it is irrational to desire something you believe is not good. BTP prohibits a particular combination of beliefs and DGP prohibits a particular combination of desire and belief. If you believe something that you believe is not true, you can avoid the irrationality entailed by BTP either by giving up the first of your beliefs or by giving up the second of your beliefs. And if you desire something that you believe is not good, you can avoid the irrationality entailed by DGP either by giving up your desire or by giving up your belief.

In the first instance, the problem of nihilism is a problem for those who think that nothing is good or bad, i.e. for nihilists about value. Total indifference—i.e. not desiring that p, for any proposition that p—would be practically disastrous for any creature remotely like us. This kind of concern has always been the principal objection to Pyrrhonian skepticism, in as much as it recommends total suspension of judgment—i.e. not believing that p, for any proposition that p. Total suspension of judgment would be practically disastrous for any creature remotely like us. The skeptic who has no beliefs about their environment would quickly fall into a ditch or be run over by a cart. Nihilism about value, in as much as it recommends total indifference, faces the same kind of objection. The nihilist who has no desires—and thus no desire not to fall into a ditch or not to be run over by a cart—would likewise quickly fall into a ditch or be run over by a cart. (Note that, as a nihilist, they could not rely on their belief that it would be bad were they to fall into a ditch or be run over by a cart.) Moreover, the situation may be even worse for the nihilist, as one way a Pyrrhonian skeptic might try to get by without beliefs is by relying on their natural desires, such as hunger and thirst, to produce action.[1] Total indifference would preclude even this potential source of action.

6.2 The Realist Solution

In response to the problem of nihilism, you might think: so much the worse for nihilism about value. Nihilism about value is false, so of course believing

[1] Sextus Empiricus, *Outlines of Scepticism* I.23–4.

it has unhappy consequences, e.g. it becomes irrational to desire anything. Granted, given DGP (§6.1), it is irrational to desire something you believe is not good. However, since some things are good, there is no "problem" concerning the rationality of having desires while believing that nothing is good or bad.

I want to grant that realists about value—i.e. those who think that some things are good—have a kind of solution to the problem of nihilism, although it is probably more accurate to say that the problem does not arise for them. Realists about value do not face the rational pressure not to desire anything that nihilists about value face.

To be clear, you are not a realist merely because you think that there are good hotels (§2.4) or because you think that sunlight is good for plants (§2.6). To be a realist, you must think that, for some proposition that p, it is good that p. In articulating AD, I presupposed no substantive account of goodness. Realism includes both the view that goodness is a non-natural property that is sometimes instantiated and the view that goodness is natural property that is sometimes instantiated. It includes the view that some things are good in virtue of the fact that we are disposed to desire some things under certain conditions. It includes the view that some things are good in virtue of the fact that it is fitting to desire some things, whether this means that some desire are accurate (cf. §3.8), that there are things we ought to desire (cf. §3.9), or that there are reasons to desire some things (cf. §3.10).

Realism about value even includes the implausible view, defended by no one, that some things are good in virtue of the fact that some things are desired. On this view, good things are good in virtue of being desired. Is "realism" really a fair name for such a view? There is, I grant, an important difference between this view, which seems thoroughly naturalistic, and the view that goodness is a non-natural property that is sometimes instantiated. But both of these views agree that some things really are good. I say "really" here, to indicate a concession: even nihilists about value can and should grant that some things *appear* good. When we think that nothing matters (§1.1), we think that, despite how things appear, nothing really matters. The view that good things are good in virtue of being desired vindicates the apparent fact that some things are good. Nihilism about value says that things are not as they appear.

You might want to reserve "realism about value" for the view that some things are *objectively* good. Of course, we are free to stipulate what we mean when we use a particular bit of jargon. However, consider, again, the view that good things are good in virtue of being desired. Is this a view on which some things are "objectively" good? I want to eat a roast beef sandwich right

124 THE EPISTEMOLOGY OF DESIRE AND THE PROBLEM OF NIHILISM

now—there is an obvious sense in which that is an objective fact. It is hardly "subjective" in the sense of being a matter of taste or opinion, such that there is no fact of the matter about whether I really do want to eat a roast beef sandwich right now. There is at least a sense of "objective" on which the realists about value canvassed above all think that some things are objectively good.

Given that realism about value is a broad church, encompassing a wide range of metaethical positions, should we take nihilism about value seriously? If nihilism about value were merely a symptom of an existential crisis, perhaps we could agree that it is simply an unfortunate consequence of having the false belief that nothing is good or bad that it makes it irrational to desire anything. However, I think nihilism about value should be taken more seriously than that. Nihilism follows from two views that should be taken seriously: the view that goodness is a non-natural property (aka metaethical non-naturalism) and the view that only natural properties are instantiated (aka philosophical naturalism). It is hardly clear that we must give up one of these views to preserve the assumption that goodness is sometimes instantiated, i.e. the assumption that some things are good.

For this reason, we cannot mitigate the problem of nihilism by appeal to a "buck-passing" account of value (§3.10). Realism about reasons, i.e. the view that there are reasons, in the context of the problem of nihilism, is no more plausible than realism about value. Reasons, in the context of the "buck-passing" account of value, are normative reasons, i.e. considerations that speak in favor of doing something. Above, I interpreted the thought that nothing matters as the thought that nothing is good or bad (§1.1), but it could just as plausibly be interpreted as the thought that there is no normative reason to do anything. The view that goodness is a non-natural property is no less plausible than the view that the property of being a reason, i.e. the property of speaking in favor of doing something, is non-natural. Philosophical naturalists should be equally suspicious of normative reasons as they are of values. Again, I want to grant that the problem of nihilism does not arise for realists about value, and likewise I want to grant that the problem of nihilism does not arise for realists about reasons. I maintain, however, that appealing to a "buck-passing" account of value makes it no easier to avoid the problem.

I have granted that the problem of nihilism does not arise for realists about value. However, even if you are a realist about value, you might wonder whether nihilism about value makes it irrational to desire anything. J.L. Mackie (1977) famously argued that "[t]here are no objective values" (p. 15)

THE PROBLEM   125

and he seems to have in mind a version of nihilism about value. Was it irrational for Mackie to believe this while wanting to take a stroll around University College? Even if he was wrong about nihilism, you might think that it was not irrational for him to both want to take a stroll and believe that it would not be good were he to take a stroll. If it was not irrational, however, then the problem of nihilism presents a puzzle even for those realists about value who are not tempted by the thought that nothing matters.

6.3 The Expressivist Solution

R.M. Hare (1957/1972) argues that the thought that nothing matters normally involves a linguistic confusion. He argues that "when we say that something matters or is important what we are doing, in saying this, is to express concern about that something" (pp. 33–4).[2] Because of this, Hare argues, you can sincerely say that nothing matters only if you are not concerned about anything (p. 35). Hare concedes that not being concerned about anything might be psychologically possible (p. 38). However, he argues, "for the majority of us to become like this is a contingency so remote so as to excite neither fear nor attraction; we just are not made like that. We are creatures who feel concern for things" (pp. 38–9). If you are concerned about anything, as any normal person is, then you cannot sincerely say that nothing matters.

For any normal person, Hare suggests, the thought that nothing matters must involve mistakenly thinking that "matters" is "intended to *describe* something that things do" rather than "to express our concern about what they do" (p. 38). For any normal person the thought that nothing matters involves confusing expressive language for descriptive language.

I proposed that to think that nothing matters is to think that nothing is good or bad (§1.1). However, what Hare says about "matters" is no less plausible, mutatis mutandis, when said about "good." If "matters" is expressive and not descriptive, then surely "good" is expressive and not descriptive.[3] If to say that something matters is to express concern about it, then to say that something is good is to express some non-cognitive attitude toward

---

[2] As Hare concedes (p. 34), this is not quite right. We can also say that something matters to indicate that someone else is concerned about it, without expressing our own concern about it. More precisely, then, the idea must be that when we say that something matters we are expressing or indicating someone's concern about it. I'll ignore this complication in what follows.

[3] I set aside "bad" for the sake of simplicity in what follows.

126 THE EPISTEMOLOGY OF DESIRE AND THE PROBLEM OF NIHILISM

it. Now, what Hare says elsewhere is that "good" is not used to describe something but rather to commend it, such that to say that something is good is to commend it.[4] It is not immediately clear what would be required, on this view, to sincerely say that nothing is good, but it seems more or less clear that it would require something just as abnormal as not being concerned about anything. If Hare is right about "good," it seems more or less clear, then you can sincerely say that nothing is good only if you are totally indifferent. And, therefore, for any normal person, the thought that nothing is good must involve confusing commendatory language for descriptive language.

If this is right, we have a kind of solution to the problem of nihilism. We could say that nihilism about value does make it irrational to desire anything, but that this is no surprise, given how confused a thought it is. Or we could say, given the fact that "good" is commendatory and not descriptive, that there is really no such thing as *believing* that nothing is good or bad, such that DGP (§6.1) cannot be applied. As in the case of realism about value (§6.2), it seems fair to say that, if Hare is right about the thought that nothing matters, the problem of nihilism does not arise.

However, I think Hare is wrong. As he points out (pp. 39–45), his account of evaluative language implies that the question of whether nihilism about value is true is a pseudo-problem, such that there is no disagreement between nihilists about value and realists about value (cf. §6.2). This is implausible.[5] There is something that realists about value affirm that nihilists about value deny. The disagreement is metaphysical, but it is a real disagreement. This is not to deny that "good" can be used to commend something rather than to describe it, but it is to insist that "good" can be used a non-commendatory way to articulate a metaphysical disagreement, as when we ask whether anything really is good. Consider Mackie's (1977) critical articulation of Platonism about goodness:

> [S]omething's being good both tells the person who knows this to pursue it and makes him pursue it. An objective good would be sought by anyone who was acquainted with it, not because of any contingent fact that this person, or every person, is so constituted that he desires this end, but just because the end has to-be-pursuedness built into it. (p. 40)

---

[4] Hare 1952, Part II, 1963b, Part I.   [5] Cf. Parfit 2006, pp. 325–30.

This represents a metaphysical claim that you might affirm or deny. Perhaps it is obvious that we should deny it. But some philosophers affirm it.[6]

There are, of course, alternative ways of articulating the distinction between nihilism about value and realism about value. They each involve different ways of conceptualizing goodness. It seems to me that the distinction can be illustrated by observing that goodness is what makes things worthy of desire. Goodness is a property such that things that have that property, and only things that have that property, are worthy of desire. I do not mean that good things are good in virtue of being worthy of desire (cf. §3.8). I mean merely that the concept of goodness is the concept of a property such that things that have that property, and only things that have that property, are worthy of desire. With the concept of goodness thus understood, is anything good? That is a metaphysical question that you might answer in the affirmative or in the negative.

None of this is meant to be decisive, of course. If you think, with Hare, that the thought that nothing matters involves a linguistic confusion, then the problem of nihilism does not arise for you. I think nihilism about value is a coherent view, even if it is mistaken. So, let us look at some alternative solutions to the problem of nihilism.

6.4 The Humean Solution, Again

Given DGP (§6.1), it is irrational to desire something you believe is not good. You might reject DGP on the grounds that desire does not admit of irrationality, because desire has no accuracy condition.

I call this the "Humean" solution to the problem of nihilism (§1.2) because it presupposes an idea first articulated by Hume: that a mental representation admits of irrationality only if it has an accuracy condition. Here is how he argues in the *Treatise of Human Nature*:

> A PASSION is an original existence, or, if you will, modification of existence, and contains not any representative quality, which renders it a copy of any other existence or modification. When I am angry, I am actually possest with the passion, and in that emotion have no more a reference to any other object, than when I am thirsty, or sick, or more than five foot

---

[6] Cf. Parfit 2006, pp. 325–30.

128 THE EPISTEMOLOGY OF DESIRE AND THE PROBLEM OF NIHILISM

> high. 'Tis impossible, therefore, that this passion can be oppos'd by, or be contradictory to truth and reason; since this contradiction consists in the disagreement of ideas, consider'd as copies, with those objects, which they represent. (2.3.3.5)
>
> REASON is the discovery of truth or falshood. Truth or falshood consists in an agreement or disagreement either to the *real* relations of ideas, or to *real* existence and matter of fact. Whatever, therefore, is not susceptible of this agreement or disagreement, is incapable of being true or false, and can never be an object of our reason. Now 'tis evident our passions, volitions, and actions, are not susceptible of any such agreement or disagreement; being original facts and realities, compleat in themselves, and implying no reference to other passions, volitions, and actions. 'Tis impossible, therefore, they can be pronounced either true or false, and be either contrary or conformable to reason. (3.1.1.9)

The Humean solution to the problem of nihilism presupposes that a mental representation admits of irrationality only if it has an accuracy condition. Since desire has no accuracy condition, the Humean concludes, it does not admit of irrationality. This suggests that desire is a mental representation that does not admit of irrationality. However, Hume suggests that desire is not a mental *representation* at all. Desires, by contrast with beliefs, are impressions, and therefore lack intentionality. The Humean solution to the problem of nihilism is not committed to this. The defender of the Humean solution can allow that desires are intentional. The practical theory of desire (§1.5) implies that desires are intentional: a disposition to act in ways that would tend to bring it about that p, according to the practical theory, is a desire *that p*, i.e. a desire whose intentional content is the proposition that p. What is distinctive of the Humean solution to the problem of nihilism is not the radical rejection of the intentionality of desire, but the modest rejection of the idea that desire has an accuracy condition.

The Humean argues that, when it comes to accuracy, desire is like imagination (§2.1). Just as it is not irrational to both imagine that you are eating lunch at a seaside café and believe that it is not true that you are eating lunch at a seaside café, it is not irrational to both want to take a walk and believe that it would not be good were you to take a walk. Just as believing that it is not true that p does not put rational pressure on you not to imagine that p, believing that it is not good that p does not put rational pressure on you not to desire that p.

You might think that the Humean solution to the problem of nihilism is a little too good to be true. If desire has no accuracy condition, it is mysterious why we were ever troubled by nihilism about value in the first place. We have been considering the idea that it is irrational both to desire that p and to believe that it is not good that p, which implies that it is irrational for a nihilist about value to desire anything. When it comes to paradigm mental representations that have no accuracy condition, nothing like this is even remotely tempting. We are not at all tempted to think that it is irrational both to imagine that p and to believe that it is not true that p, which is why we are not at all troubled by the prospect that all the things we imagine are not true. By contrast, we are troubled by the prospect that all the things we desire are not good. If desire, like imagination, has no accuracy condition, why would we find this prospect troubling?

In any event, AD is incompatible with the Humean solution to the problem of nihilism. Let us, therefore, investigate alternative solutions. However, if no alternative solution can be found, then we may have occasion to revisit the case for AD.

6.5 The Egoistic Solution

Our desires often reflect our partiality, i.e. our bias towards someone or something. If you have entered a raffle, you naturally hope that you will win. Would it be good were you to win? Perhaps it would be good were you to win, just because it would be good were anyone—or anyone equally deserving, etc.—to win. However, the more obvious thought here is that it would be good *for you* were you to win—i.e. that winning the raffle would *benefit* you. That, at least, seems like the best explanation of *why* you want to win. Moreover, it doesn't seem irrational for you to hope that you win, even if you believe that it would not be good—not good, full stop—were you to win. This suggests a solution to the problem of nihilism. DGP (§6.1) says that it is irrational to desire something you believe is not good. However, so the argument goes, in the present case, it is not irrational for you to want to win the raffle, even if you believe that it would not be good were you to win the raffle. Therefore, DGP is false.

We must keep in mind the distinction between "good" and "good for" here (§2.6). We need to set aside cases in which you believe that it would be good were you to win the raffle because winning the raffle would benefit

130   THE EPISTEMOLOGY OF DESIRE AND THE PROBLEM OF NIHILISM

you. A counterexample to DGP requires a case in which you both want to win the raffle and believe that it would not be good were you to win.

On the present proposal, it can be rationally permissible to desire something you believe is not good. In the case of the raffle, it was suggested, this has something to do with the fact that winning the raffle would benefit you. However, we would like to know: how does the fact that winning the raffle would benefit you explain why it is rationally permissible for you to want to win the raffle?

Consider:

DBP   It is irrational to both desire that p and believe that it is not good for you that p.

This would provide a kind of explanation of why it is rationally permissible for you to want to win the raffle, by explaining the relevance of the fact that winning the raffle would benefit you. However, DBP is false. Imagine that it is not you, but your best friend, who has entered the raffle. You naturally want your friend to win. Moreover, we can easily imagine that your friend's winning the raffle would not benefit you—and that you know that their winning would not benefit you. Nevertheless, your desire does not seem irrational—it is not irrational to both want your friend to win the raffle and believe that their winning would not benefit you.

6.6 The Relativistic Solution

You might want to appeal, at this point, to the distinction between agent-neutral and agent-relative value, which is based on the distinction between agent-relative and agent-neutral reasons. Thomas Nagel (1970, chapter X) distinguishes between "agent-relative reasons" (or "subjective reasons") and "agent-neutral reasons" (or "objective reasons"). In Nagel's paradigm case (pp. 90–1), if you are asked what reason you have for getting out of the way of an oncoming truck, you might cite either the fact that doing so will save *your* life—which is thus understood as an agent-relative reason—or the fact that doing so will save *someone's* life—which is thus understood as an agent-neutral reason. Elsewhere (1986; see also Parfit 1984, p. 27), Nagel articulates the distinction as follows:

> If a reason can be given a general form which does not include an essential reference to the person who has it, it is an *agent-neutral* reason. [...] If on

the other hand the general form of a reason does include an essential reference to the person who has it, it is an *agent-relative* reason. (pp. 152–3)

The idea is that although there is some reason for both of us to get you out of the way of the truck—an agent-neutral reason—there is also a reason for you, but not for me, to get you out of the way of the truck—an agent-relative reason. However, not all agent-relative reasons are prudential reasons, i.e. reasons of self-interest. Although prudential reasons are often treated as the paradigm case of agent-relative reasons,[7] those who draw the distinction between agent-neutral and agent-relative reasons generally reject the conflation of agent-relative reasons and prudential reasons, given what work they want agent-relative reasons to do, e.g. to explain why I have a special obligation to take care of my family or why I have a special obligation to keep my promises.[8] In the case of your best friend entering a raffle (§6.5), there is intuitively a reason for you, but not necessarily for anyone else, to want your friend to win the raffle. In other words, there is a non-prudential agent-relative reason for you to want your friend to win.

Notice that nothing remotely like this is plausible when it comes to reasons for belief. There cannot be reasons for belief that include an essential reference to particular people. Reasons for belief are evidence relevant to whether p (§3.10). On the present proposal, your relationship with your friend makes it the case that there is a reason for you to want your friend to win. By contrast, your relationship with your friend does *not* make it the case that there is a reason for you to believe that your friend will win—that would be wishful thinking, not believing for a reason.

Now, recall the idea that there is a reason for you, but not for me, to get you out of the way of the truck. Some argue that this difference in reasons makes for a difference in value, such that your getting out of the way of the truck has value for you that it does not have for me.[9] We might say that your getting out of the way of the truck matters for you, in a way that it does not matter for me. Corresponding to the distinction between agent-relative and agent-neutral reasons, on this view, is a distinction between agent-relative

---

[7] Cf. Nagel 1970, pp. 90–1, 1979, p. 102, 1986, p. 154, Drier 1993, pp. 35–6, Smith 2003.

[8] Cf. Nagel 1970, p. 96, Portmore 2005, p. 97, 2007, p. 43; see also Hurka 2003, p. 612, Schroeder 2007, pp. 272–3, Scanlon 2008, pp. 132–3.

[9] Garcia 1986, 1987, Smith 2003, 2009, Portmore 2005, 2007; cf. Hurka 2003, p. 611.

132 THE EPISTEMOLOGY OF DESIRE AND THE PROBLEM OF NIHILISM

and agent-neutral value. Those who posit this distinction explain it by appeal to a relativistic variant of the "fitting desire" account of value (§3.8):[10]

FD-RELATIVISTIC   It is good that p relative to S if and only if it is fitting for S to desire that p and bad that p relative to S if and only if it is unfitting for S to desire that p.

You might think that, in the original case of your entering a raffle (§6.4), it is fitting for you to want to win the raffle, and therefore, per FD-RELATIVISTIC, good relative to you that you win the raffle.

We must again ask what "fitting" and "unfitting" mean (§3.8). Given AD, we cannot appeal to the idea that to say that an attitude is fitting is to say that it is accurate and to say that an attitude is unfitting is to say that it is inaccurate. Given the implausibility of FD-REASONABLE (§3.9), we cannot appeal to the idea that to say that an attitude is fitting is to say that it is reasonable to have it and to say that an attitude is unfitting is to say that it is reasonable not have it. Might we appeal to the idea that to say that an attitude is fitting is to say that there is a reason to have it and to say that an attitude is unfitting is to say that there is a reason not to have it (§3.10)? That is a plausible enough explanation of what "fitting" and "unfitting" mean, and would make good sense in the present context: intuitively there is an agent-relative reason for you to want to win the raffle but not an agent-relative reason for me to want you to win the raffle. So, let us adopt that understanding of FD-RELATIVISTIC it is good that p relative to S if and only if there is a reason for S to desire that p and bad that p relative to S if and only if there is a reason for S not to desire that p.

How does this bear on the problem of nihilism? You might argue that nihilism is simply implausible once agent-relative value is taken into consideration. There are some things it is fitting for you to desire—on the present interpretation, there are reasons for you to desire some things—therefore, there are some things that are good relative to you. However, we saw that realism about reasons is no more plausible than realism about value (§6.2). Agent-relative reasons, like agent-neutral reasons, are normative reasons, and for that reason philosophical naturalists should be equally suspicious of

---

[10] I bracket here the idea that attributions of agent-relative value have indexical content, such that they are analogous to attributions of position-relative properties (Sen 1982, 1983; cf. Drier 1993, p. 28). The analogy is obscure (cf. Schroeder 2007, pp. 273–5) unless something like a "fitting attitudes" account of value is adopted, although see §6.7 for a discussion of visual perspective.

THE PROBLEM   133

agent-relative reasons as they are of agent-neutral reasons. Thus, the idea of agent-relative value does not make nihilism about value any less plausible.

6.7 The Perspectival Solution

Recall the evaluative perception theory of desire, on which desires are, or are analogous to, perceptions or appearances of goodness (§1.8). Nietzsche (1887/2001) writes that:

> Egoism is the *perspectival* law of feeling according to which what is closest appears large and heavy, while in the distance everything decreases in size and weight. (p. 134)

This suggests a solution to the problem of nihilism. Assume, again, that a perceptual experience of a as F is accurate if and only if a is F and inaccurate otherwise (§1.8). Consider your desire to win the raffle (§6.4), and compare your visual experience of two trees in the quad, of equal size, one more distant than the other, such that (in a sense, more on which below) the near tree looks larger than the far tree. Here is a thought: just as your visual experience inaccurately represents the near tree as larger than the far tree, your desire to win the raffle inaccurately represents your winning the raffle as good. Along these lines, Graham Oddie (2005) suggests that desires that reflect partiality are analogous to "the kind of systematic 'illusion' that is generated by the fact that our visual perceptions are perspectival," as when "the sun appears smaller than the moon, even though it is much larger" (p. 213, and see in general §3.5 and §8.3; see also Tenenbaum 2007, p. 39, p. 56). However, so we might argue, just as it is not irrational to both have a visual experience that represents the near tree as larger than the far tree and believe that the trees are the same size, it is not irrational to both want to win the raffle and believe that your winning the raffle is not good. Therefore, DGP (§6.1) is false.

The problem with this solution to the problem of nihilism is that desire, unlike perceptual experience, is susceptible to deliberation. Indeed, it is not irrational to both have a visual experience that represents the near tree as larger than the far tree and believe that the trees are the same size, just as it is not irrational to both have a visual experience that represents the Müller-Lyre lines as unequal in length and believe that they are equal in length. That is because perceptual experience is not susceptible to deliberation, and

134   THE EPISTEMOLOGY OF DESIRE AND THE PROBLEM OF NIHILISM

therefore does not admit of irrationality (§5.1). Desire, by contrast, is susceptible to deliberation, as I argued in Chapter 5. This undermines the implied analogy between perceptual experience and desire. There is a problem of nihilism because thinking that nothing is good or bad seems to put rational pressure on you not to desire anything. By contrast, thinking that the two trees are the same size clearly puts no rational pressure on you not to have a visual experience that represents the near tree as larger than the far tree. Nihilism rationally threatens our desires, whereas knowing the two trees are the same size does not rationally threaten our visual experience of them.

Moreover, it is unclear that visual perspective involves inaccurate representation in the manner alleged. Our visual experiences are perspectival in two main ways. First, our visual experiences give us a picture of our environment that is *limited* to those parts of our environment of which we are visually aware: we see only what is before our eyes, and not what is behind us or in some other place entirely. But this does not involve inaccurate representation. My present visual experience represents only what is before my eyes, as opposed to what is behind me, or how things stand right now at the Whale Pub in Hong Kong, or what was before my eyes yesterday. This does not mean that any of my visual experiences, nor my visual experiences taken collectively, are inaccurate. Not representing something does not entail misrepresenting it. Second, our visual experiences give us a picture of our environment that is drawn, as it were, from a particular *point of view*: we see objects as being near or far, above or below, and to the right or to the left. It is this aspect of visual perspective that is relevant in the case of the two trees. However, there are two plausible ways of understanding point of view, and on neither is it the case that your visual experience of the two trees is inaccurate. According to a *non-representational understanding*, visual point of view consists in your having visual experiences with certain qualitative, non-representational properties, which constitute what it's like to have said experiences.[11] The near tree "looks larger than the far tree"— this is a feature of what it's like to see the trees from a certain spot—but your visual experience does not represent the near tree as larger than the far tree, and thus is not inaccurate. According to a *representational understanding* of visual point of view, by contrast, visual point of view consists in your having visual experiences that represent spatial relations between you and the

[11] See e.g. Peacocke 1983, chapter 1.

things that you see.[12] The near tree "looks larger than the far tree," because your visual experience of the two trees represents the near tree as closer to you than the far tree. It does not represent the near tree as larger than the far tree, and thus is not inaccurate.

Could we say something similar about desire? Could we say that your desires represent certain relations between you and their objects? Consider:

AD-PROSPECTIVE S's desire that p is accurate if and only if (and because) S would be happy if it were the case that p and inaccurate if and only if (and because) S would be unhappy if it were the case that p.

This would vindicate the prospective theory of desire (§1.9). AD-PROSPECTIVE says that desire is a kind of prudential evaluation. What is distinctive of AD-PROSPECTIVE, by contrast with AD, is the idea that the accuracy condition for desire makes reference to the desirer.[13] Assuming you would be happy, and I would not be happy, were you to the win the raffle, your desire to win the raffle is accurate, whereas, were I to hope that you win the raffle, my desire would not be accurate. Given AD-PROSPECTIVE, different people's desires for the same thing might differ in accuracy.

There would be no problem of nihilism if AD-PROSPECTIVE, instead of AD, were true. When you think that nothing matters, you are not thinking that nothing would make you happy or unhappy. However, because AD and AD-PROSPECTIVE are incompatible, our defense of AD is at the same time an argument against AD-PROSPECTIVE. It would make sense to criticize your desire that the world be destroyed (§3.1), even if you would be happy if the world were destroyed. AD explains why (§3.2).

6.8 The Naturalist Solution

Hume finds compelling an extreme form of skepticism, on which he ought not believe anything.[14] However, he observes that this conclusion fails to stick. In response to the question of whether he is "really one of those

---

[12] See e.g. Harman 1990, p. 38.

[13] There are alternative ways we might achieve the same, e.g. if we said that your desire that p is accurate if and only if it is good for you that p or that your desire that p is accurate if and only if it is good for you and your associates that p.

[14] See *Treatise of Human Nature*, Book I, Part IV, *Enquiry concerning Human Understanding*, §12, Part I.

136 THE EPISTEMOLOGY OF DESIRE AND THE PROBLEM OF NIHILISM

sceptics, who hold that all is uncertain," Hume replies "that this question is entirely superfluous, and that neither I, nor any other person was ever sincerely and constantly of that opinion." He argues that:

> Nature, by an absolute and uncontroulable necessity has determin'd us to judge as well as to breathe and feel; nor can we any more forbear viewing certain objects in a stronger and fuller light, upon account of their customary connexion with a present impression, than we can hinder ourselves from thinking as long as we are awake, or seeing the surrounding bodies, when we turn our eyes towards them in broad sunshine. Whoever has taken the pains to refute the cavils of this *total* scepticism, has really disputed without an antagonist, and endeavour'd by arguments to establish a faculty, which nature has antecedently implanted in the mind, and render'd unavoidable.[15]

And he goes on to observe that his skeptical conclusions seem "strain'd and ridiculous" when he is participating in the activities of ordinary life, like playing backgammon and conversing with his friends.[16] Hume concludes, given certain skeptical arguments, that he ought not believe anything. And yet, when he returns to living his life, he finds himself believing all kinds of things. Total suspension of judgment is impossible for human beings. Hume writes that:

> It seems evident, that men are carried, by a natural instinct or preposession, to repose faith in their senses; and that, without any reasoning, or even almost before the use of reason, we always suppose an external universe, which depends not on our perception, but would exist, though we and every sensible creature were absent or annihilated. Even the animal creation are governed by a like opinion, and preserve this belief of external objects, in all their thoughts, designs, and actions.[17]

As P.F. Strawson (1985) explains:

> According to Hume the naturalist, skeptical doubts are not to be met by argument. They are simply to be neglected (except, perhaps, in so far as they supply a harmless amusement, a mild diversion of the intellect). They

---

[15] *Treatise* 1.4.1.7, see also *Enquiry* 5.2. [16] *Treatise* 1.4.7.9.
[17] *Enquiry* 12.6.

are to be neglected because they are *idle*; powerless against the force of nature, of our naturally implanted disposition to belief. (p. 13)

In a similar spirit, Thomas Reid says, of his perceptual beliefs, that they are "the immediate effect of my constitution" and that it is "not in my power" to give them up[18] and Wittgenstein (1969) describes our certainty in certain propositions as "something animal" (§359; cf. Strawson 1985, pp. 14–21).

This suggests a kind of solution to the problem of nihilism. Imagine that you conclude, given the premise that nothing is good or bad, that you ought not desire anything. Surely, just as Hume inevitably finds himself believing various things when he returns to living his life, you will find yourself desiring various things when you return to living your life. Even if you manage to achieve total indifference during your nihilistic reflections, it will not last for long, in the same way that, even if Hume manages to achieve total suspension of judgment during his skeptical reflections, it will not last for long. As Hare (1957/1972) glibly articulates the same idea, "worries about whether anything matters at all are in most cases best dispelled by Hume's well-known remedy for similar doubts about the possibility of causal reasoning – a good game of backgammon" (p. 38).

Sergio Tenenbaum (2010) suggests that (at least some) desires that reflect partiality (§6.5) constitute a species of "malignant recalcitrant illusion," analogous to the case of a superstitious person who consciously rejects the superstition that you can "jinx" your favorite sports team by speaking confidently about their chances of winning, and yet finds it hard to "shake off its influence in belief formation," such that they are reluctant to do things that might "jinx" their team (p. 218; see also §4.5, §1.4, p. 47n). Just as the superstitious person is affected by a recalcitrant belief in "jinxes," in the case of your entering a raffle you are affected by an recalcitrant desire to win the raffle. A nihilist about value might think that all of their desires are recalcitrant in this way.

Thomas Nagel (1971/1979) arrives at something like this position in his sympathetic discussion of the idea that life is absurd. He argues that:

We step back to find that the whole system of justification and criticism, which controls our choices and supports our claims to rationality, rests on responses and habits that we never question, that we should not know how to defend without circularity, and to which we shall continue to

---

[18] *Inquiry into the Human Mind on the Principles of Common Sense* 6.20.

138 THE EPISTEMOLOGY OF DESIRE AND THE PROBLEM OF NIHILISM

adhere even after they are called into question. (p. 15; see also Nagel 1986, pp. 214–23)

This is, of course, an application of the Nagelian theme (1986, 1997) of the inescapability of the "subjective point of view." In as much as having desires is part of occupying the subjective point of view, and in as much as occupying the subjective point of view is unavoidable for human beings, the nihilistic conclusion that you ought not desire anything is inevitably going to be idle. The thought that nothing matters, like the thought that we have no free will or the thought that we don't know anything, cannot have any substantial effect on how we think, act, and feel.

The present solution to the problem of nihilism seems right as far as its central contention: just as it is not possible for a human being to sustain total suspension of judgment for very long, it is not possible for a human being to sustain total indifference for very long. And perhaps that is all there is to say in response to the problem of nihilism.

We might even supplement the present solution with the claim that our inability to become totally indifferent is beneficial. "Most fortunately it happens," Hume writes, "that since reason is incapable of dispelling [skeptical doubt], nature herself suffices to the purpose."[19] Total indifference would be a disaster (§6.1), so thank goodness we are incapable of total indifference. This is perfectly compatible with nihilism about value. Indeed, inaccurate representations, even species of representation that are systematically inaccurate, can coherently be welcomed as beneficial. It is beneficial for us to be susceptible to perceptual illusions. Even if color vision involves systematic misrepresentation of objects, it is clearly beneficial for us to represent objects as colored. There is no incoherence in the social-psychological theory of "positive illusions," on which it is beneficial for us to have certain false beliefs about ourselves, or in the anthropological view that theistic beliefs are false but beneficial for religious communities. We could coherently argue that it is beneficial for us to have desires, even though our desires are systematically inaccurate.

However, because desire is susceptible to deliberation, as I argued in Chapter 5, the worry about irrationality remains.[20] It is irrational to believe

---

[19] *Treatise* 1.4.7.9; see also 2.3.3.4 and *Enquiry* 5.6; cf. Reid, *Inquiry*, 6.20.
[20] This may be the source of the appeal, for Hume, of the idea that "*belief is more properly an act of the sensitive, than of the cogitative part of our natures*" (*Treatise* 1.4.1.8) which suggests that belief is not susceptible to deliberation.

that p while believing that your belief that p is inaccurate—think again of the self-consciously superstitious person who still believes in "jinxes." It is perhaps not irrational to believe that some of your beliefs are inaccurate—although there is a puzzle about why this is not irrational—but it is clearly irrational to believe, of some particular belief of yours, that it is inaccurate. By contrast, it is not irrational to believe, of some particular perceptual experience of yours, that it is inaccurate (§5.1; cf. §6.7). However, given that desire is susceptible to deliberation, just as it is irrational to believe, of some particular belief of yours, that it is inaccurate, it is irrational to believe, of some particular desire of yours, that it is inaccurate. As Nagel (1986) argues, the problem with the thought that nothing matters is that it cannot coherently be combined with our cares and concerns: "the two attitudes have to coexist in a single person who is actually leading the life towards which he is simultaneously engaged and detached" (p. 216). The fact that total indifference is impossible for human beings—even when we add that it is beneficial for us to have desires—doesn't make the problem of nihilism go away.

6.9 Conclusion

I have articulated the problem of nihilism and canvassed a number of solutions to it. None of them, I argued, is entirely satisfactory. However, I think there is a satisfactory solution. Even though AD is true, DGP (§6.1) is false—but it will take some epistemology to see why.

The Epistemology of Desire and the Problem of Nihilism. Allan Hazlett, Oxford University Press.
© Allan Hazlett 2024. DOI: 10.1093/9780191995583.003.0006

7

Desiring the Neutral

Recall DGP (§6.1), on which it is irrational to both desire that p and believe that it is not good that p. Given DGP, it is irrational to desire something you believe is neutral, i.e. neither good nor bad. Given DGP, if you believe that nothing is good or bad, then it is irrational for you to desire anything. I said that AD makes DGP seem irresistible. However, I am going to argue, consistent with AD, that DGP is false. My leading idea is an insight from Brentano (§2.8): if something is neither good nor bad, then loving it is neither correct nor incorrect. In my preferred terminology, if it is neither good nor bad that p, then a desire that p is neither accurate nor inaccurate. This, I shall argue, explains why it can be rationally permissible to desire something you believe is not good.

7.1 Strong Incoherence

I motivated DGP by appeal to BTP (§6.1), on which it is irrational to both believe that p and believe that it is not true that p, and AD. However, just as AB does not entail BTP, AD does not entail DGP. We need to make some assumption about rationality to get from AB and AD, which are claims about accuracy, to BTP and DGP, which are claims about rationality.

Suppose you both believe that p and believe that it is not true that p. Here is something we now know, given AB: at least one of your attitudes is inaccurate. It is either true that p or it is not true that p. On the one hand, if it is true that p, then your belief that p is accurate. However, if it is true that p, then it is true that it is true that p, and therefore false that it is not true that p, and your belief that it is not true that p is inaccurate. On the other hand, if it is not true that p, then it is true that it is not true that p, and your belief that it is not true that p is accurate. However, if it is not true that p, then it is false that p, that your belief that p is inaccurate. One of your beliefs must be inaccurate. Your beliefs are strongly incoherent in the following sense:

A set of attitudes is *strongly incoherent* if and only if, necessarily, at least one of its members is inaccurate.[1]

Your belief that p and your belief that it is not true that p are strongly incoherent, because at least one of them must be inaccurate.

Now consider a principle of rationality:

No Strong Incoherence   It is irrational to have strongly incoherent attitudes.

Your belief that p and your belief that it is not true that p are strongly incoherent. Therefore, given No Strong Incoherence, it is irrational for you both to believe that p and to believe that it is not true that p. In other words, BTP is true.

I want to grant, for the sake of argument, that No Strong Incoherence, or something very much like it, is true. No Strong Incoherence needs to be amended to exclude cases of strong incoherence in which the subject cannot reasonably be expected to be aware that their attitudes are strongly incoherent. These include at least two kinds of cases. First, there are cases involving modes of presentation. It is not irrational for a naïve Lois Lane to both believe that Superman can fly and believe that Clark Kent cannot fly, even though her beliefs are strongly incoherent (cf. §5.1). (In the same way, it was not irrational for early astronomers to believe that the Morning Star and the Evening Star are two different stars, even though that belief is strongly incoherent.) Second, there are cases involving complex or obscure incoherence. It is not irrational for a beginning logic student to believe two contradictory propositions when the contradiction requires advanced logical expertise to appreciate, even though their beliefs are strongly incoherent. (In the same way, it was not irrational for Frege to believe Basic Law V, even though his belief was strongly incoherent.) The present case, however, is a case in which you can reasonably be expected to be aware that your attitudes are incoherent. If you both believe that p and believe that it is not true that p, you both have an attitude and believe something that, given AB, straightforwardly entails that said attitude is inaccurate, which seems no less irrational than having an attitude that you believe is inaccurate. Thus, the strong incoherence of believing that p

---

[1] Thus, any set of attitudes that contains a necessarily false belief is strongly incoherent.

142 THE EPISTEMOLOGY OF DESIRE AND THE PROBLEM OF NIHILISM

while believing that it is not true that p explains why it is irrational to both believe that p and believe that it is not true that p.

At first glance, it seems like we can make the same argument concerning desire. Suppose you both desire that p and believe that it is not good that p. Given AD and AB, it seems like we now know that at least one of your attitudes is inaccurate. It is either good that p or it is not good that p. On the one hand, if it is good that p, then your desire that p is accurate. However, if it is good that p, then it is true that it is good that p, and therefore false that it is not good that p, and your belief that it is not good that p is inaccurate. On the other hand, if it is not good that p, then it is true that it is not good that p, and your belief that it is not good that p is accurate. However, if it is not good that p, then it is bad that p, and your desire that p is inaccurate. Either your desire or your belief must be inaccurate, so your attitudes are strongly incoherent.

The problem with this argument is obvious: from the premise that it is not good that p, we cannot infer that it is bad that p. Because there are no alethic gaps (§2.8), from the premise that it is not true that p, we can infer that it is false that p. Because there are axial gaps, however, we cannot infer that it is bad that p from the premise that it is good that p. No proposition is neither true nor false, but some propositions are neither good nor bad— some propositions are neutral. Indeed, for the nihilist about value, such axial gaps are ubiquitous. Even given AD, your desire that p and your belief that it is not good that p are not strongly incoherent. No STRONG INCOHERENCE does not imply that it is irrational to both desire that p and believe that it is not good that p.

Given AD, desires for the bad are inaccurate (cf. §3.2), but desires for the neutral—i.e. that which is neither good nor bad—are neither accurate nor inaccurate. If it is neither good nor bad that p, then a desire that p is neither accurate nor inaccurate. If nothing is good or bad, then any desire whatsoever is neither accurate nor inaccurate.

This does not yet show that it can be rationally permissible to both desire that p and believe that it is not good that p—i.e. that DGP is false. However, we have found a difference between belief and desire that ultimately explains, as I shall argue, why it can be rationally permissible to desire something that you believe is not good.

7.2 The Risk of Contradiction

BTP says that it is irrational to desire something you believe is not true and DGP says it is irrational to desire something you believe is not good (§6.1).

DESIRING THE NEUTRAL 143

We have considered an argument for BTP that appeals to AB and No STRONG INCOHERENCE, and rejected the analogous argument for DGP (§7.1). However, there is a more plausible and straightforward way to motivate BTP, but one that also has no plausible analogue when it comes to DGP.

Suppose you both believe that p and believe that it is not true that p. Given that you believe that p, you are in a position to infer that it is true that p, since the proposition that it is true that p is entailed by the proposition that p. Suppose you do so infer, you thereby believe that it is true that p. Now you both believe that it is true that p and believe that it is not true that p, and are in a position to infer that it is true that p and not true that p. Suppose you do so infer, and thereby believe that it true that p and not true that p. You now believe something of the form <p and not-p>. Something has gone wrong. Your initial beliefs—the belief that p and the belief that it is not true that p—seem like the culprits. BTP nicely captures the thought that the irrationality of your initial state is what exposes you to the risk of inferring a contradiction.

However, desiring that p and believing that it is not good that p does not in the same way expose you to the risk of inferring a contradiction. If you believe that p you are in a position to infer that it is true that p. By contrast, if you desire that p, you are not in a position to infer that it is good that p. Inference does not operate on desire in the same way that it operates on belief. When good inference takes you from a belief that p to a belief that q, and all goes well, you believe that q because p, i.e. you believe that q on the basis of the fact that p. However, good inference cannot take you from a desire to a belief in that way. Good inference cannot take you from a desire that p to a belief that q, such that you believe that q because p. Good inference can take you from a belief that the Lakers won last night to a belief that Laker fans are happy this morning, but good inference cannot take you from a desire that the Lakers won last night to a belief that Laker fans are happy this morning.

I do not want to deny that there are circumstances in which you might reasonably transition from desiring that p to believing that it is good that p. Consider Smith, the prejudiced jailer (§4.2). Imagine that Smith realizes that her desire to go easy on her prisoners manifests compassion, rather than laziness, thereby realizing that her desire is a reliable indication that it would be good were she to go easy on her prisoners. She might, in that case, conclude that it would be good were she to go easy on her prisoners. But this kind of transition from desire to evaluative belief is not the kind of straightforward inference involved in the transition from believing that p to believing that it is true that p. When you infer that q from the premise that p,

144 THE EPISTEMOLOGY OF DESIRE AND THE PROBLEM OF NIHILISM

you presuppose an evidential connection between premise and conclusion: you presuppose that the fact that p is evidence that q. Thus, when you infer that it is true that p from the premise that p, you presuppose that the fact that p is evidence that it is true that p. Smith's imagined transition from desiring to go easy on her prisoners to believing that it would be good were she to go easy on her prisoners presupposes no such evidential connection. She does not presuppose that her going easy on her prisoners is evidence that it would be good were she to go easy on her prisoners. Any reasonable transition from desiring that p to believing that it is good that p does not presuppose that the fact that p is evidence that it is good that p. Now, given AD, the accuracy of your desire that p is evidence that it is good that p. Compare the way in which the accuracy of fear is evidence that its object is dangerous (cf. §1.11), such that you might reasonably transition from fearing something to believing that it is dangerous. In such a case, you would infer that the object of your fear is dangerous from the premise that you fear it, which presupposes that the fact that you fear it is evidence that it is dangerous, i.e. that your fear is accurate. In the same way, if you reasonably transition from desiring that p to believing that it is good that p, you infer that it is good that p from the premise that you desire that p, which presupposes that the fact that you desire that p is evidence that it is good that p, i.e. that your desire is accurate.

BTP can plausibly by motivated by the thought that both believing that p and believing that it is not true that p exposes you to the risk of inferring a contradiction. DRT, however, cannot be motivated in the analogous way, because desiring that p and believing that it is not good that p does not expose you, in the same way, to the risk of inferring a contradiction.

7.3 Weak Incoherence

Suppose you both desire that p and believe that it is not good that p. Your attitudes are not strongly incoherent (§7.1). However, here is something we now know, given AD and AB: your desire and your belief are not both accurate. It is either good that p or it is not good that p. On the one hand, if it is good that p, then your desire that p is accurate. However, if it is good that p, then it is true that it is good that p, and therefore false that it is not good that p, and therefore not true that it is not good that p, and your belief that it is not good that p is not accurate. On the other hand, if it is not good that p,

DESIRING THE NEUTRAL   145

then it is true that it is not good that p, and your belief that it is not good that p is accurate. However, if it is not good that p, then your desire that p is not accurate. Your desire and your belief cannot both be accurate. Your attitudes are weakly incoherent in the following sense:

A set of attitudes is *weakly incoherent* if and only if, necessarily, not all of its members are accurate.

Although strong incoherence entails weak incoherence, weak incoherence does not entail strong incoherence. Your desire that p and your belief that it is not good that p are weakly incoherent, because they cannot both be accurate, even though they are not strongly incoherent.

Now, consider another principle of rationality:

No Weak Incoherence   It is irrational to have weakly incoherent attitudes.

Given No Weak Incoherence, and given that your desire that p and your belief that it is not good that p are strongly incoherent, it is irrational for you to both desire that p and believe that it is not good that p. In other words, DGP (§6.1) is true.

Like No Strong Incoherence, No Weak Incoherence needs to be amended to exclude cases of weak incoherence in which the subject cannot reasonably be expected to be aware that their attitudes are weakly incoherent. Again, however, the present case is a case in which you can reasonably be expected to be aware that your attitudes are weakly incoherent. If you both desire that p and believe that it is not good that p, you both have an attitude and believe something that, given AD, straightforwardly entails that said attitude is not accurate, which seems no less irrational than having an attitude that you believe is not accurate. If No Weak Incoherence, suitably amended, is true, it is irrational to both desire that p and believe that it is not good that p.

However, as I will argue, DGP, and therefore No Weak Incoherence, is false. It can be rationally permissible to desire something you believe is not good. If you desire something you believe is not good, given AD, your desire and your belief are weakly incoherent. Thus, it can be rationally permissible to have weakly incoherent attitudes—even when you can reasonably be expected to be aware that your attitudes are weakly incoherent. No Weak Incoherence is false.

146 THE EPISTEMOLOGY OF DESIRE AND THE PROBLEM OF NIHILISM

Consider, again, your desire to take a walk (§1.4). Would it be good were you to take a walk? Imagine that you believe it would not be good were you to take a walk, e.g. that you believe that it would be neither good nor bad, that it would be neutral, were you to take a walk. We can easily imagine that this has nothing to do with nihilism about value, but is merely your considered evaluation of this particular situation. If asked whether you think it would be good were you to take a walk, your reply would be: "Not really. I just want to take a walk." Perhaps you are wrong. Perhaps you would enjoy it and your enjoyment would be good. But you reckon otherwise. Maybe you reject the non-instrumental value of enjoyment. Maybe you do not think that taking a walk will be enjoyable and find it attractive for some other reason. Must that attraction involve your believing that it would be good were you to take a walk? I think it is easy to imagine that you are attracted to taking a walk but do not believe that it would be good were you to take a walk. You want to take a walk and believe that it would not be good were you to take a walk. Does that make for an irrational combination of attitudes? Intuitively, no. It does not seem irrational to both want to take a walk and believe that it would not be good were you to take a walk. Thus, it can be rationally permissible to desire something you believe is not good. DGP is false.

Anscombe (1963) argues that you cannot "just want" a saucer of mud (pp. 70–1; cf. §3.1). Let us grant that it would be weird for someone to non-instrumentally want a saucer of mud—in other words, that if someone said they wanted a saucer of mud we would assume they instrumentally wanted a saucer of mud and if they insisted that that they non-instrumentally wanted a saucer of mud we would think they were being weird. The same cannot be said of your desire to take a walk. If you said that you did not want to take a walk *for* anything, that you just wanted to take a walk, that you just happened to want to take a walk, that would make perfect sense. Anscombe's case, it seems to me, has more to do with the abnormality of wanting a saucer of mud than with the fact that (as Anscombe and I agree) desires are evaluations (cf. §3.4).[2]

You might think that the intuition motivating the present counterexample—the intuition that it is rationally permissible for you to both want to take a walk and believe that it would not be good were you to take a walk—speaks against AD. However, the premise that it can be rationally permissible to

[2] Cf. Hare 1963a, pp. 122–7; see also Hare 1963b, pp. 108–11.

DESIRING THE NEUTRAL   147

desire something you believe is not good does not entail that AD is false. That premise would, by contrast, threaten the evaluative belief theory of desire (§1.7). Nor does the premise that it can be rationally permissible to desire something you believe is not good undermine the argument, advanced in Chapter 3, that AD provides the best explanation of why axial criticism of desires makes sense. AD, as defended here, is compatible with the rejection of DGP. Given that there are intuitive counterexamples to DGP, it should be rejected.

Above, I conceded that acedia—believing that it is good that p without desiring that p—is irrational (§5.10). Here, I have argued, against DGP, that it can be rationally permissible to desire that p while believing that it is not good that p. If acedia is irrational and DGP is false, then there is an interesting difference between believing that something is good and believing that something is not good. Assuming that acedia is irrational, believing that something is good puts rational pressure on you to desire it. It is irrational to fail to desire in accordance with your beliefs about what is good. However, assuming that DGP is false, believing that something is not good does not put rational pressure on you not to desire it. It is not irrational to fail to desire in accordance with your beliefs about what is not good.

If DGP is false, it can be rationally permissible to both desire that p and believe that it is not good that p. Given AD, if you both desire that p and believe that it is not good that p, your attitudes are weakly incoherent. Thus, No WEAK INCOHERENCE is false. It can be rationally permissible to desire something that you believe is not good, despite the fact that goodness is the accuracy condition for desire.

If I am right, we have found a counterexample to No WEAK INCOHERENCE involving desire. Assuming No STRONG INCOHERENCE (§7.1), we will not find counterexamples to No WEAK INCOHERENCE involving other attitudes—or, at least, not involving belief and intention—in the same way. Because a belief cannot be neither accurate nor inaccurate (§2.8), if two beliefs are weakly incoherent, they are also strongly incoherent. Thus, a belief that p and a belief that it is not true that p are strongly incoherent. And the same seems true of intention, if it has an accuracy condition, given the plausible candidates for that condition (§2.3), which imply that an intention cannot be neither accurate nor inaccurate.

If I am right, it can be rationally permissible to have weakly incoherent attitudes. Why? Providing an explanation here will further bolster the case against No WEAK INCOHERENCE, and thus mitigate doubts about our counterexample to DGP. This is the work of the next three sections.

7.4 James' Two Intellectual Duties

Recall NO STRONG INCOHERENCE (§7.1). Why think that it is irrational to have strongly incoherent attitudes? I compared believing that p while believing that it is not true that p to having an attitude that you believe is inaccurate. However, why think that it is irrational to have an attitude you believe is inaccurate?

It can be rationally permissible, by contrast, to make an assertion that you believe is inaccurate. What is it about attitudes that makes it irrational to have them while believing that they are inaccurate?

In an influential passage in *The Will to Believe*, William James (1897/1979) proposed that we have two distinct and equally fundamental intellectual duties:

> There are two ways of looking at our duty in the matter of opinion[.] *We must know the truth*; and *we must avoid error*, – these are our first and great commandments as would-be knowers; but they are not two ways of stating an identical commandment, they are two separable laws. [...] Believe truth! Shun error! – these, we see, are two materially different laws. (p. 24)

Consider James' second fundamental intellectual duty, the duty to avoid error. We could interpret this narrowly, as a duty to avoid having false beliefs. I am going to interpret it broadly, as a duty to avoid having inaccurate attitudes. Thus, having an attitude that you believe is inaccurate constitutes a flagrant violation of James' second duty. However, if we have an intellectual duty to avoid having inaccurate attitudes, something like NO STRONG INCOHERENCE must be true.

However, NO WEAK INCOHERENCE (§7.3) cannot be motivated in this way. It is plausible enough that we have a fundamental intellectual duty to avoid having inaccurate attitudes. But it is implausible that we have any such duty to avoid having non-accurate attitudes, i.e. attitudes that are not accurate, including attitudes that are neither accurate nor inaccurate. James' plausible suggestion is that we are enjoined to avoid *error*, i.e. to avoid having attitudes that are inaccurate. At a minimum, this leaves unmotivated the idea that we are also enjoined to avoid having attitudes that are neither accurate nor inaccurate.

Of course, James' insight is that we are not merely enjoined to avoid error. We also have his first fundamental intellectual duty, the duty to "know the truth." However, this also does not imply that we have a duty to avoid having attitudes that are not accurate. James' second duty is a negative duty; it prohibits having inaccurate attitudes. His first duty, I submit, is best understood as a positive duty, one that recommends having accurate attitudes. You could comply with James' second duty by having no attitudes at all, and the appeal of Pyrrhonian skepticism derives from the fact that suspension of judgment guarantees avoiding false belief. If James' first duty were likewise a negative duty, e.g. a duty to avoid having attitudes that are not accurate, you could likewise comply with it by having no attitudes at all. However, that is clearly not what James has in mind. He has in mind a duty that complements our duty to avoid false belief, compliance with which requires that we form at least some true beliefs. Thus, James' first fundamental intellectual duty is not a duty to avoid having attitudes that are not accurate. Again, we could interpret James' first duty narrowly, as a duty to have some true beliefs, but I am going to interpret it broadly, as a duty to have some accurate attitudes. Now, this is not yet to say exactly what compliance with James' first duty requires. It is implausible that we have a fundamental intellectual duty to believe every truth, but someone who knew only a few trivial facts would intuitively be in violation of James' first duty. As with positive duties in general, there is a "how much" question here. My point here is merely that James' insight does not imply that we have a duty to avoid having attitudes that are not accurate.

7.5 Non-Accurate Representation

Our question is why it can be rationally permissible to have weakly incoherent attitudes (§7.3). I am going argue, in this section, that there is often nothing wrong with representations that are neither accurate nor inaccurate. Thus, there is often nothing wrong with representations that are not accurate. I will then argue, in the next section, that this explains why it can be rationally permissible to have weakly incoherent attitudes.

Clear thinking about these matters is difficult because belief is our epistemological paradigm and beliefs cannot be neither accurate nor inaccurate (§2.8). Considering other species of representation will get us used to thinking about representations that are neither accurate nor inaccurate, in connection with our interest in the case of desire.

When I say that there is often "nothing wrong" with representations that are not accurate, I do not mean merely that it is often permissible to make a representation that you know is not accurate. Consider the fact that it is sometimes permissible to make a representation that you know is

150 THE EPISTEMOLOGY OF DESIRE AND THE PROBLEM OF NIHILISM

inaccurate, e.g. to assert something that you know is false (cf. §2.1). However, there is something wrong with false assertions: false assertions, even those it is permissible to make, are defective or flawed *qua* assertion; they are bad assertions, in the same way that dull knives are bad knives. False assertions are bad instances of their kind, and, in general, inaccurate representations are bad instances of their kind. For example, whatever else we might say about them, false beliefs are bad beliefs, in the sense that they are defective or flawed *qua* belief. So, when I say that there is often "nothing wrong" with representations that are not accurate, I mean to imply that non-accurate representations are often not bad instances of their kind.

If I am right, there is an important difference between attitudes that are inaccurate and attitudes that are merely not accurate, and thus an important difference between strongly incoherent attitudes (§7.1) and weakly incoherent attitudes (§7.3). If two attitudes are strongly incoherent, at least one them is inaccurate, and thus at least one of them is a bad instance of its kind. However, if two attitudes are merely weakly incoherent, no such conclusion follows, and it might be that neither attitude is a bad instance of its kind.

So, I claim that there is often nothing wrong with representations that are neither accurate nor inaccurate. Consider, first, imagination. Episodes of imagination are not the kind of thing that can be accurate or inaccurate (§2.1). Imagine that you daydream that you are eating lunch at a seaside café. Although this episode of imagination is not accurate, there is nothing wrong with it. It is not defective or flawed *qua* episode of imagination; it is not a bad episode of imagination. Thus, there can be nothing wrong with a representation that is not accurate.

Here is another example. Imagine that you are looking at the clouds floating by and see one that looks like a sailboat, such that you see the cloud as a sailboat. I think what is going on here is that you are imagining that the cloud is a sailboat. In any event, episodes of (at least this species of) "seeing-as" are not the kind of thing that can be accurate or inaccurate. Although your seeing the cloud as a sailboat is not accurate, there is nothing wrong with it. It is not defective or flawed *qua* episode of "seeing-as"; it is not a bad episode of "seeing-as." Thus, again, there can be nothing wrong with a representation that is not accurate.

Some defenders of the view that emotions are evaluations (§1.11) explain this by saying that emotions involve seeing or otherwise thinking of their objects as having certain features.[3] For example, we could say that fearing

---

[3] E.g. Roberts 1988, Goldie 2000, Nussbaum 2001.

DESIRING THE NEUTRAL 151

isopods involves seeing them as dangerous. However, at least if this idea is to be understood by reference to familiar cases of "seeing-as"—such as the case of your seeing the cloud as a sailboat—then it implies that your fear of isopods is not inaccurate, despite the fact that isopods are not dangerous. There is no inaccuracy when you see the cloud as a sailboat; accurate visual perception does not require only seeing the cloud as a cloud. Granted, there is such a thing as inaccurately visually representing something—e.g. a theater prop might look so much like a tree that you visually represent it as a tree. And, of course, there is such a thing as inaccurately believing something on the basis of visual perception—e.g. if you were to believe, of the aforementioned prop, that it is a tree. But the species of "seeing-as" involved in finding shapes in the clouds is not a species of representation that can be accurate or inaccurate.

Consider, second, asking questions. Questions are not the kind of thing that can be accurate or inaccurate. Imagine that you ask a hotel concierge the location of the nearest sushi restaurant. Although your question is not accurate, there is nothing wrong with it. It is not defective or flawed *qua* question; it is not a bad question. Thus, there can be nothing wrong with a representation that is not accurate.

This is compatible with the idea that interrogative sentences denote the set of true answers to the question they express.[4] It is also compatible with the fact that questions at least often have presuppositions. There is a sense in which a question that makes a false presupposition is inaccurate, but a question that makes no false presuppositions is not, in a corresponding sense, accurate.

This is also compatible with the plausible idea that when you ask a question you represent yourself as not knowing the answer, just as when you assert something you plausibly represent yourself as knowing it.[5] Assertions are accurate if and only if true and inaccurate if and only if false (§2.1). When you assert that p, you represent yourself as knowing that p, but if you do not know that p, your assertion is not thereby inaccurate. You may have misrepresented your epistemic status, but you did not make an inaccurate assertion unless what you asserted was false. In the same way, when you ask a question to which you do not know the answer, you accurately represent your epistemic status, but that does not make your question accurate.

---

[4] Cf. Hamblin 1958, Karttunen 1977.
[5] Cf. Unger 1975, p. 253, Davidson 1979/1984, p. 112, Slote 1979, Owens 2006.

152 THE EPISTEMOLOGY OF DESIRE AND THE PROBLEM OF NIHILISM

Consider, third, depiction. Some pictures can be assessed for accuracy. Consider Kehinde Wiley's portrait of Barack Obama (2018),[6] which is a picture of Barack Obama, seated, both in front of and within a kind of wall of leaves and flowers. We can assess whether the picture accurately represents Obama, by considering whether the man in the picture looks like Obama or whether we can see Obama in the picture. If the man in the picture does look like Obama or Obama can be seen in the picture, then the picture is accurate with respect to its representation of Obama, but if the man in the picture does not look like Obama or Obama cannot be seen in the picture, then the picture is inaccurate with respect to its representation of Obama. Wiley's portrait of Barack Obama can be assessed for accuracy.

Some pictures, however, cannot be assessed for accuracy in this way. Consider Paul Cézanne's *Seated Peasant* (*c.*1892–6),[7] which is a picture of a seated peasant. But there is no real peasant of whom it is a picture.[8] There is no one of whom we might ask whether the man in the picture looks like him or whether we can see him in the picture. Those questions of accuracy simply do not arise with this kind of picture. We can ask whether Wiley's picture accurately represents its subject, but it makes no sense to ask whether Cézanne's picture accurately represents its subject. The subject of Wiley's painting is Obama, a real human being who exists, as it were, outside of the painting, whereas the subject of Cézanne's painting is simply the peasant we see in his painting, who exists only there. We cannot coherently ask whether the painting represents him accurately or inaccurately. Cézanne's picture is neither accurate nor inaccurate with respect to its representation of its subject. However, although Cézanne's picture is not accurate, there is nothing wrong with it. It is not defective or flawed *qua* picture; it is not a bad picture. Thus, there can be nothing wrong with a representation that is not accurate.

7.6 Why Weak Incoherence Is Rationally Permissible

There is often nothing wrong with representations that are not accurate (§7.5). This, I submit, explains why it can be rationally permissible to have weakly incoherent attitudes.

---

[6] https://npg.si.edu/Barack_Obama.

[7] https://www.metmuseum.org/art/collection/search/437990.

[8] We distinguish, in this kind of case, between the subject of a painting and a model, if there was one, used by the painter. In this case, the model was a worker at the Cézanne family estate.

DESIRING THE NEUTRAL   153

Consider, again, No STRONG INCOHERENCE (§7.1). The reason it seems irrational to have strongly incoherent attitudes is that there is something wrong with representations that are inaccurate. Inaccurate representations are bad instances of their kind (§7.5). This explains the rational impermissibility of having attitudes such that, necessarily, at least one of them must be inaccurate. It does not, of course, fully explain the irrationality of having strongly incoherent attitudes, since it can be rationally permissible to assert something you believe is false. However, No STRONG INCOHERENCE presupposes that there is something wrong with representations that are inaccurate. No STRONG INCOHERENCE prohibits guaranteed inaccuracy of attitudes, which only makes sense if there is something wrong with representations that are inaccurate.

There is something wrong with representations that are inaccurate. By contrast, I have argued, there is often nothing wrong with representations that are not accurate. However, just as No STRONG INCOHERENCE presupposes that there is something wrong with representations that are inaccurate, No WEAK INCOHERENCE presupposes that there is something wrong with representations that are not accurate. No WEAK INCOHERENCE prohibits guaranteed non-accuracy of attitudes, which only makes sense if there is something wrong with representations that are not accurate. There often isn't. This explains why No WEAK INCOHERENCE is false, i.e. why it can be rationally permissible to have weakly incoherent attitudes.

There is a salient difference between the case of your both desiring to take a walk and believing that it would not be good were you to take a walk (§7.3) and the cases to which I appealed in arguing that there is often nothing wrong with representations that are not accurate (§7.5). Goodness is the accuracy condition for desire, and thus your desire has an accuracy condition. AD entails that your desire to take a walk is accurate if and only if it would be good were you to take a walk and inaccurate if and only if it would be bad were you to take a walk. Given AD, we can coherently ask whether your desire is accurate or inaccurate; indeed, if it would neither be good nor bad were you to take a walk, AD entails that your desire to take a walk is neither accurate nor inaccurate. By contrast, your daydream of eating lunch at a seaside café, your seeing the cloud as a sailboat, your question about the nearest sushi restaurant, and Cézanne's picture do not have accuracy conditions. We cannot coherently ask whether they are accurate or inaccurate.

Given this difference, you might object that No WEAK INCOHERENCE merely presupposes that there is something wrong with non-accurate representations that have an accuracy condition, which presupposition remains

154 THE EPISTEMOLOGY OF DESIRE AND THE PROBLEM OF NIHILISM

plausible. This is a difficult objection, and I am not confident about how to respond to it, which may mean we have reached the heart of the matter. There is a real difference between a merely non-accurate representation that has an accuracy condition and a merely non-accurate representation that does not have an accuracy condition. In the former case, there is a condition under which the representation would be accurate; in the latter case, there is no such condition.

Here is what I am inclined, without a great deal of confidence, to say. Recall the idea that we have two fundamental intellectual duties (§7.4): a negative duty that prohibits having inaccurate attitudes and a positive duty that recommends having accurate attitudes. Neither of these imply that there is anything wrong with merely non-accurate representations, whether they have an accuracy condition or not. Both merely non-accurate representations that have an accuracy condition and merely non-accurate representations that do not have an accuracy condition fall short of accuracy—they are all of them not accurate. That there is a condition under which the former would be accurate is no mark against them, by contrast with the latter, such that there is something wrong with the former, but not something wrong with the latter.

We may be misled here by the thought that representations that have an accuracy condition "aim" at accuracy (cf. §2.1). Compare two archers, one who aims to hit a target, whose shots are therefore attempts to hit that target, and another who shoots aimlessly, just to test their bow. If neither archer hits the target, it is clear that the former archer fails in a way that the latter archer does not fail. If you thought that representations that have an accuracy condition were analogous to the archer who aims to a hit a target, it would make sense to think that such representations fail when they are not accurate, in a way analogous to the way the first archer fails when they do not hit the target. However, I do not think that representations that have an accuracy condition are analogous to the archer who aims to a hit a target. I do not think accuracy and inaccuracy are to be understood in teleological terms.[9] If an analogy might help, consider an exclusive country club that admits only philosophy professors. Imagine that you are not a member. Does that make you a failure? Does it mean that there is something wrong with you? Hardly. And, crucially, it does not matter whether you are a philosophy professor or not. If you are a philosophy professor, there is a condition

---

[9] Cf. Hazlett 2013, chapter 6.

under which you would be a member, and if you are not a philosophy professor, then there is no such condition. In the former case, you are the kind of person who can be a member of the club; in the latter case, you are the kind of person who cannot be a member. However, either way, there is nothing wrong with you if you are not a member. I think accuracy is more like membership of an exclusive country club than it is like an archer hitting a target. For this reason, I do not think that representations that have an accuracy condition fail when they are not accurate.

7.7 Preference

Early on, we chose to study the problem of nihilism by examining the nature of desire (§1.3). Thinking that nothing matters seems to put rational pressure on you to become indifferent to everything, and we assumed that such total indifference amounts to neither desiring that p nor desiring that not-p, for any proposition that p (§6.1). However, we might just as well have chosen to study the problem of nihilism by examining the nature of preference and assumed that total indifference amounts to neither preferring that p rather than that q nor preferring that q rather than that p, for any propositions that p and that q. This suggests a problem for the proposed solution to the problem of nihilism (§7.1).

If goodness is the accuracy condition for desire, then it would be natural to conclude that betterness is the accuracy condition for preference (cf. §2.7), i.e. that a preference that p rather than that q is accurate if and only if it is better that p than that q.[10] Nihilism about value (§1.1) says that nothing is good or bad, and it seems clear that, if nothing is good or bad, then nothing is better than anything. However, if betterness is the accuracy condition for preference, thinking that nothing is better than anything seems to put rational pressure on you to have no preferences.

We have not yet articulated the conditions under which a preference is inaccurate. Consider:

CP A preference that p rather than that q is accurate if and only if it is better that p than that q, and inaccurate otherwise.

---

[10] I intend what I say here about preference to apply, mutatis mutandis, to utilities or utility functions, which I assume are to be explained in terms of preferences.

156 THE EPISTEMOLOGY OF DESIRE AND THE PROBLEM OF NIHILISM

Given CP, a preference that p rather than that q and a belief that it is not better that p than that q are strongly incoherent (§7.1). Therefore, given No STRONG INCOHERENCE, it is irrational to both prefer that p rather than that q and believe that it is not better that p than that q. Given CP and No STRONG INCOHERENCE, nihilism about value makes it irrational to have any preferences.

However, CP needs to be amended. I defended the view that goodness is the accuracy condition for desire by arguing that AD provides the best explanation of why axial criticism of desires makes sense (§3.2). In defense of the view that betterness is the accuracy condition for preference, we would like to be able to offer an analogous argument. We would like to be able to argue that CP provides the best explanation of why it makes sense to criticize a preference on the grounds that it is not better that p than that q.

It pretty clearly makes sense to criticize a preference that p rather than that q on the grounds that it is better that q than that p. That represents one kind of case in which it is not better that p than that q. If you preferred the destruction of the world to the scratching of your finger (§3.1), it would make sense to criticize your preference on the grounds that the scratching of your finger would be better than the destruction of the world.

It also pretty clearly makes sense to criticize a preference that p rather than that q on the grounds that the proposition that p and the proposition that q are equally good—i.e. that they are good to exactly the same degree (cf. §2.7). That represents another kind of case in which it is not better that p than that q. If you preferred drinking the wine on the left to drinking the intrinsically identical wine on the right, it would make sense to criticize your preference on the grounds that your drinking the wine on the left and your drinking the wine on the right would be equally good—i.e. that these two propositions are good to exactly the same degree.

However, would it make sense to criticize a preference that p rather than that q on the grounds that it is neither good nor bad that p and neither good nor bad that q? That represents yet another kind of case in which it is not better that p than that q. Suppose you prefer twiddling your thumbs counterclockwise to twiddling them clockwise. Absent further details, it is intuitively neither good nor bad that you twiddle your thumbs counterclockwise and neither good nor bad that you twiddle your thumbs clockwise. Would it make sense to criticize your preference on these grounds? I think it would not. Although it makes sense to criticize a desire for something bad, on the grounds that the desired thing is bad (§3.1), it does not make sense to criticize a preference for one neutral thing rather than another, on the grounds that the preferred thing is not better than the dispreferred thing.

I think this shows that we should amend CP to:

CP-AMENDED   A preference that p rather than that q is accurate if and only if it is better that p than that q and inaccurate if and only if it is either better that q than that p or the proposition that p and the proposition that q are equally good.

Given CP-AMENDED, a preference that p rather than that q and a belief that it is not better that p than that q are not strongly incoherent (§7.1). CP-AMENDED and No STRONG INCOHERENCE do not entail that it is irrational to both prefer that p rather than that q and believe that it is not better that p than that q. Thus, they do not entail that nihilism about value makes it irrational to have any preferences.

7.8 Why It Matters That We Already Have Desires

Imagine that your best friend has come down with a nasty case of COVID-19. You naturally hope that they recover. Would it be irrational to continue wanting your friend to recover if you came to believe—whether on account of depression or existential angst or on the basis of some philosophical argument—that it would not be good were they to recover? I have argued that it can be rationally permissible to desire something that you believe is not good, despite the fact that goodness is the accuracy condition for desire, and the present case seems like a case of rationally permissible desire for something believed not to be good.

Contrast that case with a different kind of case. Consider a question: would it be good if there were an even number of stars? The answer, presumably, is that it would not be good—it would be neither good nor bad were there an even number of stars. If you agree, you now believe that it would not be good were there an even number of stars. Now, I have argued that it can be rationally permissible to desire something that you believe is not good, despite the fact that goodness is the accuracy condition for desire. However, it hardly seems rational for you to suddenly start wishing that there are an even number of stars. Were you to spontaneously form such a desire, we would hardly have a case that seems like a case of rationally permissible desire for something believed not to be good.

Even if I am right that it can be rationally permissible to desire something that you believe is not good, there seems to be a difference between

158 THE EPISTEMOLOGY OF DESIRE AND THE PROBLEM OF NIHILISM

sustaining a desire for something you come to believe is not good and forming a desire for something you believe is not good.

In my discussion of the problem of nihilism, I have been concerned with structural rationality (§5.1). I have said nothing here about the rationality of forming desires. For all I have said, a nihilist about value (§1.1) who was indifferent to everything (§6.1) would have no way to rationally form any desires. At a minimum, given my account of orectic deliberation (§5.8), they would have no way to rationally form any desires through deliberation, because forming a desire that p through deliberation requires concluding that it is good that p, which I granted amounts to forming a belief that it is good that p (§5.4).

I want to concede that, although you can rationally sustain a desire for something you come to believe is not good, you cannot rationally form a desire for something that you believe is not good. My proposed solution to the problem of nihilism, therefore, depends on the fact that we already have desires. I have tried to explain how it could be rationally permissible for a nihilist to continue desiring things, despite coming to believe that nothing is good or bad. I have said nothing about whether it could be rational for a nihilist to form new desires. In this way, my solution to the problem of nihilism is akin to the naturalist solution (§6.8). On both approaches, the fact that we have desires is crucial. If we were starting from a position of total indifference, there may well be no way, given nihilism about value, for us to rationally come to care about anything.

7.9 Conclusion

We began with the thought that nothing matters, and the apparent rational pressure this puts on us to become indifferent to everything. I chose to understand the thought that nothing matters as the thought that nothing is good or bad, and I chose to understand indifference in terms of desire. This led us to an investigation of the nature of desire, and in particular an investigation of the relationship between desire and goodness. I argued that goodness is the accuracy condition for desire. This, I suggested, is what makes it seem that it is irrational to think that nothing matters without becoming indifferent to everything. However, I argued that it is not irrational to desire something you believe is not good, despite the fact that goodness is the accuracy condition for desire.

If I am right, the thought that nothing matters does not mandate total indifference. If there are things that you care about, thinking that nothing matters does not put rational pressure on you to stop caring about them. It is not irrational to care about something while at the same time thinking that nothing matters.

My approach has emphasized the epistemological nature of these issues in two ways. First, it seems irrational to think that nothing matters without becoming indifferent to everything because desire, like belief, has an accuracy condition—the apparent irrationality here is the same as the irrationality involved in believing something you believe is not true. Second, our investigation of the relationship between irrationality and accuracy led us to the conclusion that it can be rationally permissible to desire something you believe is not good. Because desire has an accuracy condition, that investigation had to be epistemological—our concern was with the rational permissibility of having attitudes that cannot all be accurate.

In this examination of the problem of nihilism, I have tried to avoid, and said relatively little against, two positions, which represent extremes relatively to my own. On the one hand, there is a temptation to dismiss the problem of nihilism on the grounds that desire does not admit of irrationality. This is what I called the "Humean solution" to the problem. This, it seems to me, doesn't take the problem seriously enough. It *seems* irrational to think that nothing matters without becoming indifferent to everything, which Humeans cannot grant. On the other hand, there is a temptation to think that nihilism about value is so absurdly wrong that it is no wonder that it mandates total indifference. This is what I called the "realist solution" to the problem of nihilism. This, it seems to me, takes the problem a little too seriously. Nihilism about value is more of a live option than realists allow. At least some of us inclined towards nihilism about value feel the force of the problem: we have not become indifferent to everything (as the realists think we should), but we puzzle (as the Humeans think we shouldn't) over how our failure to do so can be rational. To those who in that way are concerned with the problem of nihilism, I hope here to have provided something useful.

The Epistemology of Desire and the Problem of Nihilism. Allan Hazlett, Oxford University Press.
© Allan Hazlett 2024. DOI: 10.1093/9780191995583.003.0007

Bibliography

Adams, R.M. (2006), *A Theory of Virtue: Excellence in Being for the Good* (Oxford University Press).

Ahlstrom-Vij, K., and Grimm, S. (2013), "Getting It Right," *Philosophical Studies* 166(2), pp. 329–47.

Anscombe, G.E.M. (1963), *Intention*, second edition (Harvard University Press).

Anscombe, G.E.M. (1979), "What Is It to Believe Someone?," in C.F. Delaney (ed.), *Rationality and Religious Belief* (University of Notre Dame Press), pp. 141–51.

Armstrong, D.M. (1993), *A Materialist Theory of the Mind*, revised edition (Routledge).

Arpaly, N. (2000), "On Acting Rationally against One's Own Best Judgment," *Ethics* 110(3), pp. 488–513.

Arpaly, N. (2004), *Unprincipled Virtue: An Inquiry into Moral Agency* (Oxford University Press).

Arpaly, N., and Schroeder, T. (2014), In *Praise of Desire* (Oxford University Press).

Audi, R. (1990), "Weakness of Will and Rational Action," *Australasian Journal of Philosophy* 68(3), pp. 270–81.

Audi, R. (2010), "Moral Perception and Moral Knowledge," *Proceedings of the Aristotelian Society Supplement* 84, pp. 79–97.

Audi, R. (2013), *Moral Perception* (Princeton University Press).

Audi, R. (2018), "Moral Perception Defended," in A. Bergqvist and R. Cowan (eds.), *Evaluative Perception* (Oxford University Press), pp. 58–79.

Baehr, J. (2011), *The Inquiring Mind: On Intellectual Virtues and Virtue Epistemology* (Oxford University Press).

Bengson, J., and Moffett, M.A. (2007), "Know-how and Concept Possession," *Philosophical Studies* 136, pp. 31–57.

Bengson, J., and Moffett, M.A. (2012), "Nonpropositional Intellectualism," in J. Bengson and M.A. Moffett (eds.), *Knowing How: Essays on Knowledge, Mind, and Action* (Oxford University Press), pp. 161–95.

Bennett, J. (1974), "The Conscience of Huckleberry Finn," *Philosophy* 49(188), pp. 123–34.

Bennett, J. (1990), "Why Is Belief Involuntary?," *Analysis* 50(2), pp. 87–107.

Berker, S. (2022), "The Deontic, The Evaluative, and the Fitting," in C. Howard and R.A. Rowland (eds.), *Fittingness: Essays in the Philosophy of Normativity* (Oxford University Press), pp. 23–57.

Besser-Jones, L. (2008), "Social Psychology, Moral Character, and Moral Fallibility," *Philosophy and Phenomenological Research* 76(2), pp. 310–32.

Boghossian, P. (2003), "The Normativity of Content," *Philosophical Issues* 13, pp. 31–45.

Boghossian, P. (2005), "Is Meaning Normative?," in C. Nimtz and A. Beckermann (eds.), *Philosophy—Science—Scientific Philosophy: Main Lectures and Colloquia of GAP.5* (Mentis), pp. 205–18.

162 BIBLIOGRAPHY

Boyd, R. (1988), "How to be a Moral Realist," in G. Sayre-McCord (ed.), *Essays on Moral Realism* (Cornell University Press), pp. 187–228.

Bradley, R., and List, C. (2009), "Desire-as-Belief Revisited," *Analysis*, 69(1), pp. 31–7.

Bradley, R., and Stefánsson, H.O. (2016), "Desire, Expectation, and Invariance," *Mind* 125(499), pp. 691–725.

Brady, M.S. (2013), *Emotional Insight: The Epistemic Role of Emotional Experience* (Oxford University Press).

Brandt, R.B. (1946), "Moral Valuation," *Ethics* 56(2), pp. 106–21.

Brandt, R.B. (1979), *A Theory of the Right and the Good* (Oxford University Press).

Bratman, M. (2009a), "Intention, Belief, and Instrumental Rationality," in D. Sobel and S. Wall (eds.), *Reasons for Action* (Cambridge University Press), pp. 13–36.

Bratman, M. (2009b), "Intention, Belief, Practical, Theoretical," in S. Robertson (ed.), *Spheres of Reason: New Essays in the Philosophy of Normativity* (Oxford University Press), pp. 31–60.

Brentano, F. (1874/1973), *Psychology from an Empirical Standpoint*, trans. A.C. Rancurello, D.B. Terrell, and L. McAlister (Humanities Press).

Brentano, F. (1889/1969), *The Origin of Our Knowledge of Right and Wrong*, trans. R. Chisholm and E.H. Schneewind (Routledge & Kegan Paul).

Brentano, F. (1956), *Die Lehre vom Richtigen Urteil* (Francke Verlag).

Brink, D.O. (1989), *Moral Realism and the Foundations of Ethics* (Cambridge University Press).

Brink, D.O. (2008), "The Significance of Desire," *Oxford Studies in Metaethics* 3, pp. 5–45.

Broad, C.D. (1930), *Five Types of Ethical Theory* (Harcourt, Brace, and Company).

Broad, C.D. (1954), "Emotion and Sentiment," *Journal of Aesthetics and Art Criticism* 13(2), pp. 203–14.

Brogaard, B. (2009), "What Mary Did Yesterday: Reflections on Knowledge-*wh*," *Philosophy and Phenomenological Research* 78(2), pp. 439–67.

Brogaard, B. (2012), "Knowledge-How: A Unified Account," in J. Bengson and M.A. Moffett (eds.), *Knowing How: Essays on Knowledge, Mind, and Action* (Oxford University Press), pp. 136–60.

Broome, J. (1991), "Desire, Belief, and Expectation," *Mind* 100(2), pp. 265–7.

Broome, J. (1999), "Normative Requirements," *Ratio* 12, pp. 398–419.

Broome, J. (2007), "Does Rationality Consist in Responding Correctly to Reasons?," *Journal of Moral Philosophy* 4, pp. 349–74.

Broome, J. (2013), *Rationality through Reasoning* (Wiley-Blackwell).

Byrne, A. (2012), "Knowing What I Want," in J. Perry and J. Liu (eds.), *Consciousness and the Self: New Essays* (Cambridge University Press), pp. 165–83.

Byrne, A. (2015), "The Epistemic Significance of Experience," *Philosophical Studies* 173, pp. 947–67.

Byrne, A., and Hájek, A. (1997), "David Hume, David Lewis, and Decision Theory," *Mind* 106(423), pp. 411–28.

Callahan, L.F. (2018), "Moral Testimony: A Re-Conceived Understanding Explanation," *Philosophical Quarterly* 68(272), pp. 437–59.

BIBLIOGRAPHY 163

Callard, A. (2017), "Everyone Desires the Good: Socrates Protreptic Theory of Desire," *Review of Metaphysics* 70, pp. 617–44.

Cappelen, H. (2012), *Philosophy without Intuitions* (Oxford University Press).

Carter, J.A., and Pritchard, D. (2015), "Knowledge-How and Cognitive Achievement," *Philosophy and Phenomenological Research* 91(1), pp. 181–99.

Cath, Y. (2009), "The Ability Hypothesis and the New Knowledge-How," *Noûs* 43(1), pp. 137–56.

Cath, Y. (2012), "Knowing How without Knowing That," in J. Bengson and M.A. Moffett (eds.), *Knowing How: Essays on Knowledge, Mind, and Action* (Oxford University Press), pp. 113–35.

Chan, T. (ed.) (2013), *The Aim of Belief* (Oxford University Press).

Chappell, T. (2008), "Moral Perception," *Philosophy* 83(326), pp. 421–37.

Charles, D. (1982/3), "Rationality and Irrationality," *Proceedings of the Aristotelian Society* 83, pp. 191–212.

Chisholm, R. (1977), *Theory of Knowledge*, second edition (Prentice-Hall).

Chisholm, R. (1986), *Brentano and Intrinsic Value* (Cambridge University Press).

Coady, C.A.J. (1992), *Testimony: A Philosophical Study* (Oxford University Press).

Coleman, M.C. (2008), "Directions of Fit and the Humean Theory of Motivation," *Australasian Journal of Philosophy* 86(1), pp. 127–39.

Connolly, K. (2017), "Perceptual Learning," *Stanford Encyclopedia of Philosophy* (Summer 2017 Edition), Edward N. Zalta (ed.), https://plato.stanford.edu/archives/sum2017/entries/perceptual-learning/.

Cowan, R. (2015), "Perceptual Intuitionism," *Philosophy and Phenomenological Research* 90(1), pp. 164–93.

Crisp, R. (2000), Review of J. Kupperman, *Value...And What Follows* (Oxford University Press), *Philosophy* 75(3), pp. 452–62.

Cullison, A. (2009), "Moral Perception," *European Journal of Philosophy* 18(2), pp. 159–75.

Cullity, G. (2018), *Concern, Respect, and Cooperation* (Oxford University Press).

D'Arms, J., and Jacobson, D. (2000a), "The Moralistic Fallacy: On the 'Appropriateness' of Emotions," *Philosophy and Phenomenological Research* 61(1), pp. 65–90.

D'Arms, J., and Jacobson, D. (2000b), "Sentiment and Value," *Ethics* 110(4), pp. 722–48.

Dancy, J. (2010), "Moral Perception," *Proceedings of the Aristotelian Society Supplement* 84, pp. 99–117.

Davidson, D. (1963/2001), "Actions, Reasons, and Causes," reprinted in *Essays on Actions and Events* (Oxford University Press), pp. 3–19.

Davidson, D. (1970/2001), "Mental Events," reprinted in *Essays on Actions and Events* (Oxford University Press), pp. 207–27.

Davidson, S. (1978/2001), "Intending," reprinted in *Essays on Actions and Events* (Oxford University Press), pp. 83–102.

Davidson, D. (1979/1984), "Moods and Performances," in A. Margalit (ed.), *Meaning and Use* (Reidel), reprinted in D. Davidson, *Inquiries into Truth and Interpretation* (Oxford University Press), pp. 109–21.

164 BIBLIOGRAPHY

Davis, W.A. (1986), "The Two Senses of Desire," in J. Marks (ed.), *The Ways of Desire: New Essays in Philosophical Psychology on the Concept of Wanting* (Precedent Publishing), pp. 63–82.

De Sousa, R. (1974), "The Good and the True," *Mind* 83(332), pp. 541–51.

De Sousa, R. (1987), *The Rationality of Emotion* (MIT Press).

Deonna, J., and Teroni, F. (2012), *The Emotions: A Philosophical Introduction* (Routledge).

Devitt, M. (2011), "Methodology and the Nature of Knowing How," *Journal of Philosophy* 108(4), pp. 205–18.

Döring, S. (2003), "Explaining Action by Emotion," *Philosophical Quarterly* 53(211), pp. 214–300.

Döring, S. (2007), "Seeing What To Do: Affective Perception and Rational Motivation," *dialectica* 61(3), pp. 363–94.

Döring, S., and Eker, B. (2017), "Desires without Guises: Why We Need Not Value What We Want," in F. Lauria and J.A. Deonna (eds.), *The Nature of Desire* (Oxford University Press), pp. 79–118.

Dretske, F. (1988), *Explaining Behavior: Reasons in a World of Causes* (MIT Press).

Drier, J. (1993), "Structures of Normative Theories," *The Monist* 76(1), pp. 22–40.

Drier, J. (1996), "Rational Preference: Decision Theory as a Theory of Practical Rationality," *Theory and Decision* 40(3), pp. 429–76.

Drier, J. (2001), "Humean Doubts about Categorical Imperatives," in E. Millgram (ed.), *Varieties of Practical Reasoning* (MIT Press), pp. 27–47.

Driver, J. (2001), *Uneasy Virtue* (Cambridge University Press).

Driver, J. (2003), "The Conflation of Moral and Epistemic Virtue," *Metaphilosophy* 34(3), pp. 367–83.

Drucker, D. (2022), "Reasoning Beyond Belief Acquisition," *Noûs* 56(2), pp. 416–42.

Enoch, D. (2011), *Taking Morality Seriously* (Oxford University Press).

Ewing, A.C. (1947), *The Definition of Good* (Macmillan).

Ewing, A.C. (1959), *Second Thoughts on Moral Philosophy* (Macmillan).

Fantl, J. (2012), "Ryle's Regress Defended," *Philosophical Studies*, 156(1), pp. 121–30.

Fantl, J., and McGrath, M. (2007), "On Pragmatic Encroachment in Epistemology," *Philosophy and Phenomenological Research* 75(3), pp. 558–89.

Fantl, J., and McGrath, M. (2009), *Knowledge in an Uncertain World* (Oxford University Press).

Feldman, R. (2003), *Epistemology* (Prentice-Hall).

Feldman, S.D., and Hazlett, A. (2021), "Fitting Inconsistency and Reasonable Irresolution," in B. Brogaard and D.E. Gatzia (eds.), *The Philosophy and Psychology of Ambivalence: Being of Two Minds* (Routledge), pp. 131–46.

Fletcher, G. (2016), "Moral Testimony: Once More with Feeling," *Oxford Studies in Metaethics* 11, pp. 45–73.

Foley, R. (1993), *Working without a Net: A Study of Egocentric Rationality* (Oxford University Press).

Foley, R. (2012), *When Is True Belief Knowledge?* (Princeton University Press).

Foot, P. (1961), "Goodness and Choice," *Proceedings of the Aristotelian Society Supplement* 35, pp. 45–60.

Frege, G. (1918–19/1956), "The Thought: A Logical Inquiry," trans. P.T. Geach, *Mind* 65(259), pp. 289–311.

BIBLIOGRAPHY 165

Fricker, E. (2006), "Second-Hand Knowledge," *Philosophy and Phenomenological Research* 123(3), pp. 592–618.

Friedman, J. (2020), "The Epistemic and the Zetetic," *Philosophical Review* 129(4), pp. 501–36.

Friedrich, D. (2017), "Desire, Mental Force, and Desirous Experience," in F. Lauria and J.A. Deonna (eds.), *The Nature of Desire* (Oxford University Press), pp. 57–76.

Frijda, N.H. (1986), *The Emotions* (Cambridge University Press).

Frost, K. (2014), "On the Very Idea of Direction of Fit," *Philosophical Review* 123(4), pp. 429–84.

Fumerton, R. (2006), *Epistemology* (Blackwell).

Garcia, J.L.A. (1986), "Evaluator Relativity and the Theory of Value," *Mind* 95(378), pp. 242–5.

Garcia, J.L.A. (1987), "Goods and Evils," *Philosophy and Phenomenological Research* 47(3), pp. 385–412.

Geach, P.T. (1956), "Good and Evil," *Analysis* 17(2), pp. 33–42.

Gettier, E. (1963), "Is Justified True Belief Knowledge?," *Analysis* 23(6), pp. 121–3.

Gibbard, A. (1990), *Wise Choices, Apt Feelings: A Theory of Normative Judgment* (Oxford University Press).

Glick, E. (2011), "Two Methodologies for Evaluating Intellectualism," *Philosophy and Phenomenological Research* 83(2), pp. 398–434.

Glick, E. (2012), "Abilities and Know-How Attributions," in J. Brown and M. Gerken (eds.), *Knowledge Ascriptions* (Oxford University Press), pp. 120–39.

Glick, E. (2015), "Practical Modes of Presentation," *Noûs* 49(3), pp. 538–59.

Goldie, P. (2000), *The Emotions: A Philosophical Exploration* (Oxford University Press).

Goldie, P. (2004), "Emotion, Feeling, and Knowledge of the World," in R.C. Solomon (ed.), *Thinking about Feeling: Contemporary Philosophers on Emotions* (Oxford University Press), pp. 91–106.

Goldman, A. (1967), "A Causal Theory of Knowing," *Journal of Philosophy* 64(12), pp. 357–72.

Goldman, A. (1976), "Discrimination and Perceptual Knowledge," *Journal of Philosophy* 73(20), pp. 771–91.

Goldman, A. (2007), "Philosophical Intuitions: Their Target, Their Source, and Their Epistemic Status," *Grazer Philosophische Studien* 74(1), pp. 1–26.

Gordon, E.C. (2017), "Social Epistemology and the Acquisition of Understanding," in S.R. Grimm, C. Baumberger, and S. Ammon (eds.), *Explaining Understanding: New Perspectives from Epistemology and Philosophy of Science* (Routledge), pp. 293–317.

Graham, P. (1997), "What Is Testimony?," *Philosophical Quarterly* 47(187), pp. 227–32.

Graham, P. (2021), "Typing Testimony," *Synthese* 199(3–4), pp. 9463–77.

Greco, J. (1999), "Agent Reliabilism," *Philosophical Perspectives* 13, pp. 273–96.

Greco, J. (2003), "Knowledge as Credit for True Belief," in M. DePaul and L. Zagzebski (eds.), *Intellectual Virtue: Perspectives from Ethics and Epistemology* (Oxford University Press), pp. 111–34.

Greco, J. (2010), *Achieving Knowledge: A Virtue-Theoretic Account of Epistemic Normativity* (Oxford University Press).

166 BIBLIOGRAPHY

Greco, J. (2016), "What Is Transmission?," *Episteme* 13(4), pp. 481–98.

Greenspan, P. (1980), "A Case of Mixed Feelings: Ambivalence and the Logic of Emotion," in A.O. Rorty (ed.), *Explaining Emotions* (University of California Press), pp. 223–50.

Greenspan, P. (1988), *Emotions and Reasons: An Inquiry into Emotional Justification* (Routledge).

Greenspan, P. (2004), "Emotions, Rationality, and Mind/Body," in R.C. Solomon (ed.), *Thinking about Feeling: Contemporary Philosophers on Emotions* (Oxford University Press), pp. 125–34.

Gregory, A. (2012), "Changing Direction on Direction of Fit," *Ethical Theory and Moral Practice* 15, pp. 603–14.

Gregory, A. (2013), "The Guise of Reasons," *American Philosophical Quarterly* 50(1), pp. 63–72.

Gregory, A. (2017), "Might Desires Be Beliefs about Normative Reasons for Action?," in F. Lauria and J.A. Deonna (eds.), *The Nature of Desire* (Oxford University Press), pp. 201–17.

Gregory, A. (2018), "Why Do Desires Rationalize Actions?," *Ergo* 5.

Gregory, A. (2021), *Desire as Belief: A Study of Desire, Motivation, and Rationality* (Oxford University Press).

Grimm, S. (2006), "Is Understanding a Species of Knowledge?," *British Journal for the Philosophy of Science* 57(3), pp. 515–35.

Grimm, S. (2011), "What Is Interesting?," *Logos & Episteme* 2(4), pp. 515–42.

Grimm, S. (2014), "Understanding as Knowledge of Causes," in Abrol Fairweather (ed.), *Virtue Epistemology Naturalized: Bridges between Virtue Epistemology and Philosophy of Science* (Springer), pp. 239–45.

Haddock, A., Millar, A., and Pritchard, D. (eds.) (2009), *Epistemic Value* (Oxford University Press).

Hájek, A., and Pettit, P. (2004), "Desire beyond Belief," *Australasian Journal of Philosophy* 82(1), pp. 77–92.

Hamblin, C. (1958), "Questions," *Australasian Journal of Philosophy* 36(3), pp. 159–68.

Hare, R.M. (1952), *The Language of Morals* (Oxford University Press).

Hare, R.M. (1957/1972), "'Nothing Matters': Is 'the Annihilation of Values' Something That Could Happen?," in *Applications of Moral Philosophy* (University of California Press), pp. 32–47.

Hare, R.M. (1963a), "Descriptivism," *Proceedings of the British Academy* 49, pp. 115–34.

Hare, R.M. (1963b), *Freedom and Reason* (Oxford University Press).

Harman, G. (1990), "The Intrinsic Quality of Experience," *Philosophical Perspectives* 4, pp. 31–52.

Hart, W.D. (1988), *Engines of the Soul* (Cambridge University Press).

Hawkins, J. (2008), "Desiring the Bad Under the Guise of the Good," *Philosophical Quarterly* 58(231), pp. 244–64.

Hawley, K. (2003), "Success and Knowledge-How," *American Philosophical Quarterly*, 40(1), pp. 19–31.

Hawley, K. (2010), "Testimony and Knowing How," *Studies in History and Philosophy of Science* 41, pp. 397–404.

BIBLIOGRAPHY 167

Hawthorne, J. (2004), *Knowledge and Lotteries* (Oxford University Press).

Hawthorne, J., and Stanley, J. (2008), "Knowledge and Action," *Journal of Philosophy* 110(10), pp. 571–90.

Hazlett, A. (2013), *A Luxury of the Understanding: On the Value of True Belief* (Oxford University Press).

Hazlett, A. (2017a), "Imagination that Amounts to Knowledge from Fiction," in E. Sullivan-Bissett, H. Bradley, and P. Noordhof (eds.), *Art and Belief* (Oxford University Press), pp. 119–34.

Hazlett, A. (2017b), "Towards Social Accounts of Testimonial Asymmetries," *Noûs* 51(1), pp. 49–73.

Hazlett, A. (2018), "Understanding and Structure," in S. Grimm (ed.), *Making Sense of the World: New Essays on the Philosophy of Understanding* (Oxford University Press), pp. 135–58.

Heathwood, C. (2006), "Desire Satisfaction and Hedonism," *Philosophical Studies* 128(3), pp. 539–63.

Helm, B.W. (2001), *Emotional Reason: Deliberation, Motivation, and the Nature of Value* (Cambridge University Press).

Helm, B.W. (2009), "Emotions as Evaluative Feelings," *Emotion Review* 1(3), pp. 248–55.

Henderson, D., and Greco, J. (2015), *Epistemic Evaluation: Purposeful Epistemology* (Oxford University Press).

Hieronymi, P. (2005), "The Wrong Kind of Reason," *Journal of Philosophy* 102(9), pp. 437–57.

Hieronymi, P. (2006), "Controlling Attitudes," *Pacific Philosophical Quarterly* 87, pp. 45–74.

Hills, A. (2009), "Moral Testimony and Moral Epistemology," *Ethics* 120(1), pp. 94–127.

Hills, A. (2016), "Understanding Why," *Noûs* 50(4), pp. 661–88.

Hills, A. (2020), "Moral Testimony: Transmission Versus Propagation," *Philosophy and Phenomenological Research* 101(2), pp. 399–414.

Hinchman, E. (2005), "Telling as Inviting to Trust," *Philosophy and Phenomenological Research* 120(3), pp. 562–87.

Hopkins, R. (2007), "What Is Wrong With Moral Testimony?," *Philosophy and Phenomenological Research* 74(3), pp. 611–34.

Hornsby, J. (2012), "Ryle's *Knowing-How*, and Knowing How to Act," in J. Bengson and M.A. Moffett (eds.), *Knowing How: Essays on Knowledge, Mind, and Action* (Oxford University Press), pp. 80–100.

Howell, R. (2014), "Google Morals, Virtue, and the Asymmetry of Deference," *Noûs* 48(3), pp. 389–415.

Hulse, D., Read, C.N., and Schroeder, T. (2004), "The Impossibility of Conscious Desire," *American Philosophical Quarterly* 41(1), pp. 73–80.

Humberstone, I.L. (1987), "Wanting as Believing," *Canadian Journal of Philosophy* 17(1), pp. 49–62.

Humberstone, I.L. (1992), "Direction of Fit," *Mind* 101(401), pp. 59–82.

Hurka, T. (2001), *Virtue, Vice, and Value* (Oxford University Press).

Hurka, T. (2003), "Moore in the Middle," *Ethics* 113(3), pp. 599–628.

168 BIBLIOGRAPHY

Hursthouse, R. (1999), *On Virtue Ethics* (Oxford University Press).

Jackson, F. (1985), "Internal Conflicts in Desires and Morals," *American Philosophical Quarterly* 22(2), pp. 105–14.

James, W. (1897/1979), *The Will to Believe and Other Essays in Popular Philosophy* (Harvard University Press).

Jenkin, Z. (2020), "The Epistemic Role of Core Cognition," *Philosophical Review* 129(2), pp. 251–98.

Jenkin, Z. (2022), "Crossmodal Basing," *Mind* 131(524), pp. 1163–94.

Johnston, M. (2001), "The Authority of Affect," *Philosophy and Phenomenological Research* 63(1), pp. 181–214.

Johnston, M. (2011), "On a Neglected Epistemic Virtue," *Philosophical Issues* 21, pp. 165–218.

Joyce, R. (2001), *The Myth of Morality* (Cambridge University Press).

Kallestrup, J. (2009), "Knowledge-wh and the Problem of Convergent Knowledge," *Philosophy and Phenomenological Research* 78(2), pp. 468–76.

Karttunen, L. (1977), "Syntax and Semantics of Questions," *Linguistics and Philosophy* 1(1), pp. 3–44.

Kavka, G. (1983), "The Toxin Puzzle," *Analysis* 43(1), pp. 33–6.

Kelly, T. (2003), "Epistemic Rationality and Instrumental Rationality: A Critique," *Philosophy and Phenomenological Research* 66(3), pp. 612–40.

Kenny, A. (1963), *Action, Emotion, and Will* (Routledge & Kegan Paul).

Kieswetter, B. (2017), *The Normativity of Rationality* (Oxford University Press).

Kolodny, N. (2005), "Why Be Rational?," *Mind* 114(455), pp. 509–63.

Kolodny, N. (2007), "How Does Coherence Matter?," *Proceedings of the Aristotelian Society* 107, pp. 29–63.

Konek, J. (2016), "Probabilistic Knowledge and Cognitive Ability," *Philosophical Review* 125(4), pp. 509–87.

Kraus, O. (1937), *Die Werttheorien: Geschichte und Kritik* (Verlag Rulolph M. Rohrer).

Kraut, R. (2011), *Against Absolute Goodness* (Oxford University Press).

Kvanvig, J. (2003), *The Value of Knowledge and the Pursuit of Understanding* (Cambridge University Press).

Kvanvig, J. (2009), "The Value of Understanding," in D. Pritchard, A. Haddock, and A. Millar (eds.), *Epistemic Value* (Oxford University Press), pp. 95–112.

Lauria, F. (2017), "The 'Guise of the Ought-to-Be': A Deontic View of the Intentionality of Desire," in F. Lauria and J.A. Deonna (eds.), *The Nature of Desire* (Oxford University Press), pp. 139–64.

Lewis, D. (1979), "Attitudes *De Dicto* and *De Se*," *Philosophical Review* 88(4), pp. 513–43.

Lewis, D. (1986), *On the Plurality of Worlds* (Blackwell).

Lewis, D. (1988), "Desire as Belief," *Mind* 97(387), pp. 323–32.

Lewis, D. (1989), "Dispositional Theories of Value," *Proceedings of the Aristotelian Society Supplement* 63, 113–37.

Lewis, D. (1996), "Desire as Belief II," *Mind* 105(418), pp. 303–13.

Littlejohn, C., and Turri, J. (eds.) (2014), *Epistemic Norms: New Essays on Action, Belief, and Assertion* (Oxford University Press).

Lord, E. (2018), *The Importance of Being Rational* (Oxford University Press).

BIBLIOGRAPHY 169

Lyons, W. (1980), *Emotion* (Cambridge University Press).

McBrayer, J.P. (2010a), "A Limited Defense of Moral Perception," *Philosophical Studies* 149(3), pp. 305–20.

McBrayer, J.P. (2010b), "Moral Perception and the Causal Objection," *Ratio* 23(3), pp. 291–307.

McDowell, J. (1985/1998), "Values and Secondary Qualities," reprinted in *Mind, Value, and Reality* (Harvard University Press), pp. 131–50.

McGrath, M. (2013), "Phenomenal Conservativism and Cognitive Penetration: The 'Bad Basis' Counterexamples," in C. Tucker (ed.), *Seemings and Justification: New Essays on Dogmatism and Phenomenal Conservativism* (Oxford University Press), pp. 225–47.

McGrath, M. (2021a), "Being Neutral: Agnosticism, Inquiry, and Suspension of Judgment," *Noûs* 55(2), pp. 463–84.

McGrath, M. (2021b), "Epistemic Norms for Waiting (and Suspension)," *Philosophical Topics* 49(2), pp. 173–202.

McGrath, S. (2004), "Moral Knowledge by Perception," *Philosophical Perspectives* 18, pp. 209–28.

McGrath, S. (2011), "Scepticism about Moral Expertise as a Puzzle for Moral Realism," *Journal of Philosophy* 108(3), pp. 111–37.

McGrath, S. (2018), "Moral Perception and Its Rivals," in A. Bergqvist and R. Cowan (eds.), *Evaluative Perception* (Oxford University Press), pp. 161–82.

McHugh, C. (2011), "What Do We Aim at When We Believe?," *Dialectica* 65(3), pp. 369–92.

McHugh, C., and Way, J. (2016), "Fittingness First," *Ethics* 126, pp. 575–606.

MacIntyre, A. (1990), "Is Akratic Action Always Irrational?," in O. Flanagan and A. Rorty (eds.), *Identity, Character, and Morality: Essays in Moral Psychology* (MIT Press), pp. 379–400.

Mackie, J.L. (1977), *Ethics: Inventing Right and Wrong* (Penguin Books).

Magalotti, T., and Kriegel, U. (2021), "Emotion, Epistemic Assessability, and Double Intentionality," *Topoi* 41, pp. 183–94.

Maguirre, B., and Woods, J. (2020), "The Game of Belief," *Philosophical Review* 129(2), pp. 211–49.

Marks, J. (1982), "A Theory of Emotion," *Philosophical Studies* 42(2), pp. 227–42.

Marks, J. (1986), "The Difference between Motivation and Desire," in J. Marks (ed.), *The Ways of Desire: New Essays in Philosophical Psychology on the Concept of Wanting* (Precedent Publishing), pp. 133–47.

Millgram, E. (1995), "Was Hume a Humean?," *Hume Studies* 21(1), pp. 75–94.

Millgram, E. (1997), *Practical Induction* (Harvard University Press).

Miracchi, L. (2015), "Competence to Know," *Philosophical Studies* 172(1), pp. 29–56.

Moore, G.E. (1903), *Principia Ethica* (Cambridge University Press).

Moran, R. (2001), *Authority and Estrangement: An Essay on Self-Knowledge* (Princeton University Press).

Moran, R. (2005), "Getting Told and Being Believed," *Philosopher's Imprint* 5(5), pp. 1–29.

Moss, J. (2012), *Aristotle on the Apparent Good: Perception, Phantasia, Thought, and Desire* (Oxford University Press).

170 BIBLIOGRAPHY

Moss, S. (2018), *Probabilistic Knowledge* (Oxford University Press).

Mulligan, K. (1998), "From Appropriate Emotions to Values," *The Monist* 81(1), pp. 161–88.

Nagel, J. (2012), "Experiments and Intuitions: A Defense of the Case Method in Epistemology," *Philosophy and Phenomenological Research* 85(3), pp. 495–527.

Nagel, T. (1970), *The Possibility of Altruism* (Princeton University Press).

Nagel, T. (1971/1979), "The Absurd," reprinted in *Mortal Questions* (Cambridge University Press), pp. 11–23.

Nagel, T. (1979), *Mortal Questions* (Cambridge University Press).

Nagel, T. (1986), *The View from Nowhere* (Oxford University Press).

Nagel, T. (1997), *The Last Word* (Oxford University Press).

Nichols, S., Stich, S., and Weinberg, J.M. (2003), "Meta-Skepticism: Meditations in Ethno-Epistemology," in S. Luper (ed.), *The Skeptics* (Ashgate), pp. 227–47.

Nickel, B. (2001), "Moral Testimony and Its Authority," *Ethical Theory and Moral Practice* 4(3), pp. 253–66.

Nietzsche, F. (1887/2001), *The Gay Science*, trans. J. Nauckhoff (Cambridge University Press).

Noë, A. (2004), *Action in Perception* (MIT Press).

Noë, A. (2005), "Against Intellectualism," *Analysis* 65(4), pp. 278–90.

Noordhof, P. (2018), "Evaluative Perception as Response-Dependent Representation," in A. Bergqvist and R. Cowan (eds.), *Evaluative Perception* (Oxford University Press), pp. 80–108.

Norman, R. (1971), *Reasons for Actions: A Critique of Utilitarian Rationality* (Blackwell).

Nozick, R. (1981), *Philosophical Explanations* (Harvard University Press).

Nussbaum, M. (2001), *Upheavals of Thought: The Intelligence of Emotions* (Cambridge University Press).

O'Callaghan, C. (2019), Review of S. Siegel, *The Rationality of Perception*, *The Philosophical Review* 128(1), pp. 126–30.

Oddie, G. (1994), "Harmony, Purity, Truth," *Mind* 103(412), pp. 451–72.

Oddie, G. (2001), "Hume, the *BAD* Paradox, and Value Realism," *Philo* 4(2), pp. 109–22.

Oddie, G. (2005), *Value, Reality, and Desire* (Oxford University Press).

Oddie, G. (2017), "Desire and the Good: In Search of the Right Fit," in F. Lauria and J.A. Deonna (eds.), *The Nature of Desire* (Oxford University Press), pp. 29–56.

Oddie, G. (2018), "Value Perception, Properties, and the Primary Bearers of Value," in A. Bergqvist and R. Cowan (eds.), *Evaluative Perception* (Oxford University Press), pp. 239–58.

Olson, J. (2004), "Buck-Passing and the Wrong Kind of Reasons," *Philosophical Quarterly* 54(215), pp. 295–300.

Olson, J. (2014), *Moral Error Theory: History, Critique, Defense* (Oxford University Press).

Owens, D.J. (2003), "Does Belief Have an Aim?," *Philosophical Studies* 115, pp. 283–305.

Owens, D.J. (2006), "Testimony and Assertion," *Philosophical Studies* 130, pp. 105–29.

Parfit, D. (1984), *Reasons and Persons* (Oxford University Press).

BIBLIOGRAPHY 171

Parfit, D. (1997), "Reasons and Motivation," *Proceedings of the Aristotelian Society Supplement* 71, pp. 99–130.

Parfit, D. (2001), "Rationality and Reasons," in D. Egonsson, B. Petersson, J. Josefsson, and T. Rønnow-Rasmussen (eds.), *Exploring Practical Philosophy: From Action to Values* (Ashgate), pp. 17–39.

Parfit, D. (2006), "Normativity," *Oxford Studies in Metaethics* 1, pp. 325–80.

Parfit, D. (2011), *On What Matters*, Volume One (Oxford University Press).

Peacocke, C. (1983), *Sense and Content: Experience, Thought, and Their Relations* (Oxford University Press).

Peacocke, C. (2018), "Are Perceptions Reached by Rational Inference? Comments on Susanna Siegel, *The Rationality of Perception*," *Res Philosophica* 95(4), pp. 751–60.

Pearson, G. (2012), *Aristotle on Desire* (Cambridge University Press).

Peters, R.S. (1970), "The Education of the Emotions," in M.B. Arnold (ed.), *Feelings and Emotions: The Loyola Symposium* (Academic Press), pp. 187–203.

Pettigrew, R. (2016), *Accuracy and the Laws of Credence* (Oxford University Press).

Pettit, P. (1987), "Humeans, Anti-Humeans, and Motivation," *Mind* 96(384), pp. 530–3.

Piller, C. (2000), "Doing What Is Best," *Philosophical Quarterly* 50(199), pp. 208–26.

Piller, C. (2006), "Content-Related and Attitude-Related Reasons for Preferences," *Royal Institute of Philosophy Supplement* 59, pp. 155–81.

Platts, M. (1997), *Ways of Meaning*, second edition (MIT Press).

Portmore, D. (2005), "Combining Teleological Ethics with Evaluator Relativism: A Promising Result," *Pacific Philosophical Quarterly* 86(1), pp. 95–113.

Portmore, D. (2007), "Consequentializing Moral Theories," *Pacific Philosophical Quarterly* 88(1), pp. 39–73.

Poston, T. (2016), "Know How to Transmit Knowledge?," *Noûs* 50(4), pp. 865–78.

Price, C. (2015), *Emotion* (Polity).

Price, G. (1989), "Defending Desire-as-Belief," *Mind* 98(389), pp. 119–27.

Price, H.H. (1954), "Belief and Will," *Proceedings of the Aristotelian Society Supplement* 28, pp. 1–26.

Pritchard, D. (2010), "Knowledge and Understanding," in D. Pritchard, A. Millar, and A. Haddock, *The Nature and Value of Knowledge: Three Investigations* (Oxford University Press), pp. 3–87.

Quine, W.V.O. (1956/1966), "Quantifiers and Propositional Attitudes," reprinted in *The Ways of Paradox and Other Essays* (Random House), pp. 183–94.

Quinn, W. (1993), "Putting Rationality in Its Place," in R. Frey and C. Morris (eds.), *Value, Welfare, and Morality* (Cambridge University Press), pp. 26–50.

Rabinowicz, W., and Rønnow-Rasmussen, T. (2004), "The Strike of the Demon: On Fitting Pro-attitudes and Value," *Ethics* 114(3), pp. 391–423.

Railton, P. (1986), "Moral Realism," *The Philosophical Review* 95(2), pp. 163–207.

Railton, P. (1997), "On the Hypothetical and Non-Hypothetical in Reasoning about Belief and Action," in G. Cullity and B. Gaut (eds.), *Ethics and Practical Reason* (Oxford University Press), pp. 53–79.

Railton, P. (2007), "Humean Theory of Practical Rationality," in D. Copp (ed.), *The Oxford Handbook of Ethical Theory* (Oxford University Press), pp. 265–81.

172 BIBLIOGRAPHY

Railton, P. (2012), "That Obscure Object, Desire," *Proceedings of the American Philosophical Association* 86(2), pp. 22–46.

Railton, P. (2017), "Learning as an Inherent Dynamic of Belief and Desire," in F. Lauria and J.A. Deonna (eds.), *The Nature of Desire* (Oxford University Press), pp. 249–76.

Raz, J. (1999), "Agency, Reason, and the Good," in *Engaging Reason: On the Theory of Value and Action* (Oxford University Press), pp. 22–45.

Raz, J. (2010), "On the Guise of the Good," in S. Tenenbaum (ed.), *Desire, Practical Reason, and the Good* (Oxford University Press), pp. 111–35.

Raz, J. (2016), "The Guise of the Bad," *Journal of Ethics and Social Philosophy* 10(3), pp. 1–14.

Ridge, M. (2014), *Impassioned Belief* (Oxford University Press).

Roberts, R.C. (1988), "What An Emotion Is: A Sketch," *Philosophical Review* 97(2), pp. 183–209.

Roberts, R.C. (2003), *Emotions: An Essay in Aid of Moral Psychology* (Cambridge University Press).

Roland, J. (1958), "On 'Knowing How' and 'Knowing That'," *Philosophical Review* 67(3), pp. 379–88.

Ross, A. (1986), "Why Do We Believe What We Are Told?," *Ratio* 28, pp. 69–88.

Ross, W.D. (1930/2002), *The Right and the Good* (Oxford University Press).

Rumfitt, I. (2003), "Savoir Faire," *Journal of Philosophy* 100, pp. 158–66.

Ryle, G. (1946), "Knowing How and Knowing That," *Proceedings of the Aristotelian Society* 46, pp. 1–16.

Scanlon, T.M. (1998), *What We Owe to Each Other* (Harvard University Press).

Scanlon, T.M. (2007), "Structural Irrationality," in G. Brennan, R. Goodin, F. Jackson, and M. Smith (eds.), *Common Minds: Themes from the Philosophy of Philip Pettit* (Oxford University Press), pp. 84–103.

Scanlon, T.M. (2008), *Moral Dimensions: Permissibility, Meaning, Blame* (Harvard University Press).

Scarantino, A. (2014), "The Motivational Theory of Emotions," in J. D'Arms and D. Jacobson (eds.), *Moral Psychology and Human Agency: Philosophical Essays on the Science of Ethics* (Oxford University Press), pp. 156–85.

Schafer, K. (2013), "Perception and the Rational Force of Desire," *Journal of Philosophy* 110(5), pp. 258–81.

Schaffer, J. (2007), "Knowing the Answer," *Philosophy and Phenomenological Research* 75(2), pp. 383–403.

Schaffer, J. (2009), "Knowing the Answer Redux: Replies to Brogaard and Kallestrup," *Philosophy and Phenomenological Research* 78(2), pp. 477–500.

Schiffer, S. (2002), "Amazing Knowledge," *Journal of Philosophy* 99(4), pp. 200–2.

Schroeder, M. (2007), "Teleology, Agent-Relative Value, and 'Good'," *Ethics* 117(2), pp. 265–95.

Schroeder, M. (2021), *Reasons First* (Oxford University Press).

Schroeder, T. (2004), *Three Faces of Desire* (Oxford University Press).

Schroeder, T. (2017), "Empirical Evidence against a Cognitivist Theory of Desire and Action," in F. Lauria and J.A. Deonna (eds.), *The Nature of Desire* (Oxford University Press), pp. 221–48.

BIBLIOGRAPHY 173

Schroeder, T., and Arpaly, N. (2014), "The Reward Theory of Desire in Moral Psychology," in J. D'Arms and D. Jacobson (eds.), *Moral Psychology and Human Agency: Philosophical Essays on the Science of Ethics* (Oxford University Press), pp. 186–214.

Schueler, G.F. (1991), "Pro-Attitudes and Direction of Fit," *Mind* 100(400), pp. 277–81.

Schueler, G.F. (1995), *Desire: Its Role in Practical Reason and the Explanation of Action* (MIT Press).

Searle, J. (1969), *Speech Acts: An Essay in the Philosophy of Language* (Cambridge University Press).

Searle, J. (1983), *Intentionality: An Essay in the Philosophy of Mind* (Cambridge University Press).

Searle, J. (1992), *The Rediscovery of the Mind* (MIT Press).

Sen, A. (1982), "Rights and Agency," *Philosophy and Public Affairs* 11(1), pp. 3–39.

Sen, A. (1983), "Evaluator Relativity and Consequential Evaluation," *Philosophy and Public Affairs* 12(2), pp. 113–32.

Setiya, K. (2007), *Reasons without Rationalism* (Princeton University Press).

Setiya, K. (2010), "Sympathy for the Devil," in S. Tenenbaum (ed.), *Desire, Practical Reason, and the Good* (Oxford University Press), pp. 82–110.

Shafer-Landau, R. (2003), *Moral Realism: A Defence* (Oxford University Press).

Shah, N. (2003), "How Truth Governs Belief," *Philosophical Review* 112(4), pp. 447–82.

Shah, N. (2006), "A New Argument for Evidentialism," *Philosophical Quarterly* 56(225), pp. 481–98.

Shah, N. (2008), "How Action Governs Intention," *Philosophers' Imprint* 8(5), pp. 1–19.

Shah, N., and Velleman, D. (2005), "Doxastic Deliberation," *Philosophical Review* 114(4), pp. 497–534.

Sidgwick, H. (1907), *The Methods of Ethics*, seventh edition (Hackett Publishing).

Siegel, S. (2011), *The Contents of Visual Experience* (Oxford University Press).

Siegel, S. (2017), *The Rationality of Perception* (Oxford University Press).

Sliwa, P. (2012), "In Defense of Moral Testimony," *Philosophical Studies* 158(2), pp. 175–95.

Sliwa, P. (2015), "Understanding and Knowing," *Proceedings of the Aristotelian Society* 140(1), pp. 57–74.

Slote, M. (1979), "Assertion and Belief," in J. Dancy (ed.), *Papers on Language and Logic: Proceedings of the Conference on Language and Logic Held at the University of Keele, April, 1979* (Keele University Library), pp. 177–90.

Slote, M. (2001), *Morals from Motives* (Oxford University Press).

Smith, M. (1987), "The Humean Theory of Motivation," *Mind* 96(381), pp. 36–61.

Smith, M. (1993), "Realism," in P. Singer (ed.), *A Companion to Ethics* (Blackwell), pp. 399–410.

Smith, M. (1994), *The Moral Problem* (Blackwell).

Smith, M. (2003), "Neutral and Relative Value After Moore," *Ethics* 113(3), pp. 576–98.

Smith, M. (2009), "Two Kinds of Consequentialism," *Philosophical Issues* 19, pp. 257–72.

174 BIBLIOGRAPHY

Snowdon, P. (2003), "Knowing How and Knowing That: A Distinction Reconsidered," *Proceedings of the Aristotelian Society* 104(1), pp. 1–29.

Sobel, D., and Copp, D. (2001), "Against Direction of Fit Accounts of Belief and Desire," *Analysis* 61(1), pp. 44–53.

Solomon, R.C. (1973), "Emotions and Choice," *Review of Metaphysics* 27(1), pp. 20–41.

Solomon, R.C. (1993), *The Passions: Emotions and the Meaning of Life* (Hackett Publishing).

Solomon, R.C. (2004), "Emotions, Thoughts, and Feelings: Emotions as Engagements with the World," in R.C. Solomon (ed.), *Thinking about Feeling: Contemporary Philosophers on Emotions* (Oxford University Press), pp. 76–88.

Solomon, R.C. (2007), *True to Our Feelings: What Our Emotions Are Really Telling Us* (Oxford University Press).

Sosa, E. (1988), "Methodology and Apt Belief," *Synthese* 74(3), pp. 415–26.

Sosa, E. (2007), *A Virtue Epistemology: Apt Belief and Reflective Knowledge, Volume 1* (Oxford University Press).

Sosa, E. (2009a), "A Defense of the Use of Intuitions in Philosophy," in M. Bishop and D. Murphy (eds.), *Stich and His Critics* (Blackwell), pp. 101–12.

Sosa, E. (2009b), "Knowing Full Well: The Normativity of Beliefs as Performances," *Philosophical Studies* 142, pp. 5–15.

Sosa, E. (2015), "Mind-World Relations," *Episteme* 12(2), pp. 155–66.

Sosa, E. (2021), *Epistemic Explanations: A Theory of Telic Normativity and What It Explains* (Oxford University Press).

Stalnaker, R. (1987), *Inquiry* (MIT Press).

Stampe, D. (1986), "Defining Desire," in J. Marks (ed.), *The Ways of Desire: New Essays in Philosophical Psychology on the Concept of Wanting* (Precedent Publishing), pp. 149–73.

Stampe, D. (1987), "The Authority of Desire," *Philosophical Review* 96(3), pp. 225–81.

Stanley, J. (2005), *Knowledge and Practical Interests* (Oxford University Press).

Stanley, J. (2011), *Know How* (Oxford University Press).

Stanley, J., and Williamson, T. (2001). "Knowing How," *Journal of Philosophy* 98(8), pp. 411–44.

Stefánsson, H.O. (2014), "Desires, Beliefs, and Conditional Desirability," *Synthese* 191, pp. 4019–35.

Steglich-Petersen, A. (2006), "No Norm Needed: On the Aim of Belief," *Philosophical Quarterly* 56, pp. 499–516.

Steglich-Petersen, A. (2009), "Weighing the Aim of Belief," *Philosophical Studies* 145, pp. 395–405.

Steup, M., and Neta, R. (2020), "Epistemology," *Stanford Encyclopedia of Philosophy* (Fall 2020 Edition), Edward N. Zalta (ed.), https://plato.stanford.edu/archives/fall2020/entries/epistemology/.

Stocker, M. (1979), "Desiring the Bad: An Essay in Moral Psychology," *Journal of Philosophy* 76(12), pp. 738–53.

Stokes, D. (2013), "Cognitive Penetrability of Perception," *Philosophy Compass* 8(7), pp. 646–63.

Strawson, G. (2010), *Mental Reality*, second edition (MIT Press).

BIBLIOGRAPHY 175

Strawson, P.F. (1985), *Skepticism and Naturalism: Some Varieties* (Columbia University Press).
Suikkanen, J. (2004), "Reasons and Value: In Defence of the Buck-Passing Account," *Ethical Theory and Moral Practice* 7(5), pp. 513–35.
Sussman, D. (2009), "For Badness' Sake," *Journal of Philosophy* 106(11), pp. 613–28.
Tappolet, C. (2012), "Emotions, Perceptions, and Emotional Illusions," in C. Calabi (ed.), *Perceptual Illusions: Philosphical and Psychological Essays* (Palgrave Macmillan), pp. 205–22.
Tappolet, C. (2016), *Emotions, Values, and Agency* (Oxford University Press).
Taylor, C.C.W. (1986), "Emotions and Wants," in J. Marks (ed.), *The Ways of Desire: New Essays in Philosophical Psychology on the Concept of Wanting* (Precedent Publishing), pp. 217–31.
Taylor, G. (1975), "Justifying the Emotions," *Mind* 84(335), pp. 390–402.
Tenenbaum, S. (2003), "*Accedie*, Evaluation, and Motivation," in S. Stroud and C. Tappolet (eds.), *Weakness of Will and Practical Irrationality* (Oxford University Press), pp. 147–71.
Tenenbaum, S. (2007), *Appearances of the Good: An Essay on the Nature of Practical Reason* (Cambridge University Press).
Tenenbaum, S. (2008), "Appearing Good: A Reply to Schroeder," *Social Theory and Practice* 34(1), pp. 131–8.
Thompson, J.J. (2008), *Normativity* (Open Court).
Turri, J. (2011), "Manifest Failure: The Gettier Problem Solved," *Philosophers' Imprint* 11(8), pp. 1–11.
Unger, P. (1975), *Ignorance: A Case for Scepticism* (Oxford University Press).
Velleman, D. (1992), "The Guise of the Good," *Noûs* 26(1), pp. 3–26.
Velleman, D. (1996), "The Possibility of Practical Reason," *Ethics* 106, pp. 694–726.
Velleman, D. (2000), "On the Aim of Belief," in *The Possibility of Practical Reason* (Oxford University Press), pp. 244–81.
Wanderer, J. (2012), "Addressing Testimonial Injustice: Being Ignored and Being Rejected," *Philosophical Quarterly* 62(246), pp. 148–69.
Watson, G. (1975), "Free Agency," *Journal of Philosophy* 72(8), pp. 205–20.
Wedgwood, R. (2002), "The Aim of Belief," *Philosophical Perspectives* 16, pp. 267–97.
Weinberg, J.M., Nichols, S., and Stich, S. (2001), "Normativity and Epistemic Intuitions," *Philosophical Topics* 29(1/2), pp. 429–60.
Werner, P.J. (2016), "Moral Perception and the Contents of Experience," *Journal of Moral Philosophy* 13, pp. 294–317.
Wiggins, D. (1987/1998), "A Sensible Subjectivism?," in *Needs, Values, Truth: Essays in the Philosophy of Value*, third edition (Oxford University Press), pp. 185–214.
Williams, B. (1970/1973), "Deciding to Believe," reprinted in *Problems of the Self* (Cambridge University Press), pp. 136–51.
Williams, B. (1980/1981), "Internal and External Reasons," reprinted in *Moral Luck: Philosophical Papers, 1973–1980* (Cambridge University Press), pp. 101–13.
Williams, B. (1985/2006), *Ethics and the Limits of Philosophy* (Routledge).
Williams, B. (1989/1995), "Internal Reasons and the Obscurity of Blame," reprinted in *Making Sense of Humanity and Other Philosophical Papers, 1982–1993* (Cambridge University Press), pp. 35–45.

176 BIBLIOGRAPHY

Williams, B. (2002), *Truth and Truthfulness: An Essay in Genealogy* (Princeton University Press).

Wilson, A. (2017), "Avoiding the Conflation of Moral and Epistemic Virtues," *Ethical Theory and Moral Practice* 20(5), pp. 1037–50.

Wittgenstein, L. (1958), *Philosophical Investigations*, trans. G.E.M. Anscombe, second edition (Blackwell).

Wittgenstein, L. (1969), *On Certainty*, trans. D. Paul and G.E.M. Anscombe (Harper & Row).

Yablo, S. (1993), "Is Conceivability a Guide to Possibility?," *Philosophy and Phenomenaological Research* 53(1), pp. 1–42.

Zagzebski, L. (1996), *Virtues of the Mind: An Inquiry into the Nature of Virtue and the Ethical Foundations of Knowledge* (Cambridge University Press).

Zagzebski, L. (2001), "Recovering Understanding," in M. Steup (ed.), *Knowledge, Truth, and Duty: Essays on Epistemic Justification, Responsibility, and Virtue* (Oxford University Press), pp. 235–51.

Zagzebski, L. (2003), "The Search for the Source of Epistemic Good," *Metaphilosophy* 34(1/2), pp. 12–28.

Zagzebski, L. (2008), *On Epistemology* (Wadsworth).

Zagzebski, L. (2010), "Exemplarist Virtue Theory," *Metaphilosophy* 41(1/2), pp. 41–57.

Zagzebski, L. (2012), *Epistemic Authority: A Theory of Trust, Authority, and Autonomy in Belief* (Oxford University Press).

Zagzebski, L. (2017), *Exemplarist Moral Theory* (Oxford University Press).

Zangwill, N. (1998), "Direction of Fit and Normative Functionalism," *Philosophical Studies* 91(2), pp. 173–203.

Index

Because the index has been created to work across multiple formats, indexed terms for which a page range is given (e.g., 52–53, 66–70, etc.) may occasionally appear only on some, but not all, of the pages within the range.

accuracy 28, 30, 32–3
  non-accurate representations 149–52
acedia 15, 112–5, 117–18, 147
acquaintance 84
"aim of belief" 29–30, 154–5
  "aim of desire" 31
akrasia 103, 105, 112–5, 116–7
Anscombe, G.E.M. 10–13, 13–14, 20, 50–1, 56–7, 146
Aristotle 99, 107
Arpaly, Nomy 112 n.26
attitudes 98–9, 118
assertion 28, 119, 149–51
Augustine 48
aversion 38–9
axial gaps 43–5, 142
axial gluts 45–7, 47–8, 55, 64 n.11

badness 39
belief
  accuracy condition for 14, 20, 27–30, 53–4
  alethic criticism of 51–2, 63–4
  degree of 42–3, 84
  evaluative belief 15, 33–4
benefit see prudential value
Berker, Selim 43 n.33
Brandt, Richard 65
Brentano 44–5, 47, 64 n.11, 140
"buck passing" account of value 70–1, 124

Charles, David 33 n.11
Chisholm, Roderick 44
credence see degree of belief
correctness 29–30

Davidson, Donald 6–7, 14
deliberation 18–19, 21, 23, 94, 97–8
  doxastic 94, 100–1, 110, 116
  orectic 94, 99, 108–9, 115–8, 138–9, 158
  practical 102–3, 106, 111, 116–19

depiction 152
desire 5–7
  axial criticism of 51–3
  as a propositional attitude 31, 34–7
  accuracy condition for 14, 20, 23–4, 30–4, 40, 54, 63, 119, 121–2, 153–4
  evaluative belief theory of 15–8, 21, 146–7
  evaluative perception theory of 18–9, 21
  "guise of the good" 14, 15, 33–4
  instrumental vs. non-instrumental 7–10, 32, 45 n.36, 56, 99, 106–8, 111–12, 146
  not essentially practical 12–13, 36–7
  practical theory of 10–3, 21, 22, 61–2
  prospective theory of 19–20, 21, 135
  strength of 41–3
  testimonial 88–9
Descartes 21, 39
direction of fit 10–12, 33

emotion 21–4, 96, 150–1
epistemic luck 90–3
epistemology 24–6
expressivism 125–7

Feldman, Richard 25
fittingness 29–30, 64–9, 132
  fitting attitudes account of value 64, 123, 131–2
Foley, Richard 90–1
Foot, Phillipa 56–7
Fumerton, Richard 25

Geach, P.T. 37
Gettier cases see epistemic luck
goodness 38, 109, 111–12, 123, 127
  agent-relative 131–3
  as propositional 37–8
  degrees of 40

178 INDEX

goodness (*cont.*)
  not a property 38
  see also axial gaps, axial gluts, instrumental value, prudential value, relative value

Hare, R.M. 56–7, 125–7, 137
Hieronymi, Pamela 101–4
Hobbes 21–2
Hume 4, 13–15, 21, 51, 56, 127–8, 135–7, 138
Humean theory of practical
  rationality 4–5, 13
Humberstone, L. 19

incoherence 140–7, 152–5
instrumental value 7, 32, 45, 99–100
intention 36–7, 102–5, 118–19
imagination 28, 128–9, 150–1, 153

James, William 148–9

Kenny, Anthony 22
knowledge
  of goodness 76–7
  orectic 75, 84–6
  phenomenal 84 n.17
  practical 80–1
  propositional 76, 80–3
  virtue-theoretic account of 81
Kraus, Oskar 44–5

Lewis, David 17 n.41

Nagel, Thomas 130–1, 137–9
Neta, Ram 25
Nietzsche 133

Mackie, J.L. 124–5, 126–7
modes of presentation 96, 141–2
Moore, G.E. 99–100
moral realism 122–5
moral testimony 87–8
Müller-Lyre illusion 96 n.6, 133–4

nihilism about value 1–4, 52, 86, 121,
  124–5, 155

perceptual experience 18–19, 28, 28 n.5, 84,
  96–8, 119, 133–5, 138–9, 150–1

practical reasoning *see* deliberation, practical
preference 42, 155–7
prudential value 2, 19–20, 39–40, 47–8, 111,
  114–15, 123, 129–30

rational control *see* deliberation
Railton, P. 19
rationality 29–30, 53, 68–9
  of desire 3–4, 4–5, 9–10, 14–15,
    114–5, 121–2
  structural 95, 122, 158
reasons 71, 95, 132–3
  agent-relative 130–2
  for belief 72
  for desire 69, 72–3
  practical 50
reasoning *see* deliberation
Reid, Thomas 137
relative value 2–3, 37, 47–8, 111, 114–15, 123
Ross, W.D. 37, 46–7

Searle, John 11
Scanlon, T.M. 94, 95
Schafer, Kurt 112 n.26
Schroeder, Timothy 19 n.48, 112 n.26
Shah, Nishi 71, 104
Slote, Michael 59–60
Spinoza 22, 99
Smith, Michael 11–12
Stalnaker, Robert 11–12
Steup, Matthias 25
Strawson, Galen 12–13
Strawson, P.F. 136–7

Taylor, C.C.W. 12 n.22
Tenenbaum, Sergio 137

understanding 80–1, 87–9

virtue ethics 58–60, 86–7

weakness of will *see* akrasia
well-being *see* prudential value
Williams, Bernard 83–4
Wittgenstein 84 n.18, 137
"wrong kind of reasons" problem 71–3

Zagzebski, Linda 25, 59–60, 90–1